John Keats:
The Poems

JOHN BLADES

D0348203

palgrave

2324143   821.7 KEA
BLA

© John Blades 2002

All rights reserved. No reproduction, copy or transmission of
this publication may be made without written permission.

No paragraph of this publication may be reproduced, copied or
transmitted save with written permission or in accordance with
the provisions of the Copyright, Designs and Patents Act 1988,
or under the terms of any licence permitting limited copying
issued by the Copyright Licensing Agency, 90 Tottenham Court
Road, London W1T 4LP.

Any person who does any unauthorised act in relation to this
publication may be liable to criminal prosecution and civil
claims for damages.

The author has asserted his right to be identified as
the author of this work In accordance with the Copyright, Designs
and Patents Act 1988.

First published 2002 by
PALGRAVE
Houndmills, Basingstoke, Hampshire RG21 6XS and
175 Fifth Avenue, New York, N.Y. 10010
Companies and representatives throughout the world

PALGRAVE is the new global academic imprint of
St. Martin's Press LLC Scholarly and Reference Division and
Palgrave Publishers Ltd (formerly Macmillan Press Ltd).

ISBN 0–333–94894–7 hardcover
ISBN 0–333–94895–5 paperback

This book is printed on paper suitable for recycling and
made from fully managed and sustained forest sources.

A catalogue record for this book is available
from the British Library.

Library of Congress Cataloging-in-Publication Data

Blades, John.
    John Keats / John Blades.
        p. cm.—(Analysing texts)
    Includes bibliographical references and index.
    ISBN 0–333–94894–7—ISBN 0–333–94895–5 (pbk.)
        1. Keats, John, 1795–1821—Criticism and interpretation. I. Title.
    II. Analysing texts (Palgrave (Firm))

PR4837 .B56 2002
821'.7—dc21

                                                    2002025333

10 9 8 7 6 5 4 3 2 1
11 10 09 08 07 06 05 04 03 02

Printed in China

For Doug and Ruth Stephens

Contents

PART 2:   THE CONTEXT AND THE CRITICS

General Editor's Preface

This series is dedicated to one clear belief: that we can all enjoy, understand and analyse literature for ourselves, provided we know how to do it. How can we build on close understanding of a short passage, and develop our insight into the whole work? What features do we expect to find in a text? Why do we study style in so much detail? In demystifying the study of literature, these are only some of the questions the *Analysing Texts* series addresses and answers.

The books in this series will not do all the work for you, but will provide you with the tools, and show you how to use them. Here, you will find samples of close, detailed analysis, with an explanation of the analytical techniques utilised. At the end of each chapter there are useful suggestions for further work you can do to practise, develop and hone the skills demonstrated and build confidence in your own analytical ability.

An author's individuality shows in the way they write: every work they produce bears the hallmark of that writer's personal 'style'. In the main part of each book we concentrate therefore on analysing the particular flavour and concerns of one author's work, and explain the features of their writing in connection with major themes. In Part 2 there are chapters about the author's life and work, assessing their contribution to developments in literature; and a sample of critics' views are summarised and discussed in comparison with each other. Some suggestions for further reading provide a bridge towards further critical research.

Analysing Texts is designed to stimulate and encourage your critical and analytic faculty, to develop your personal insight into the author's work and individual style, and to provide you with the skills and techniques to enjoy at first hand the excitement of discovering the richness of the text.

NICHOLAS MARSH

Introduction

Part 1 of this study of Keats involves detailed practical analysis of examples of his poetry. My general approach here has been to select a poem, or an extract from each poem under review, commenting on interesting themes and significant stylistic features and, where relevant, drawing out connections between the extract and other verse by Keats.

For the shorter lyrics I have generally used the whole of a poem but for the narrative verse I have adopted a slightly different approach, taking a short passage as a starting point for an investigation of the whole work and arranging my analysis around the key themes and techniques which the passage reveals. Accordingly, you will find it useful to have before you a copy of each of the longer poems under scrutiny. For my references and quotations I have used John Barnard's very comprehensive edition, *John Keats: The Complete Poems*, published by Penguin.

In Part 2, I have set out to locate Keats's poetry in the context of his life and period, chiefly through a survey of his letters (Chapter 6) but also through a detailed analysis of the Romantic movement in the nineteenth century (Chapter 7). The final chapter takes a close look at some critical attitudes to Keats's verse by reviewing the work of four important critics, and at the same time showing how critical attitudes have changed over the past two centuries.

If you are new to the study of Keats's work or to Romantic poetry in general then you may like to begin by reading Chapters 6 and 7. At the same time if you are unfamiliar with the terminology of literary studies then a couple of useful reference books on this are *The Penguin Dictionary of Literary Terms and Literary Theory*, edited by J. A. Cuddon, and *Practical Criticism*, by John Peck and Martin Coyle (Macmillan Press – now Palgrave Macmillan). For those whose technical appetite is not readily satisfied by these two works, then Katie Wales's *A Dictionary of Stylistics* (Longman) should do the trick.

Principal Events in John Keats's Life

1795 **31 October** John Keats born in Finsbury, London, to Thomas and Frances Keats (Thomas was manager and ostler at the Swan and Hoop Inn, Moorgate).

1797 Birth of brother George.

1799 Birth of brother Tom.

1801 Birth of brother Edward (who died before his fourth birthday).

1803 Birth of sister, Frances Mary (Fanny).
August Keats goes to Clarke's School, London, a liberal and progressive institution where he strikes a close and enduring friendship with the headmaster's son, Charles Cowden Clarke.

1804 **April** Father dies in riding accident.
June Mother remarries. The Keats children are sent to live with their grandparents.

1810 Mother dies from tuberculosis.

1811 Keats leaves school to become apprenticed to Thomas Hammond, surgeon and apothecary.
Completes a prose translation of *The Aeneid* begun at school.

1814 'Imitation of Spenser' (first known poem), 'On Peace' etc.
December Fanny Keats goes to live in the care of the Keats family legal guardian, Richard Abbey (who later disapproved of Keats's career as a poet).

1815 **February** Composes sonnet on release of the poet Leigh Hunt from prison (he had been convicted of libel against the Prince Regent).

October Enters Guy's Hospital as a student and later becomes surgeon's dresser.

1816 **July** Qualifies as an apothecary, physician or surgeon.
Summer vacation with Tom in Margate, Kent.
September John, Tom and George share lodgings in London.
October Meets the poets Leigh Hunt and John Reynolds, and the painter Benjamin Haydon. In this circle Keats's political and artistic views reach maturity.
Composes 'On First Looking into Chapman's Homer' and 'Keen, fitful gusts...'.
December '*I stood tip-toe...*' and *Sleep and Poetry*.

1817 **March** *Poems*, Keats's first volume of poetry, is published to almost complete critical silence, though it is highly praised by his associates.
April Moves to Margate where Tom later joins him. Starts writing *Endymion*.
May In Hastings, Keats meets Mrs Isabella Jones; a well-read and highly attractive woman, worldly, with modern views on sexuality, Mrs Jones became the model or inspiration for some of Keats's independent and assertive female characters.
November Completes *Endymion*.
December Keats attends the 'immortal dinner' at Haydon's; Wordsworth and Charles Lamb are among the guests.

1818 **January** Visits Wordsworth.
March–April Nurses Tom in Teignmouth, Devon, where he writes *Isabella*.
April *Endymion* published.
May Brother George marries Georgiana Wylie.
June They leave for America; Keats sets off on a walking tour of the Lake District and Scotland (plus N. Ireland) with

his friend Charles Brown. Keats hoped to find experience and material to 'get Wisdom' and enrich his writing.

August   Sore throat forces Keats's return to London where he nurses Tom.

September   Has begun *Hyperion*. Meets Fanny Brawne.

October   'Letter A' to George and Georgiana.

December   Tom dies of tuberculosis. Keats moves in with Brown at Wentworth Place, Hampstead.

December–January   'Letter B.'

1819   **January**   Keats visits Chichester and begins *The Eve of St Agnes*.

February   Writes *The Eve of St Mark*.

February–May   'Letter C'.

March   Abandons *Hyperion*. Early signs that he has contracted tuberculosis.

April   The Brawnes family moves next door to Keats. Meets Coleridge. Writes *La Belle Dame sans Merci*.

April/May   Composes the major odes: 'To Psyche', 'To a Nightingale', 'On a Grecian Urn', 'On Melancholy', and 'On Indolence'. George reveals the extent of his monetary difficulties and Keats becomes increasingly anxious about the family's precarious financial situation.

June   In love with Fanny Brawne but departs London to be free to compose poetry.

June–October   First visits Portsmouth, then Winchester – composes *Lamia*: begins *The Fall of Hyperion*.

September   Composes 'To Autumn'. Discards *The Fall of Hyperion* on the grounds that it is influenced too much by Milton.

December   Becomes engaged to Fanny Brawne.

1820   **February**   Keats suffers severe lung haemorrhage. Revises *Lamia*.

July   Collection of verse later known as *Poems 1820* published.

August   Nursed by Fanny and Mrs Brawne. Shelley invites Keats to Italy but he declines the offer.

September Leaves for Italy in the care of the painter and steadfast friend Joseph Severn in the hope of recovering his health.

October Arrives at Naples where his ship is held in quarantine for ten days.

November Travels to Rome, and takes lodgings at the 'Spanish Steps'.

1821 **February 23** Keats dies of tuberculosis and is buried in Rome.

PART 1

ANALYSING
KEATS'S POETRY

1

'Standing on tip-toe': Keats's Early Verse

In this chapter we will be examining some of the poems from Keats's first published volume of poetry, titled simply *Poems*, and published in 1817, when Keats was aged 21. What I am particularly interested in discovering are Keats's interests or concerns at this early stage of his life, looking at the themes as well as the style in a selection of his poems. The pieces I have chosen to look at in detail are 'On First Looking into Chapman's Homer', 'Keen, fitful gusts are whispering here and there', '*I stood tip-toe upon a little hill*', and *Sleep and Poetry*.

'On First Looking into Chapman's Homer'

We can begin our discussion by looking immediately at one of the most famous of the early poems, 'On First Looking into Chapman's Homer', often regarded as a key marker in Keats's early development.

'On First Looking into Chapman's Homer'

Much have I travelled in the realms of gold,
   And many goodly states and kingdoms seen;
   Round many western islands have I been
Which bards in fealty to Apollo hold.
Oft of one wide expanse had I been told   5

> That deep-browed Homer ruled as his demesne;
> Yet did I never breathe its pure serene
> Till I heard Chapman speak out loud and bold:
> Then felt I like some watcher of the skies
> When a new planet swims into his ken;　　　　　　10
> Or like stout Cortez when with eagle eyes
> He stared at the Pacific – and all his men
> Looked at each other with a wild surmise –
> Silent, upon a peak in Darien.

Even a cursory reading of this will notice its many references to travel, exploration, discovery, and its allusions to great names of the distant past, Apollo, Homer, Cortez, Chapman. In general terms it speaks of states and kingdoms, as well as of reactions to events: seen, heard, felt, silent. And while the 'I' narrator claims to be an experienced traveller he has been humbled by this new encounter and a new perspective.

These are, of course, only a few of my own first impressions and it is important to remember that each reader will have different responses to the same material: there is not merely one, exclusive meaning to be extracted from the text. However, through these tentative impressions I have found a way into the poem, and can begin to fill them out.

The opening four lines point to the narrator's own personal experiences at first hand (travelled, seen, been), as well as to the sorts of locations of these (realms, states, kingdoms, islands). He creates the unmistakable impression of restlessness, a wanderer rather than a settler. He is a searcher, too, after something particular, undefined, and yet an explorer of old places rather than a discoverer of new ones.

And the title? How does it fit with all this? The title is important, I think, in a number of ways. It provides a strongly focused hint as to the precise meaning of the new experience but, at the same time, it creates a mild thrill of adventure, of danger even. The 'Chapman's Homer' of the title refers to the translation of Homer's ancient Greek epic poems by an Elizabethan writer, George Chapman. A friend of Keats had shown him a rare copy of the translation – and the impact on Keats was so strong that he wrote his poem practically in one sitting on the following morning.

I think that in this poem Keats has in mind Homer's *The Odyssey* because this depicts the vagrant wanderings of Odysseus/Ulysses around the islands and realms of the Mediterranean. And line 4 points directly at Homer as literally one of those 'bards in fealty to Apollo', one of the great poets inspired by Apollo, the classical god of writing.

So when Keats talks here of his extensive travels he is, of course, speaking metaphorically, using travel as a figure for reading, in the realms of gold – which implies the imagination and its capacity to expand in time as well as place. With this key figure of 'travel-as-reading' at the heart of the poem the next four lines come into sharper focus: although he is a voracious reader, Keats is admitting that he had only heard of the great reputation of 'deep-browed' Homer, never ventured into the works themselves. And then line 8 draws us to a momentary pause,

> Till I heard Chapman speak out loud and bold....

This prepares the reader for a change of voice in the final six lines. For one thing the closing section sets out Keats's response to his discovery of this brilliant translation, opening up his mind to exciting new visions as well as fresh perspectives on his own life. In a series of lively similes he is at once like an astronomer stumbling on a new planet, and then like a great explorer, 'stout Cortez', beholding a new horizon. Moreover, the many references in this part to seeing (in lines 9, 11, 12 and 13) clearly suggest his eyes having been suddenly opened up to undreamed-of realms. And the fact that he compares himself to a searching astronomer and to an explorer with a mission reveals to us that Keats now regards himself as purposive, directed, instead of a passive wanderer, merely drifting from place to place, from one random book to the next with no sense of a genuine objective in life.

Once we have focused on the metaphor of travel as reading it is easier to understand that at the heart of the poem is Keats's deeply felt sensitivity to literature. There is his profound belief too in the power of a text to transform the reader, to engage the reader's imagination and move him or her in unexpected ways. And for

Keats personally there is ultimately more: the power of the text to stir his own imagination to write poetry. Which is exactly what reading Chapman's Homer has caused him to do – to write this poem.

These points are also important because they touch on one of the key topics in Keats – his inquiry into the mysterious workings of the imagination, what he refers to as the 'realms of gold'. Ironically the theme of imagination also underlies what I have identified as the central metaphor of the poem. The success of the poem itself depends on the imagination of us too, the readers – it depends on our continuously drawing in impressions, actively making connections, challenging our interpretations.

And this is another reason why Keats equates the act of reading with that of travelling. By doing this he skilfully draws the reader into the poem in a way similar to that in which he himself was originally drawn into Chapman's translation of Homer. So, in a complex interaction the reader and the writer are drawn together by a shared experience.

Clearly, too, literature itself is a major theme of this poem. This is interesting for a variety of reasons. As a poet Keats became deeply self-conscious and self-critical about his own writing, and this poem offers an early insight onto this side of his artistic life. After the opening lines with their brash, ebullient claims, the writer is quickly humbled by the reality of his new vision.

In this way literature itself frequently figures as a key theme in his work as a whole. This fact is interesting here because of the way that the poem deftly brings into focus the role of the reader as a sort of traveller, navigating on a sea of literature. At the same time, in its references to other poets, it also invites a discussion of the role and place of the writer in relation to society and to other writers (and symbolically Homer is often venerated as the first poet).

From early on in his artistic life Keats's driving ambition was to achieve lasting fame as a poet. From this point of view, the daunting spectre of the 'deep-browed' Homer looming over the poem acts for Keats as an heroic objective as well as a sort of presiding judge. He is described as ruling his 'demesne' (or jurisdiction) and thus presents an image of something slightly menacing. Indeed the references to domains (realms, states, kingdoms, as well as demesne) together with the word 'fealty' create an aura of exclusion and tyranny, in which Keats has been made to feel like an intruder, out of his range. Until, that is, Chapman became his sage companion, urging Keats to speak out 'loud and bold' (line 8) as if to energise him to meet the challenge and to embrace the power of Apollo.

Keats's own emotions are very apparent here too. The poem announces an emotional awakening as well as an intellectual one. In line 9 he refers directly to feeling and, coming at this key point in the piece, this emphasises the change in attitude brought about by Chapman's translation. While the early part of the poem is emotionally quite subdued, the overall effect of Chapman's 'loud and bold' is to fire up the poem (as well as the poet) with the prospect of new and heightened experiences. Now there are 'eagle eyes' and 'wild surmise', and the emotion builds up towards the end of the poem until it reaches that pause created in the final line by the word 'Silent' and the comma which follows it. The result is to parallel the awe that Keats's own imagination had felt, moved deeply by the effect of literature reaching down into his poetic soul. At the end of the poem the themes of literature and emotion merge together.

We should turn now to look at some aspects of Keats's style and see how it is intimately linked with the subject matter. We have already considered something of the structure of the poem – a sonnet – and the change in direction and attitude at about lines 8 and 9. The sonnet was one of Keats's favourite poetic forms and the type he uses here is the Petrarchan sonnet, named after the Italian Renaissance poet Francesco Petrarca, or simply Petrarch. This type has a strong sense of structure, the fourteen lines being divided into eight (the octet or octave) and six (the sestet), and if you examine the rhyme scheme you can see how this too reflects the underlying thematic structure of the poem (ABBA ABBA – CDCDCD). With this in mind, notice the effect of the pivotal word 'Then' at the start of the sestet. On one level it operates to stress the narrative sequence: X happened then Y. But it also helps to signal the change in focus and feeling: in terms of emotion, the word has the effect of checking the subdued drift of the poem. It does this because it is a stressed word (just as the word 'Much' in line 1 is a stressed word, seizing the reader's attention at the outset). To test the stress of this word

('Then') try reading line 9 as 'I felt then like some watcher of the
skies': it simply does not create the same tenacity.

Keats is especially scrupulous in both the choice and positioning
of his words. Let us examine other examples. In the opening line his
expression 'the realms of gold' is a memorable phrase in the mind.
But what does it mean? I have already suggested that it refers
metaphorically to the imagination but we can equally look at it in
more simple terms. Gold? The best, of course, precious, uncor-
rupted. He is referring to books, to the classics, ageless, great or
famous, and they are 'gold' because of their reputation . . . even if they
are not quite popular with everyone.

Or 'gold' may refer to the gold leaf on the pages of the book and
on the spine in luxury bindings. So Keats has read the best, or
thought he had, but what he took to be the best turns out to be
overshadowed by the new experience of reading Chapman's translation. The phrase then takes on a rapture of its own, extending into
the golden recesses of the imagination. And the imagination is crucial
as a defining characteristic of nineteenth-century Romanticism as a
whole as well as of Keats's own verse. Physical journeys can be great
adventures but they rarely compare in excitement and power to those
invoked by the imagination.

Keats has a soft spot for archaic words too. Sometimes this is the
result of his reading English classics like Shakespeare, Chaucer and
Edmund Spenser, and their diction rubs off on his poetry – usually
consciously. Sometimes however, he deliberately drops in an out-
dated term just to give his verse the patina of age, or to make it sound
erudite (and in Keats's day there was also a fashion for medieval verse
– with some poets even trying to pass off their work as genuinely
medieval). In the present poem, 'goodly', 'oft', 'demesne' and 'ken'
have a decorative function as well as carrying important meanings.
Taking 'demesne', for example, it is important here because by
suggesting a private world it underlines the idea that Keats feels
himself to be an intruder in the closeted world of literature, an
outsider.

Less obscure words can be just as fruitful. For example, why is
Homer 'deep-browed'? Why does Cortez have 'eagle eyes'? And what
is the effect of 'serene' – used in line 7 as a noun, not as an adjective?

Syntax and sentence type are also important. We have noted the structural effect of the words 'Much' and 'Then'. The octet consists of four fairly flat statements, a catalogue of experiences. But after the narrator's discovery of Chapman's text the sentence structure becomes more complex: the sestet contains a pair of extended sentences that build up towards a climax, a climax which is brilliantly suspended until the final line and that dramatic pause after the word 'Silent'. Notice, too, the differences in punctuation in the two sections of the poem; how do these parallel the themes and moods in each part?

You will have spotted the reversal of normal syntax in lines 1 and 3 ('have I'), line 5 ('had I'), line 7 ('did I') and line 9 ('felt I'), and while Keats undoubtedly used these to fit the rhythm or 'metre' of the lines he was also, I think, attracted to the poetic aura which they create. They echo the rhetoric of some classical models (such as Milton) and thus help to bolster up what is after all quite a youthful poem.

As we might expect, many of the individual words carry strong metaphorical effect. We have already noted the central metaphor of 'reading-as-travel'. The references to real people – Chapman, Homer, Cortez and the unnamed astronomer – all work on the literal level but as great names they also carry metaphorical force as giants of Western culture and as icons of fame. So at the same time they are both intimidating yet also enticing to someone in pursuit of fame. In the latter respect the mention of Apollo is significant too. As the Greek god of verse he represents for Keats a personal deity and so his appearance here can be seen as Keats signalling to his readers that he has real poetic ambitions, enlisting the god as a sort of totem, a badge or talisman.

Keats is as scrupulous about the sounds of the poem – including rhythm and rhyme – as he is about their meaning, perhaps more so. He has the ear as much as the eye. For this reason you will always get more from a Keats poem if it is read aloud. For instance, try lines 5 and 6, or 11 and 12, and note what is interesting about their sounds.

Alliteration alone makes the poem a pure delight. Take a look at the sounds in the opening two lines and note the repetition of the 'm' sound. Its effect? Perhaps it gives the start an underlying insistence, a resolve. And then lines 4 and 5 have a number of 'w' sounds (including that at the end of 'Apollo'). Together with the open vowels in those lines the 'w' supports the sense of awe at the spaces referred to. Then, particularly in the sestet, the alliterative /s/ makes a significant contribution to the sonnet. Try reading it aloud and note the result.

In terms of assonance, or the vowel sounds, the long /ee/ predominates and this, together with other repeated long vowels, perhaps enhances the muscular determination which coils through the poem.

In more general terms sound has quite a range of functions. On a fairly simple level the sheer variety of sounds gives the poem intense musical interest, adding an extra dimension to the overall experience. At the same time, Keats manipulates sound (as well as pauses, or 'caesurae') for special local effect as we saw in the reversals above and in the poeticisms 'Oft' and 'stout'. The names in the poem, too, carry rhetorical effect in addition to their literal meaning. The richness of the poem's sounds complements the exotic settings in it, the 'realms of gold', the aura of a historic period, hinting at magic and adventure. Moreover, Keats indulges in sound play purely and simply for the exquisite effects on the ear, as in the phrase 'pure serene' (7), a taste of the many aural delights to come in his later work.

We now need to draw together all of these critical strands to make an appraisal of the poem. A large measure of the poem's appeal lies in its simplicity, which works through the plainness of its diction. It is an elegant, honest affirmation of the poet's discovery of the charm of literature and the potency of the imagination. He delights in the ability of literature to open up the imagination to new worlds, to jolt the reader's complacency sideways.

I mentioned earlier how Keats composed the poem almost immediately after reading Chapman's translation of Homer's epic tales. The freshness of his rising excitement still comes breaking through the measured restraint of the octet. His frankness is both clear and succinct. This is a landmark poem, heralding Keats's mastery of the sonnet form, and as such declares his arrival as a gifted and committed artist; the poem itself announces this explicitly but its technical accomplishments confirm it with deep conviction. It is the first of

Keats's genuinely original poems, revealing his versatility in summoning a range of poetic techniques – form, diction, sound, and theme – towards a deeply held purpose.

However, there are one or two awkward moments: for example, the phrases 'Oft of one' (line 5) and 'swims into his ken' (10) grate a little, and it was not Cortez but Vasco de Balbao who led the first Europeans to view the Pacific from South America. Yet none of this detracts materially from the breathtaking success of the poem.

Against this, and finally, Keats holds our interest through a host of striking techniques: the bold intimacy of the 'I' narrator; the easy manipulation of sounds and silences; and the poem's skill in synthesising a diversity of references – classical mythology, a renaissance Spanish explorer, an Elizabethan translator and an eighteenth-century scientist. All within the space of fourteen lines! The poem bubbles with ripening self-confidence.

I have suggested that 'On First Looking into Chapman's Homer' signals a turning point in Keats's development as a poet. To fully appreciate the extent of his achievement here, though, it is illuminating to take a look at some of the earliest verse by Keats; for example, try 'On Peace' (written in spring 1814) or 'Ode to Apollo' (February 1815), both of which show the young writer's promise, yet to me they are loosely constructed, too derivative and lack the sharp focus of 'Chapman's Homer'.

We have made a positive start to our study of Keats's verse and I think it would be useful to follow this with discussion of another sonnet, written at about the same time, though our discussion will be somewhat briefer.

'Keen, fitful gusts are whispering here and there'

'Keen, fitful gusts are whispering here and there' was written in the same month as 'On First Looking into Chapman's Homer' (October 1816) and was included by Keats in his first published volume of poetry. My approach in discussing the two sonnets here is not to rank them one above the other but simply to draw out the characteristics

of Keats's early verse while at the same time broadening the range of
our own critical techniques and terminology.

> Keen, fitful gusts are whispering here and there
> Among the bushes half leafless, and dry;
> The stars look very cold about the sky,
> And I have many miles on foot to fare.
> Yet feel I little of the cool bleak air,   5
> Or of the dead leaves rustling drearily,
> Or of those silver lamps that burn on high,
> Or of the distance from home's pleasant lair:
> For I am brimful of the friendliness
> That in a little cottage I have found;   10
> Of fair-haired Milton's eloquent distress,
> And all his love for gentle Lycid drowned:
> Of lovely Laura in her light green dress,
> And faithful Petrarch gloriously crowned.

First impressions? Again it is told by a first-person narrator, 'I'. It
is dominated by two principal images: a bleak natural scene in cold
night air, followed by memories of a contrasting warm interior, a
cottage visited by the poet. The octet focuses on the imminent
ordeal of a lonely return home, while the sestet rings with convivial
society and references to literature. The diction in general is clear and
accessible but certain words stand out (such as 'keen', 'lair', 'gentle
Lycid' and 'crowned') and these may call for individual discussion.
Interestingly, although it is a short simple poem it does contain
strong elements of narrative together with Keats's more familiar
lyrical effects.

It is not difficult to spot that nature is one of the poem's cardinal
points, both as setting and as theme. But what we need to consider
here is Keats's attitude to nature. Overtly, lines 2 and 5 recall a cold
and desolate scene, and line 6 links it with death. On the other hand,
it is not especially wild (the wind 'whispering' and dead leaves 'rustling') since it permits Keats to reflect lucidly on the evening's discussion. Yet the poet's acute sensitivity to the details of the location allows
him to select key impressionistic features that will spark the reader's
own imagination into filling out the scene.

It is a poem of contrasts too. As an example, note the contrast between that narrow space at his feet where the leaves are rustling and the vast reaches of the distant stars (those 'silver lamps', line 7). This opens up a distinct feeling of expansiveness which in turn magnifies his isolation. Notice too the contrast of dark and light in the two parts of the sonnet, each a foil to the other: combined with the great expanse of space, it points up the emotional gap between the two scenes.

Keats's response to the natural scene in the octet is characteristically a *felt* one. Having said that, he does take up an unexpected angle on the scene. The night outside is cold and harsh and he is alone; yet in spite of this he is resolute and self-possessed. He faces the prospect of his 'many miles on foot' with composure and is surprisingly uplifted by the memory of the 'friendliness' of the evening's conviviality. The cold air envelops and yet increases his inner warmth and well-being: 'Yet feel I little of the cool bleak air' (line 5).

As we would now expect, Keats uses the octet–sestet division in the sonnet as a turning point in both setting and theme. In the sestet, homeward bound, the poet recalls a very sociable evening at his friend's cottage (in fact the home of Leigh Hunt). Their eager talk has been of literature; *Lycidas* is a poem written by John Milton in memory of a young drowned poet, while Laura was the cherished subject of Petrarch's sonnets. Keats is 'brimful of friendliness' but obviously also brimful of literary talk. The cold night urges him on while the warm intoxicating effect of the evening, its words still buzzing excitedly in his mind, fills him with inner radiance.

On this literal level, then, Keats superbly evokes that warm afterglow from conversations held late into the night, weary but with words still echoing inside. On the metaphorical level there are some thematic reminders of the sonnet 'On First Looking into Chapman's Homer': particularly in terms of the journey and the literary subject, and we should now take a deeper look at these.

Conversation about literary matters has, of course, fired up Keats's poetic imagination (in fact, it has led to the writing of this sonnet). Furthermore it has, I believe, pricked his conscience about his own poetic ambition. Thus the journey can be understood as an oblique reference, like 'Chapman's Homer', to Keats's proposed career as a poet.

Like many poets, Keats makes special use of key positions or
markers in a poem to draw attention to particular words or ideas;
an obvious example is the first or last words in a poem or section. So
here the words 'keen' (hinting at ambition) and 'crowned' (hinting at
the success of that ambition) occupy significant positions and help to
hold the poem together. In this way the poem itself represents a
movement or journey, from ambition to success – or so Keats
intends it to be anyway.

This metaphor can be opened up further. How, for example, are
we to interpret the 'whisperings' on this route: as self-doubt? or as
the hostility of critics? It is certain to be a test of endurance, for 'I
have many miles on foot to fare' (line 4). As a young poet Keats is
very much aware of his own inexperience and uncertainty but at the
same time is encouraged by his literary friends and their bookish
talk; observe the contrast between the bleak 'half leafless' reality of
where he stands now and the cheer suggested by Laura's 'light green
dress' (line 13), a figure for the eventual achievement of his poetic
goal.

Meanwhile there lurk other threats to his endeavour. The reference
to 'Lycid' in line 12 recalls the premature death of another aspiring
poet, mourned by Milton as a symbol of unfulfilled promise. It is, of
course, both a warning and a spur to Keats to bring his growing
talents to ripeness.

As I have indicated above, Keats's ear and eye for the right word are
acute. Individual words have a habit of unlocking rich new veins of
meaning and thus they invite our close attention. 'Keen, fitful gusts', as
we have just seen, offers good examples of this. In general terms
Keats's diction is simple and clear, without archaisms, and his syntax is
on the whole regular (with just the one reversal, in line 5). He creates a
relaxed conversational atmosphere with the same air of freshness as if
he had only just spoken these words before parting. His buoyant
mood is supported by the poem's use of an intimate first person, 'I',
narrator and the poem is in effect a sort of dramatic soliloquy.

On the other hand, the word 'lair' stumbles on the modern ear (it
can mean simply bed or haven) and the adjective 'gentle' in line 12 is
perhaps too demure. They are examples of those minor blips of
inexperience that the poem itself hints at.

Sentences too are conversational in style and rhythm. The conjunctions 'yet' and 'for' point to the logical progression of a simple argument. However, the repetition of the conjunction 'Or' at the beginning of lines 6, 7 and 8 has a more complex outcome: while denying the unpleasant conditions of the cold bleak night, each line actually sets them up firmly in the reader's mind. Then the word 'Or' is balanced by the word 'Of', in lines 11 and 13 in the sestet, implying that the bleakness is cancelled out by the poet's happy memory of the evening.

The poem is so well crafted that Keats smoothly combines the nature imagery in the octet with the literary references in the sestet without any great sense of either being forced. Other imagery is equally subtle. Note the allusions to sound – in 'whispering', 'rustling', 'eloquent', and yet at the same time a peculiar stillness inhabits the poem (as frequently happens in the best of Keats's verse).

The sonnet itself seems to whisper intimately to the reader through its own recurring consonant sounds, especially the sibilant /s/ and /f/. The repetition of the brittle /l/ consonant also tries to emulate the rustling of the dry crumbling leaves, echoed again in the sestet, in lines 12 and 13. In line 9 the change in mood is paralleled by the change in vowel sounds, which in general become more open (see lines 11 to 14) after the mainly /ee/ and /er/ syllables in the octet. The effect is to point up the rise in spirit which climaxes in the final word 'crowned'.

Our discussion of 'Keen, fitful gusts' has necessarily been limited to a few key areas. However, the poem undoubtedly rewards more detailed analysis of its style. At the same time our brief investigation has focused on separate elements of the poem and it is important to go back and re-read it in order to get a more complete picture and to understand how these elements work together.

We have noted how Keats uses the 8 + 6 sonnet structure to set up contrasts (light/dark, solitude/companionship) and to draw out the drama of these contrasts. Yet we do not feel it is a divided production. For one thing the poem is, of course, united by the 'I' voice throughout and there are subtle touches like the repetition of the word 'little' (lines 5 and 10) and the twin references to light (7 and 13). The pivotal word 'For' (9) acts as a connective, looking both ways, as well as offering a new starting point (compare the word 'Then' in 'Chapman's Homer'). Keats produces unity too in the different ways that he generates the reader's interest; for example, the poem opens with some mystery, then there are two surprise lines (5 and 9), and there is the gradually uplifting mood, which gathers pace through to that climactic word 'crowned'. (To compare a slightly different, more emotional treatment of a similar theme take a look at the sonnet 'On Leaving some Friends at an Early Hour', which was written in the same month as 'Keen, fitful gusts'.)

Keats's success in this poem springs from his precision on the one hand and his lightness of touch on the other. His judgement is finely tuned. The result is a marvellous lyric, achieved in a mere fourteen lines, pulling together theme, setting, feeling and sound into a nicely balanced form. But as well as its obvious lyrical attitude it also presents a small-scale narrative, anticipating two of Keats's more fully worked accounts in this first collection, namely '*I stood tip-toe upon a little hill*' and *Sleep and Poetry*.

'I stood tip-toe upon a little hill'

Sometime during June 1816 Keats took a stroll to visit an acquaintance in what was then the rural hamlet of Hampstead, just outside London. Pausing by a gate he became enraptured by the mood of the occasion. It was for him a sublime instant, in which the rural scene of sky, meadow and woodland coalesced with a sudden burst of joy. It was also a time when he had become aware of and resolute in his destiny as a poet. So, not surprisingly, it created a moment of powerful significance for him – and it was followed by other such euphoric moments that summer. Together they worked to convince Keats that he had made the right decision in abandoning a career in medicine for one in literature. And one of the immediate outcomes of this was the poem '*I stood tip-toe upon a little hill*'.

By this point in his literary life Keats was thoroughly adept at composing sonnets – he could and did rattle them off to order (frequently in timed competitions with the poets Shelley and Leigh Hunt). But he was convinced that the best verse was long verse.

Sonnets offered a decent formal challenge but the great poets had always, he believed, written at length. In his first volume of verse, *Poems* (1817), the two longest poems are '*I stood tip-toe upon a little hill*' and *Sleep and Poetry* and significantly they were placed at the beginning and the end respectively of the collection. Clearly their author intended them to play an important role as the sentinels of the volume.

'*I stood tip-toe*' is composed as a series of connected sections which together form a sort of narrative development as well as a loosely threaded argument. Using a first-person narrator once again, Keats gives full rein to his brilliant lyrical skill in the depiction of the natural landscape but, significantly, he makes use of this graphic setting to explore ideas on poetic sensitivity and the imagination, themes which recur throughout the whole of his work. It also marks an early appearance for some mythological figures which receive important treatment later: Psyche, Pan, Diana and Endymion, as well as Apollo.

The section I have chosen to explore is one of the most interesting and complex in the poem, lines 93–132. Compared with his lyric verse, Keats's longer and narrative poems present a different sort of challenge for analysis and so I will also be using the passage as a starting point for a wider discussion of the poem as a whole.

> Were I in such a place, I sure should pray   93
> That naught less sweet, might call my thoughts away,
> Than the soft rustle of a maiden's gown
> Fanning away the dandelion's down;
> Than the light music of her nimble toes
> Patting against the sorrel as she goes.
> How she would start, and blush, thus to be caught
> Playing in all her innocence of thought.   100
> O let me lead her gently o'er the brook,
> Watch her half-smiling lips, and downward look;
> O let me for one moment touch her wrist;
> Let me one moment to her breathing list;
> And as she leaves me may she often turn
> Her fair eyes looking through her locks auburn.
> What next? A tuft of evening primroses,

O'er which the mind may hover till it dozes;
O'er which it well might take a pleasant sleep,
But that 'tis ever startled by the leap   110
Of buds into ripe flowers; or by the flitting
Of diverse moths, that aye their rest are quitting;
Or by the moon lifting her silver rim
Above a cloud, and with a gradual swim
Coming into the blue with all her light.
O Maker of sweet poets, dear delight
Of this fair world, and all its gentle livers;
Spangler of clouds, halo of crystal rivers,
Mingler with leaves, and dew and tumbling streams,
Closer of lovely eyes to lovely dreams,   120
Lover of loneliness, and wandering,
Of upcast eye, and tender pondering!
Thee must I praise above all other glories
That smile us on to tell delightful stories.
For what has made the sage or poet write
But the fair paradise of Nature's light?
In the calm grandeur of a sober line,
We see the waving of the mountain pine;
And when a tale is beautifully staid,
We feel the safety of a hawthorn glade: 130
When it is moving on luxurious wings,
The soul is lost in pleasant smotherings.

This important section follows Keats's keynote reference to
Apollo (line 50) with its strong hint that he is concerned as much
to discuss the art of poetry itself as the many charms of nature. These
charms are evoked in the highly controlled impressions of the stream
and its banks. In lines 63 to 69, through a careful alignment of diction
(chiefly its adjectives) he conjures an almost tangible vision of the
tranquil bower, cool, moist, abundant with plant and animal life,
whose lives are all bound together in organic unity.

So, on one level, nature is associated with bliss and harmony. In
his emphasis on the mood of the picture Keats draws attention
of course to the capacity of nature to affect individual human
emotion and psychology. In line 108 he talks of how 'the mind

may hover till it dozes' and later of how the bubbling stream 'Charms us away from all our troubles' (138). Where in the sonnet 'Keen, fitful gusts are whispering here and there' Keats talked of his mood in spite of nature, here he explores his harmony with it. Yet he does not merge fully with nature (as some Romantic poets strove to do); he remains lucidly conscious of its effects on himself and of his relationship with it (in spite of nature's own 'pleasant smotherings', line 132).

This awareness of relationship is important too in another way: that is, in terms of Keats's ideas about poetic creativity. Here, and in other early poems, we continually encounter his image of the woven bower of bliss, a centre of calm and escape from the clamour and demands of the everyday urban world. This, for Keats, is where nature comes alive spiritually (and morally) to refresh the mind and the body. Yet, for the poet it is also the point at which he or she becomes energised to create art; the tranquillity induces a form of sacred silence in which their creative energy can be tellingly released (lines 125–6).

Moreover, this religious concept of bliss-in-nature ties in with Keats's use of mythology in the poem. To prepare us for this he has already referred to a couple of classical figures: Mercury (line 24) and Apollo (line 50). Yet at first it seems odd that in a beautifully lyrical poem about an English woodland walk he should even mention Greek and Roman mythology at all. However, Keats's justification of this lies at the very centre of his theory of the imagination in this poem.

At about line 93 Keats's mind reaches that state of blissful harmony which I have just described. At this moment his imagination takes over in a faintly erotic fantasy concerning a nymph who drifts sensuously across his path. Blushing at her discovery, she denies his vague urgings ('O let me') because, as Diana, she is here the goddess of chastity, re-materialising later as the moon, 'her silver rim / Above a cloud...' (113–14). Her 'appearance' prepares the way for that of other mytho-logical characters following this extract – and leads eventually to the tale of Endymion and Diana herself.

Keats visualises this tranquil natural scene as a kind of gateway by which human beings can become spiritually vitalised. He uses the phrase 'tip-toe' in the poem's opening line, and in other poems, to suggest a condition of being poised between two differing states, amphibious. Then, through the active process of the imagination, humans are thus able to transcend this mundane world of the senses to enter the realm of the spirit (metaphorically, at least). At that point the individual comes alive to a new, higher layer of experience in nature. Mythology represents for Keats this higher, spiritual layer, which becomes accessible through the imagination, and the appearance of the nymph in line 95 may suggest this.

Because this is a higher realm, Keats sees it in moral terms too. Since they are both regions of calm, nature and mythology can symbolise order, even perfect order, so that under their inspiration the poet is able to conceive verse of a sublime power,

> For what has made the sage or poet write
> But the fair paradise of Nature's light?
>
> (125–6)

And when poetry is inspired in this way, when it achieves a 'calm grandeur' or is 'beautifully staid' (that is, steady or balanced, line 129), it can intoxicate the reader too. In this way literature can share with nature the power to beguile the soul of man:

> When it is moving on luxurious wings,
> The soul is lost in pleasant smotherings.
>
> (131–2)

Keats's strategy here is highly sophisticated. Observe how he moves almost imperceptibly from the natural setting in a wood (93–115), to a theory of literature (116–26), and on to suggestions of religious belief (lines 127 on). What he outlines is a view of the poet as a visionary – a gifted individual who is able to see beyond the appearances of the physical world into the reality that underlies it. In this way he strongly aligns himself with the ancient poets who invented the stories of mythology to make sense and order out of what they took to be a world of chaos, 'bringing / Shapes from the invisible world' (185–6).

In our two previous poems Keats had looked at poetry from the point of view of the reader but here (and in *Sleep and Poetry*) he focuses on the theory and process of *creativity*; that is, from the point of view of the writer. He knew that it was a great challenge for any nineteenth-century poet to recover and refresh the ancient myths and he sets out to achieve this by recapturing the exact vision that inspired the classical writers themselves. We shall need to evaluate Keats's achievements in this ambitious project but, before we do, let us next examine more closely some aspects of his style in this section of the poem.

Here, as in the rest of the poem, Keats fluctuates between descriptions of natural settings and accounts of ghostly mythological figures. This approach hints at the interrelationship between the two but later, from line 141 on, it even permits Keats to steer the reader's attention towards the realm of myth but also towards an outline of his theory of poetics. At the same time the variation in viewpoint helps to maintain the reader's involvement by setting up a resonance between the physical world of nature and of the senses, and the transcendental world of the gods.

Here more than in earlier sections Keats's own voice and emotions are held under strict control. He seems tentative, an explorer once again, tremulously testing out the exotic (and erogenous) zones bordering on the spirit world. All the same, we feel that strong emotions are never far from the surface and they do eventually emerge more fully after this section in an oxymoron which aims at expressing the narrator's complex feelings,

> . . . a half heard strain,
> Full of sweet desolation – balmy pain.

> (161–2)

Throughout his writing, Keats repeatedly draws attention to the complex moment of almost simultaneous joy and sorrow. In the extract we can hear a gradual crescendo of joy in the words 'pleasant' (109), 'delight' (116), 'lovely' (120 twice), 'glories' (123), and 'luxurious wings' (131). But immediately following this the mood quickly swoons into melancholy, the pang of sensual pleasure (hinted at here

in the exclamatory 'O' in lines 101, 103, and 116). As an intricate
emotion (of 'balmy pain') this sweet melancholy is personified by
Narcissus, who appears in lines 163 to 180, a complex entanglement
of sensual indulgence, torment and desire (see also 'Ode to a Nightingale', stanza I).

The poem as a whole has numerous references to 'lovely' and to
physical sensuality, and the imagery in general expresses the profuse
pleasures of Keats's setting: for example its sounds (see lines 95 and
97), touch (103), and the many references to visual delights as well as
to vision itself (such as in line 106). Literature luxuriates in 'pleasant
smotherings', with its characteristic Keatsian undertones of release
and abandon, eroticised here by the cool restraint of the quiet stream
(101) and the pale chastity of Diana (95).

In more general terms the imagery as a whole enmeshes neatly
with these themes, as we would expect it to. For example, release and
abandon are paralleled here and in other sections through the imagery of escape, of birds and flight (see especially lines 111 and 131).
Escape is suggested too by references to drowsiness and sleep (for
example, lines 108–9 and 120) while desolation is made coolly explicit
in the allusion to solitude in line 121.

Keats's great excitement in the rich fabric of sense detail is
unmistakable, bringing his scenes alive and up-tempo, with a voice
which itself seems occasionally to be 'on tip-toe'. In this way the
drama of the poem is enacted through the release of energies briefly
constrained within this rich fabric; in other words the diversity of the
imagery helps to give the poem much of its dramatic interest while
holding out the exhilarating promise of freedom.

And, of course, it *is* freedom; it is not anarchy. Yet if this is
freedom then how does Keats manage to control his creation? One
source of control is the poet's own conscious and unifying narrative
voice throughout the poem. Another is the more formal control
found in the regularity of the verse itself, its rhyme and rhythm.
Keats uses traditional heroic couplets here, pairs of rhymed lines in
iambic pentameter, presenting a very ordered, consistent texture. If
you are unfamiliar with this verse form then the following is a good
example of a regular couplet, taken from the beginning of the passage
(the stressed syllables are highlighted):

> Were **I** in **such** a **place**, I **sure** should **pray**
> That **naught** less **sweet**, might **call** my **thoughts** away
>
> (93–4)

(for another regular example, see lines 129–30).

This poetic form provides a methodical discipline or framework for the verse. Having said that, however, I should note that Keats still tries to inject some variety and a more conversational tone by breaking the routine of the iambic line with irregular stresses (see lines 112 and 118 for instance) and by varying the number of syllables within the line (check lines 111 and 125; and see also lines 48 and 50).

In terms of the rhyme, too, a regular heroic couplet runs the risk of sliding into tedious repetition – and at its worst it can sound a bit like a sort of pantomime refrain. So, as we might expect, Keats adopts a range of devices to lessen the impact of the final syllable of a line. One simple device is the use of enjambement or run-over lines, allowing a sentence to flow over two or more lines (for examples, see lines 97–8, 110–11 and so on). Another is to make use of caesurae – mid-line breaks – to minimise the pause on the line end, the rhyming syllable, as in lines 93–4. In addition, a very effective technique used extensively and successfully by Keats is internal rhyme. This can best be seen over a series of lines, for example,

> We see the waving of the mountain pine;
> And when a tale is beautifully staid,
> We feel the safety of a hawthorn glade.
>
> (128–30)

Notice here how Keats repeats that /ai/ sound in 'waving', 'tale', 'staid', 'safety', 'glade', and the /ee/ of 'see', 'beautifully', and 'safety'. As well as taking some attention away from the end-line rhymes this cross-rhyme also creates melody and helps to hold the verse together, networking the sounds into a web. There are numerous other examples in the poem but you could look at lines 103–6 and trace the pattern there; also, look back at the two sonnets we analysed earlier and compare Keats's technique there with that in '*I stood tip-toe*'.

We can now draw all these various observations together. By far the
most beautiful part of the poem is the first 180 or so lines. It bursts
with a brilliantly sinewy lyricism of minute detailed observation. It is
loaded with more and still more music and pictorial charm – or at
least as much as any poem can reasonably bear without buckling
under the weight of its own copious imagery. Keats's excitement and
freshness continually break through the detail,

> Open afresh your round of starry folds,
> Ye ardent marigolds!
> Dry up the moisture from your golden lids,
> For great Apollo bids...
>
> (47–50)

It is without doubt an ambitious poem. It is also a young man's
poem and it has the faults of youthful verse (as well as some of its
virtues). There are discomforts such as the clumsy choice of 'aye'
(lines 70 and 183), and those dainty adjectives like 'gently', 'sweet' and
'little' are too twee for modern ears. Most of the faults are in fact the
result of Leigh Hunt's sentimental influence (the dedicatory quotation comes from his *The Story of Rimini*). On the other hand, Hunt was
surely right when he reviewed the poem as a 'piece of luxury',
displaying 'all that fertile power of association and imagery which
constitutes the abstract poetical faculty'.

By comparison with other verse written by Keats at this time, '*I
stood tip-toe*' is emotionally restrained – its burgeoning feelings are
curbed by the stubborn momentum of the verse and the rationalism
of its themes, as well as by the structural demands of the verse form,
which we have already noted.

There is some urgency about these feelings however, which seems
to me to be wholly truthful. In addition Keats does well to convince us
of the values in his themes. The boldness of his project testifies to his
growing self-confidence as a poet (at a time when he was subject to
some gnawing self-doubts about his talents). Not merely does he set
out to reinstate some outmoded classical figures in a contemporary
narrative but he drives this unlikely material into a very credible theory

of poetics, uniting nature and mythology within it. In the same breath he boldly ventures to generate poetry that will match nature itself in terms of its 'pleasant smotherings', seducing and subverting the reader. And the 'tip-toe' of the title directly points us to this stealing ambition.

That said, however, the poem's glaring weaknesses come about as a direct result of its author's overreaching ambition, in particular his drive to write a fashionably long piece. The result overall is a loose and rambling production. To be kind we might say that its length permits Keats to capture the freshness and spontaneity of the original experiences as well as the unsorted aura of discovery. And equally, we could say that the plot is less concerned with external events than with the internal, the subtle progress of a burgeoning mind (a scenario that Keats takes up again in *The Fall of Hyperion*).

But it cannot be denied that the early energy and focus of the poem are sadly dissipated by its length. Its many strands become increasingly divergent and their purposes masked by growing wordiness until Keats eventually, and abruptly, dumps it. It is as though he had suddenly become distracted by the more thrilling prospect of working up the Endymion/Diana story into a full and separate treatment (as indeed he was soon to do).

Unhappily, most of Keats's early attempts at narrative verse are also undermined by their excessive length (see, for example, *Calidore. A Fragment* and *Sleep and Poetry*). Yet in '*I stood tip-toe*' he successfully sustains the reader's interest, for most of the poem anyway. For one thing, there is the poem's imaginative richness, its images and settings, and for another there is the frankness and sharpness of the poet's responses to these scenes and to 'events'. Keats's own particular point of view is also something new here – in both its style and its concepts. And we should not overlook the significance of the poem's conflict between desire and frustration among the immortals (a parallel to that of Keats's own aspirations behind the poem) even if by the end this conflict remains largely unresolved.

We can also measure Keats's achievements in this poem by setting it alongside another poem of similar ambition, *Sleep and Poetry*, which was completed in the same month as '*I stood tip-toe*'. The author himself appears to have regarded it as a companion piece and, not surprisingly, it shares similar interests as well as similar techniques. I

would therefore like to complete this chapter with a discussion of
some of the themes and the style of *Sleep and Poetry*, though I have not
taken any particular extract for detailed study.

Sleep and Poetry

Like '*I stood tip-toe*', *Sleep and Poetry* is constructed in a series of sections
and Keats again employs heroic couplets. The opening sections extol
the benefits of sleep in all its mysterious facets, such as its tranquillity,
its regenerative powers and the ability to induce strong imaginative
visions. Keat prostrates himself before the figure of Poesy, humbly
confessing his inexperience, and then pays homage to Apollo his
protective spirit. With Apollo's encouragement and sanction he
would endeavour to 'seize the events of the wide world' (81) and
through his verse give them 'Wings to find out an immortality' (84;
compare this with '*I stood tip-toe*', lines 130–1).

Once again, Keats clearly sets out his desire to win poetic fame, yet
now he is acutely conscious of the transience of human life (symbolised by the butterfly at line 343): 'life is but a day; / A fragile dew-
drop...' (85–6). Ironically, though, this brief span is what gives
intensity to life's rich pleasures and, in a famous passage, he begs
for a guarantee of life, 'O for ten years' (96), in which to dedicate
himself to the service of Poesy.

As if in answer to his prayer, a mysterious charioteer now enters
the poem. It is another manifestation of Apollo, now the sun-god.
But the charioteer also personifies the faculty of the imagination.
With this established Keats launches his attack on the British poets of
the eighteenth century, chiefly for their scorn of the imagination and
for their over-formulaic approach to composition: 'lined out with
wretched rule / And compass vile...' (195–6).

Poetry, he argues, is more than simply the discussion of themes. It
requires music too and imagination, if it is to fulfil its greatest endeavour, 'To soothe the cares, and lift the thoughts of man' (247). Embracing
the rising generation of Romantic poets, Keats defiantly claims his place
among the fellowship of readers and writers: the essence of artistic
creativity is to be achieved by recognising the community of mankind.

At length his passion subsides, surrounded by the busts and books in Leigh Hunt's library where Keats had slept the night, and the poem closes in that peace and refreshment which had originally stirred him to write.

In comparison with the previous poem, *Sleep and Poetry* is both a more abstract and a more passionate composition, particularly in its discussion of Keats's poetic theory. However, his arguments are frequently obscured by his poeticisms and by the weight of questions which he explicitly raises (see the opening eleven lines and lines 270–5). But what we are clear about by the end is both the conviction and the anger in Keats's voice.

Perhaps because it was motivated by a night in a library rather than by a summer walk, *Sleep and Poetry* is a much less lyrical, less congenial composition than '*I stood tip-toe*'. The questions it raises (as well as the answers it offers) are more arid, usually referring to literary or bookish matters, for example: What is the proper subject of poetry? What are the role and nature of a poet, particularly with regard to his society and the claims on his talents? And what is the importance in poetry of nature, the imagination and mythology?

There is no doubt about the gravitas of these issues. Yet, as Keats himself points out, poetry has got to offer more than just academic discussion about intellectual themes ('themes / Are ugly clubs', line 234); it should be 'sweet music' and 'fine sounds' too (223–8). So on his own terms his poem ought to offer us more than this, must give us the 'sweet music' too. His poem can be judged in part by this.

The poem raises other questions too. Chief among them is the question of what Keats means by 'sleep'. On a fairly simple level, sleep here is rest; it is ease and escape, refreshing the mind and body after work and offering relief from the hard realities of daily life (see lines 11 to 15). It offers relief from the ever-present consciousness and is therefore 'higher beyond thought' (line 19). On this level it is worth comparing here the much later poem 'To Sleep', a brilliantly succinct treatment of a similar theme.

Sleep is important too for the creative mind; it is 'The silence when some rhymes are coming out' (321). Which links with a similar idea in '*I stood tip-toe*', the idea that a state of calm is an essential state of mind if the Romantic imagination is to function to its best.

Silence too is referred to throughout the poem as an adjunct to sleep (see lines 68, 120 and 278) and in the later verse it is often associated with good health. This carried great personal importance for Keats, living as he did in the noise and grime of urban London. By contrast, Hunt's Hampstead cottage was a bower of bliss (a 'bowery nook', line 63) and its library a cultural idyll.

Furthermore, sleep is a relief from the turmoil of passion. Not just from sexual yearnings but also from the grinding agitation of conscience, change, uncertainty, politics, ambition, all threatening to overthrow his artistic poise. And, typically, Keats closely relates 'sleep' and silence with solitude, as here in this poem.

In this specialised sense of a 'higher consciousness' sleep is another metaphor of the imagination. We are once again in the 'realms of gold'. Yet what, exactly, does Keats mean here by linking sleep with the imagination? Is it dreams, or the fancy, or simply the unconscious? Samuel Taylor Coleridge, a highly influential Romantic poet and philosopher, conceived of the imagination as a dynamic centre of the creative mind, actively shaping and ordering perceptions and ideas. However, Keats has not worked out his own concept to the same degree, and his personification of the charioteer/imagination tends to obscure his full intentions. What he seems to be getting at in his own idea of the imagination lies in the substance behind these lines.

> And many a verse from so strange influence
> That we must ever wonder how, and whence
> It came. Also imaginings will hover
> Round my fire-side, and haply there discover
> Vistas of solemn beauty...
>
> (69–73)

To put it simply, for Keats the imagination is a relatively passive mechanism, similar to dreaming, beyond his control, and hence 'we must ever wonder how'. Yet, at the same time, it works a mysterious creativity deep in the unconscious. It is something that must be allowed space and tranquillity to 'meander' (74) and to blossom in full. In Keats's major odes and his mature narrative verse, dreams are synonymous with profound insights made possible by the imagination, usually through a redrafting of reality. (For Keats's later view on this aspect of the imagination, see the poem 'Fancy').

We have observed how Keats angrily blasts his predecessors for their desertion of the imagination. He accuses them of preferring the strait jacket of reason and argument, so that 'Imagination cannot freely fly / As she was wont...' (164). By doing this he also strongly identifies imagination or sleep with freedom, and Keats's own poetry is itself his testimony to this freedom. At the same time, freedom goes hand in hand with that great feeling of light which habitually infuses his verse, especially when we compare it with the dull and staid conceits of, say, Pope or Swift, who are among the chief targets of his wrath. By contrast, Keats cites Spenser, Shakespeare, Milton, Chatterton and Wordsworth among his ideals of music and imaginative art (206–9).

But there's a problem. If the imagination exists beyond the conscious control of a poet then we can reasonably ask what it is the poet actually does in composing a poem; that is, is he anything more than just a passive vehicle for dreams and experiences to work through?

Naturally Keats regards the poet as more engaged than this, more active, and he provides some answers under the heading of 'Poesy'. He uses this term in at least three different ways. First, Poesy is basically the practice of writing poetry, to which Keats dedicates himself in the lines

> O Poesy! for thee I hold my pen
> That am not yet a glorious denizen
> Of thy wide heaven...
>
> (47–9)

And at line 96 he begs for the indulgence and freedom of ten years to perfect the art of 'glorious' poetry (with awful irony, given the unripeness of his actual death some four years later, in 1821). However, he intends more than simply the process of sitting down and writing verse, and this first meaning of 'Poesy' includes the poet's apprenticeship in the methods and ways of poetry (for more on this, see lines 101 on).

The second meaning of 'Poesy' is Keats's view of the creative
process itself: the internal, subjective, aesthetic mechanism by which
the artist converts experience into a work of art. It is, of course, a
complex process,

> Then the events of this wide world I'd seize
> Like a strong giant, and my spirit tease
> Till at its shoulders it should proudly see
> Wings to find out an immortality.
>
> (81–4)

It involves first a direct experience of nature, love etc. (see lines 64–7)
and then reflection on this in tranquillity (lines 71–80) until through
the mysterious actions of the imagination and artistic judgement the
writer creates the poem, novel, painting or whatever it might be.

The third sense of 'Poesy' is a more general but equally more
controversial one. Towards the end of *Sleep and Poetry*, surrounded by
books and sculpture in Leigh Hunt's library, he is filled with youthful
awe and euphoria at the sheer power of art. In particular he has in
mind again Petrarch's Italian sonnets about Laura, declaring

> For over them was seen a free display
> Of out-spread wings.
>
> (392–3)

And there are those wings again. His line of argument here is not a
direct one, but what Keats is striving to hit at is, I think, that most
enigmatic property which any work of art may be said to possess and
which qualifies it as 'art'. Using the metaphor of 'wings' he tries to
suggest both the property itself as well as its elusiveness. Not all
critics would agree that such a quality exists. But if it does exist, then,
as Keats says, this is what elevates words, pictures, musical sounds
and so on to the status of ART. 'Poesy' would be this property. So in
this third sense 'Poesy' applies not exclusively to poetry or even to
writing but to any field of art.

Whether or not you agree with Keats (or with me for that matter)
is another thing. The poem does, however, convey the strong im-

pression of a young poet coming to terms with the theoretical issues of his vocation. He announces, 'I've seen / The end and aim of Poesy' (292–3) and it is a sacramental discovery, a sort of poetic annunciation to him: he has experienced an insight onto his destiny as a poet (in this respect compare the rapture of Cortez's men gazing at the Pacific in 'On First Looking into Chapman's Homer'). At the same time he remains coolly aware of the practical implications of his discovery, including the duty to submit himself at the altar of poetry in all its wondrous facets (and the poem uses much imagery of religion), even to the extent of forgoing worldly diversions,

> And can I ever bid these joys farewell?
> Yes, I must pass them for a nobler life.
>
> (122–3)

Gifted with the power of the imagination Keats's poet becomes a great visionary figure. It is a curious power, a gift from God perhaps ('his great Maker', line 43), here in the guise of Apollo the charioteer, and Keats avoids a specifically Christian interpretation. Sometimes a blessing, often a dire curse (see lines 307–10), the gift is an 'inward frown / Of conscience' (304–5).

For Keats, woman too has a crucial function in the mysterious process. Laura is cited as the archetypal figure here: she begins as simply the material object of sexual interest, but for the poet she becomes both the quintessence of poetic beauty (390–1) and at the same time the inspirational spirit of art (see lines 394–5).

Then the enigmatic appearance of the charioteer hurtling towards the centre of the poem imposes a shadowy, retributive presence over the whole piece. It comes as an awesome reminder for Keats – and for all writers – of the neglected powers of the imagination and to 'keep alive / The thought of that same chariot' (160–1). Yet, while its music is 'ever-fleeting' (141), elusive, its aftermath is unmistakable, trailing behind 'Shapes of delight, of mystery, and fear' (138). Such is the breathtaking force of the imagination.

Surprisingly, the chariot is both swift and light, attended by calm. However, it has a troubling, unsettling effect on Keats since it visits him as a remembrance of a lost virtue. In contrast to this calm, a strange ominous thunder rumbles intermittently through the poem (explicitly so in lines 27, 231 and 274, but grumbling throughout) and it seems to be a portent of change. Resolute against this mysterious force, Keats deftly holds together the two polarised moods of calm and turmoil in uneasy tension until in the library section they eventually subside and resolve themselves ... into a slumber.

Apart from Keats's own voice, it is the charioteer/Apollo who exerts the most substantial presence in *Sleep and Poetry*. Its function as the central metaphorical feature is to be a sort of hub about which the whole poem turns, an uneasy still point in the wide arc of the poem. As the presiding genius the figure of Apollo also has the task of drawing together some of the loose strands in this quite loose poem. Accordingly Keats assigns to the charioteer some of the most beautiful lyrical verse in the whole piece (lines 122–80).

On the other hand, as the climax to the poem, the charioteer/Apollo section really arrives too soon and what follows has a struggle to retain the reader's interest imaginatively. Thematically too this figure is lacking. In spite of his important central role Apollo does not actually take a full part in the poem and it is left too much to the reader to make the necessary connections and to fill out his significance.

Sleep and Poetry is an ambitious poem and, while this calls for special, mature skills, its length does allow Keats to develop some important thoughts towards a theory of poesy/poetry. This is interesting in itself of course but Keats's method of getting emotionally involved in the issues also generates an engaging conflict here. This is particularly apparent in his account of the dead poetry of the previous century set against his own ideals for the new Romantic verse. In turn, this dramatised conflict is also a fruitful source of tension in the poem, arising principally from the frankness of Keats's own voice. Time and again through his poetry Keats uses this tension of opposites to create dramatic interest for the reader.

For many readers, the poet's voice itself will be central to the poem's fascination. The poem achieves this by presenting such a great variety of tones, moods and emotions. For example, these include awe and exuberance at the effects of sleep, ecstatic adulation to the god of poetry, a tentative petition for ten years of poetic life, scorn for the Neo-Classicist writers, as well as affirmation of his own calling. At length, his fever gives way to calm resolution, equanimity, composure and, finally, joy. The emotions are, on the whole, finely judged and in addition to their versatility they convey an unmistakable sense of conviction which itself helps to extend the reader's involvement. All of which attests to Keats's increasing maturity of style as well as to a confidence in his own voice.

In this respect, there is no denying that Keats's own commitment and assurance carry the poem forward. This is important because *Sleep and Poetry* does not have that same idea of an unfolding narrative as in '*I stood tip-toe*'. In both poems Keats struggles to master the formal requirements of the long poem. Unfortunately *Sleep and Poetry* lacks the redeeming elegance and charm of '*I stood tip-toe*', its poise of musicality. Its melody is less rich and sinewy and, perhaps due to its abstractions, it lacks the same degree of delightful lyrical freshness. Where *Sleep and Poetry* gives us the narrow joy of the poet, '*I stood tip-toe*' gave us the joy of the human being as a whole.

Clearly, its loose structure and the attenuated length are the poem's two weakest features. It is a free-flow, rambling assemblage, a vehicle in which Keats can hammer out his theories of poetry and imagination. But at its centre the theory is too often obscured by its wordiness and it struggles for coherence. For momentum it relies too often on the slender effects of the poet's own voice and these become dissipated by the great length. Equally, the main thrust is often diverted and finally it is blunted. The end is, like that of '*I stood tip-toe*', hurried and sudden, with more than a hint in the final line that Keats had become exasperated with his sprawling progeny of a poem and simply abandoned its cadences:

> I leave them as a father does his son.
>
> (404)

Having said all this, what are the poem's virtues? We have already noticed the engaging commitment and frankness of Keats's voice together with its versatility. These are important too for our later discussion. While it falls short of a successful production we are certainly left with a strong sense of Keats's deeply felt excitement: in the prospects of a literary destiny, in the ecstatic pride in youth too,

as well as in the adventure of an uncertain future. And around him
we can feel the presence of shadowy forces and powerful energies
urging him forward.

Sleep and Poetry was written after a fitful night's sleep at Leigh
Hunt's on a make-shift bed in the library, Keats's mind still buzzing
with the heady ideas of a long evening's discourse. The poem fully
exposes the exhilarating effects of this as well as his frustrating
knowledge of his own unripeness (Byron derided him as a 'tadpole
of the Lakes'), not yet a 'glorious denizen' among the important poets
of his day; the poem represents a personal resolution to become one.
At the same time Keats's constant alertness to life's frailty injects his
impatience with a poignant urgency (and this prefigures one of the
major concerns of his mature verse, especially the great odes).

It is in this respect, of the future, that the poem poses its strongest
interest. By placing *Sleep and Poetry* at the end of his first volume of
poems, Keats makes an unmistakable pledge to his readers of greater
things to come.

Conclusions

Two general features that have emerged here from this survey of
Keats's early published writing are the poet's growing self-confidence
and his burgeoning ambition. These may help to account for Keats's
early readiness to take on a variety of poetic forms and to drive himself
to the limits of his ability. These are also the characteristics that
prevailed throughout the whole of his short life as a poet. At this
early stage they are really a sign of his struggle to establish his own
unique voice amid the gathering force of Romanticism – and in the face
of some severely harsh criticism of his work from the literary press.

In particular we have seen suppleness and adventure in Keats's
exploration of different metres and forms, such as heroic couplets,
experiments in iambic pentameter, the sonnet and longer narrative
modes. We have seen too how Keats adapts these traditional forms
to suit his own structural purposes and themes, especially in the light
of his early theory of poetics, which was as much a reaction away
from the strictures of Neo-Classicism as it was the full-bodied

embrace of Romanticism (for more on these movements, see Chapter 7). Central to this embrace is the great importance placed by Keats on the role of the imagination, both in the creation as well as in the apprehension of beauty.

In terms of technique we have examined many of those individual features that help to define Keats's style at this early stage of his career; for example, an acute sensitivity to the sound and bearing of words and forms, a strong awareness of the power of myth and imagery for suggesting alternative forms of existence, and his conception of the poet as a visionary.

In more general terms, we have counted among Keats's strengths the poise and sensuality of his lyrics and noted too some youthful imperfections such as a tendency towards long-windedness and diffusion in the early attempts at narrative verse. Above all, I have suggested that as a highly self-conscious and self-critical mind Keats is an intensely reflective poet and one aware of his own shortcomings, perhaps severely so.

On the whole, though, it is fair to ask whether, if Keats had died at the end of 1817, his volume of *Poems* would still be read today; and the answer is, almost certainly, no. Its chief interest remains in the freshness and genius shown by a minority of these early poems (including the two sonnets we have discussed) and, in these, lies the promise of the magnificent riches to follow.

Further Research

To consolidate the insights we have achieved in this chapter I suggest that you apply these to a study of two further poems from Keats's first volume of poetry. The two I recommend for your analysis are 'On the Sea' and 'To Emma'.

As you work through these poems, make a detailed note of your early impressions of them and then attempt to identify familiar themes and stylistic features, while also noting new areas for discussion. Try to express what you feel are the strengths and weaknesses of the two poems, comparing them where relevant with the ones discussed above.

When you consider 'On the Sea', examine in particular the role that imagery and the senses play in it. Also try to assess the import-ance of the poetic form in the meaning of the poem (it may help to look back at my comments on 'On First Looking into Chapman's Homer' and 'Keen, fitful gusts'). 'To Emma' is a relatively light work, a sort of seduction. What means does the poet use to entice the woman of the title? Also, how does Keats develop the poem's different emotional states?

For each poem, discuss the poet's use of sounds, both in his selection of individual words or phrases as well as in his patterns of rhyme and rhythm. Finally, try to link your findings about sound with the themes and other observations arising from your analysis.

2

The 'beautiful mythology of Greece': *Endymion* and *Lamia*

This chapter will concentrate on two long narrative poems which use Greek mythology for their setting. Where, in the opening chapter, we discussed Keats's poems in the order in which they were composed, here and in subsequent chapters we will discuss poems by grouping them together around a common setting or style or genre. Here we tackle *Endymion: A Poetic Romance* (written in 1817) and *Lamia* (completed in 1820). As well as each having a Greek setting these poems deal with some common themes – though their treatments of them are widely different.

Endymion: A Poetic Romance

Endymion: A Poetic Romance is both a passionate love poem and a Romantic fantasy quest in which the hero undergoes a succession of ordeals on a journey of self-discovery. It is the sequence of these ordeals which gives the poem its structural outline. The plot sets out to make a close connection between human love and the essence of both natural and artistic beauty. However, neither the course of the hero's journey nor the interconnection of these features runs smooth and they are continually disrupted or questioned by the intervention into the mortal world of the goddess Diana (or Cynthia, as she is sometimes called).

The plot of *Endymion* is relatively clear. In Book I, Endymion, a Latmian shepherd chieftain, has become deeply enchanted and disturbed by visions of a mysterious goddess and the competing uncertainties of reality and dream have reduced him to anxiety and helplessness. Where Book I introduces Endymion to the realm of *heavenly* mysteries, Book II initiates him into the secrets of the *earth* as he pursues a butterfly/nymph into labyrinthine passages of the underworld. There he encounters the dormant figure of Adonis, whose lover, the goddess Venus, offers hope to Endymion in his own quest. In a flash he is suddenly transposed onto the bed of the ocean to be introduced, in Book III, to the ways of the *watery* deep by Glaucus, an old man who is at last freed from a witch's curse through Endymion's help. Book IV opens with Endymion suddenly falling in love with an Indian maid after hearing her Song of Sorrow. A brief sojourn in the Cave of Quietude offers him momentary respite before he rejoins the maid. Forced to choose between the mortal beauty of the Indian girl and the dream beauty of Diana he chooses the former. The dilemmas of reality versus dream and of mortal love versus immortal are resolved when the maid and Diana merge, and reappear as the same woman. Endymion is redeemed by this his final ordeal and he achieves immortality.

In this brief summary of the poem I have highlighted key words to indicate some of its cardinal points, which are reinforced in some of the poem's major deities too: air (Diana), earth (Pan), sea (Neptune). Another set of cardinal points around which Keats structures his epic is made explicit in the prefaces to each of its books: namely, (I) beauty, (II) love, (III) power, (IV) the poetic imagination, or poetry itself.

However, before we go into detail I have selected a passage from Book I for close analysis and as the starting point for a wider discussion of the poem. The passage selected is lines 769 to 802 and represents one of the most controversial sections of *Endymion*:

'Peona! ever have I longed to slake
My thirst for the world's praises: nothing base,   770
No merely slumbrous phantasm, could unlace
The stubborn canvas for my voyage prepared –
Though now 'tis tattered, leaving my bark bared
And sullenly drifting: yet my higher hope
Is of too wide, too rainbow-large a scope,   775
To fret at myriads of earthly wrecks.
Wherein lies happiness? In that which becks
Our ready minds to fellowship divine,
A fellowship with essence; till we shine,
Full alchemized, and free of space. Behold   780
The clear religion of heaven! Fold
A rose leaf round thy finger's taperness,
And soothe thy lips: hist, when the airy stress
Of music's kiss impregnates the free winds,
And with a sympathetic touch unbinds   785
Aeolian magic from their lucid wombs;
Then old songs waken from enclouded tombs;
Old ditties sigh above their father's grave;
Ghosts of melodious prophesyings rave
Round every spot where trod Apollo's foot;   790
Bronze clarions awake, and faintly bruit,
Where long ago a giant battle was;
And, from the turf, a lullaby doth pass
In every place where infant Orpheus slept.
Feel we these things? – that moment have we stepped   795
Into a sort of oneness, and our state
Is like a floating spirit's. But there are
Richer entanglements, enthralments far
More self-destroying, leading, by degrees,
To the chief intensity: the crown of these   800
Is made of love and friendship, and sits high
Upon the forehead of humanity...'.

Immediately before this passage Peona has drawn her brother
away from the festive sacrifice to Pan and questioned him about
his dejection and his neglect of his duties as their chief. Endymion

recounts his strange dream of soaring into the moonlit heavens and of falling in love with the vision of a beautiful woman. On waking he has become completely perplexed and unable to decide whether the encounter had been simply a human dream or an illusion contrived by a goddess. Peona coldly dismisses her brother's experience as 'nothing but a dream' and the above extract is part of his reply to her.

I have selected this passage because it foregrounds some of the poem's major themes, and in any case it displays some beautiful rich verse – almost every line sings a rich melody. In dramatic terms it is significant too because it reveals the deep conflicts turning over in Endymion's mind, threatening to disrupt its insecure equilibrium. These conflicts are clearly mirrored in the emotional diction of the passage (unlace, tattered, drifting, wrecks, rave, battle) and they represent issues that preoccupy the bulk of the poem, and press it forward.

The discord inside Endymion at this moment can be understood as the clash between matters of the human or mortal sphere (such as fame, friendship, happiness, love and natural beauty) and those of the spirit, the immortal sphere (including divine love and immortal beauty). And underlying this awesome clash, intensifying its dilemma, are Endymion's profound uncertainties about the differences between reality, dream and illusion.

We can proceed by examining issues of the mortal and immortal life under three thematic headings: the nature of Endymion's identity, love, and beauty.

At the heart of Endymion's dilemma is a radical uncertainty about the nature of his own 'self'; that is, a sort of crisis about his own identity and about his relationships with other people. The extract begins with an admission that his life has been the selfish pursuit of fame,

> Peona! ever have I longed to slake
> My thirst for the world's praises ...

> (I.769–70)

However, love, the 'unsating food' (I.816), has now harassed him into taking stock of his confused life by blunting his egoistic ambition.

Even a cursory reading of Book I reveals that Endymion's composure has received quite a serious jolt. When he first appears in the poem, robed in the garments of a 'chieftain king', there is an obvious gulf between his outward, regal show, and the neglect of his tribal duties. While his people, his community, throng in exultant celebration of Pan he sits disconsolate and at some distance, alone. As shepherd-king his role personifies the theme of power in the poem – or at least it ought to do. But here Keats uses the idea of kingship principally to magnify Endymion's solitude especially in regard of the neglect of duties in the 'congregated world' (I.818).

By establishing this uncertainty at the core of Endymion's consciousness the poem sets up the hero's narrative as a quest of self-discovery. Ironically but inevitably it seeks to do this by focusing on the self. Endymion is set to find out what sort of person he is through his love of another (namely the goddess Diana) and through his kinship with the rest of humanity. As in 'Chapman's Homer', the journey is the central literary figure:

> The journey homeward to habitual self!
>
> (II.276)

Again the stimulus for the poem is Keats's own situation since during the composition of his epic he had himself undergone something of a crisis of identity as an aspiring but as yet unproved poet. However, his own ordeal was probably less traumatic than the despair suffered by Endymion,

> I have clung
> To nothing, loved a nothing, nothing seen...
> Or felt but a great dream!
>
> (IV.636–8)

The impassioned exposure of his soul to his sister Peona is the first stage of the journey.

The love of Peona for her brother is only one element in the broad band of love themes, which stretches from platonic love and 'fellowship divine' (I.779) to worldly sexual desire. In broader terms,

Endymion's melancholy is slowly eased by his realisation of the fellowship of people both with themselves and with the objects of nature,
combined together as a unity of being, 'Into a sort of oneness' (I.796).
Bereft of this crown of friendship in the festival of Pan, Endymion does
not recover it until, as a prelude to his spiritual apotheosis later, he
merges with the glorious throng in Neptune's palace in Book III. And
in the passage above it is significant that while he starts out with the
first-person pronouns 'I' and 'my', by the close he speaks of 'we'.

All the same, whilst he is aware of this community as an eventual
ideal he is at this moment in no position to achieve it. Essentially he has
become a victim of his own passion, fretted by fantasies of sex and lust-
fulfilment. Consequently, tormented libido, failure and despair have
shunted his vexed hopes and pride back and forth until he becomes
frustrated and lost. All his attempts at imposing his free will on the ego
have become a nonsense, a form of tragic nihilistic joke. On the very
fringes of sanity, Endymion has now been compelled into a reassess-
ment and a re-definition of his identity in the world of others. The
above passage is important because it marks the start of this process.

The exact starting point seems to be the question 'Wherein lies
happiness?' (line 777), and then Endymion submits himself to the
realisation that the answer is in 'fellowship'. But what it is that triggers
off this paradigmatic sort of realisation is unclear. Keats is convinced
that there must be some agency, a something, but a something in-
effable: 'for which no wording can be found' (IV.962). In the above
passage this indefinable entity charms the reader with 'music's kiss' and
the 'Eolian magic', as a sort of conducive aura collects and moves us,

> Feel we these things? – that moment have we stepped
> Into a sort of oneness...

(795–6)

For Endymion, as for Keats himself, solitude and separation are
anathema to his conception of mankind. And yet this fellowship
with mankind (it's 'entanglements') is only the start,

> leading, by degrees,
> To the chief intensity: the crown of these

> Is made of love and friendship, and sits high
> Upon the forehead of humanity.
>
> (799–802)

Friendship is the crowning splendour of mankind, but also a step on the ascent that leads to the ultimate, to love, the 'chief intensity', radiant like a fierce 'drop / Of light' (806–7) as Endymion conceives it. This is the very pinnacle and end of human existence. So much so that, with affinities to some eastern religions, the process is actually self-effacing, which is paradoxical given that this is the moment of discovery of one's self within a community of others.

This theme is, of course, developed further in that part of Endymion's speech which follows our extract, and we will need to trace it for a little distance. One important consequence of this highly rarefied form of love is a tendency to merge into the rest of humanity, 'we blend / Mingle and so become part of it' (I.810). For Keats at this time this condition represents what it is to be truly human, and love is its 'proper pith' (I.814). Quintessentially the capacity for love is what marks us out from the rest of the universe.

However, Endymion also possesses sufficient presence of mind to be wary of the traps of mendacious or false prophets. In the section following our extract he vents his ire on 'men-slugs and human serpentry' (I.821), those counterfeits, parasites, and reactionaries conspiring to diminish society's true visionaries, men and women who promote liberal or progressive ideas in the service of mankind. In particular Keats has in mind the Tory critics who disparaged Romanticism as a movement and had attacked his own early verse in particular.

There is, though, a peril here. Love embodies too the power to 'let occasion die' (I.822), to en-thrall, so much so that even the most resolute, the most ambitious are prone to succumb to its allure and thus let the ripe opportunity slip away under the spell of 'love's elysium' (I.823). This for Keats is of course a difficult conundrum, and one that remained with him – see his later ballad *La Belle Dame sans Merci* for a more austere treatment of this theme.

In spite of this, Endymion refuses to scorn love's tendency to entangle. In the process he also broadens out his theme, uniting the idea of private love with that of love as fellowship or concord, the balm of humanity (as Keats believed poetry to be too). He cherishes love, this 'ardent listlessness', on the grounds that it 'might bless / The world with benefits unknowingly' (I.826–7), that love magnifies the well-being of all of us by chance and indifference. He goes on to hit home his argument by the compelling metaphor of the nightingale: that although she sings 'but to her love', everyone else who hears the song may benefit by it (I.828–35).

Endymion is, in part at least, trying to come to terms with the deep frustrations caused by his encounter with the elusive mystery woman (a figure that recurs throughout Keats's verse and may represent his faith in the accidental nature of love, and of life as a whole). The parallels between Endymion's situation and those of others such as Pan and Syrinx, Alpheus and Arethusa, Glaucus and Scylla help to relieve this ache, of course, but not finally. The question which the above extract focuses on and which nags Endymion throughout is: Why love at all? Why get involved with these 'entanglements, enthralments' (798) when they incur so much pain?

As we have already noted, one answer is that love as a humanising force enriches the whole of mankind. But, as if this were not enough, he adds a further couple of points. Love and especially sex unites the whole of organic creation; it is the force that drives the whole of life. And the other point is that the human capacity for love together with an innate sensitivity enables mankind to marvel at the beauty, the 'entanglements' that encompass the universe. In short it is the basic creative instinct of mankind (but especially of poets) that actively brings nature alive for us through our capacity for love (on this issue see Endymion's brilliant image of the chain of nature in lines 835–42 of Book I and compare it with Oceanus's speech in *Hyperion. A Fragment*, II.173 on).

But there is a down side to all this. Such an exquisite sensitivity is for Endymion a double-edged distinction, a source of deep melancholy as well as of soaring joy at other times. It is a theme which runs throughout Keats's poetry: for instance, that 'balmy pain' in *I stood tip-toe* (line 162), and in *Lamia* the 'pleasure, and the ruddy strife / Of hearts and lips' (I.40). Endymion's problem lies, in part, in coming to terms with a passionate love which, while highly enticing, is extremely painful in its frustrations. He feels the need to reach beyond to a more spiritual state of love, one that might offer bliss and mental healing.

To the question 'Wherein lies happiness?' (777) he points in the direction of the transcendent, of a 'fellowship divine', towards a 'clear religion' (781), and a 'sort of oneness' (796). The imagery in the above extract and immediately following it reveals that Endymion's solution to his 'ruddy strife' lies in the more spiritual disciplines of medieval courtly love. This is a code of chivalric love with conventions of physical ordeals, ascetic sufferings, melancholy and sickness – all beneath the indifferent gaze of a largely unresponsive mistress, and all tending to magnify the lover's despondency still more, even to the brink of death. Thus is it for Endymion, especially so because he remains ignorant of his mistress's true identity.

In another convention of courtly love, the frustrated lovelorn knight is often driven to a death-wish to relieve his pains. Endymion too, in spite of his denials, exhibits this facet and thoughts of dying are never far from the surface both here and elsewhere in the poem – for example, the tombs and ghosts (787–9) and the 'floating spirit' (797) more than suggest that he is half in love with easeful death.

Like death, love is the human theme. In Book III, at Glaucus's wedding, Venus asks of Endymion,

> What, not yet
> Escaped from dull mortality's harsh net?
>
> (906–7)

And the key word 'Escaped' points us to the double theme: dull mortality with its inevitable death coupled with the ache and strife of love. On the other hand, and curiously, love is actually a salient feature in the lives of the immortal gods despite their separation from our earthly turmoil by the 'fragile bar' (I.360). Hence Diana's struggle to win Endymion's love.

This, of course, presents Keats with a logical problem. But it is one made necessary by his insistence on the special role of love in the narrative, a role that he makes explicit when Endymion speculates on the potential influence of love,

Now, if this earthly love has power to make
Men's being mortal, immortal...

(I.843–4)

In other words, such is the capacity of this mysterious force of love
that it can even enable human beings to transcend the 'fragile bar', to
'shake Ambition' and the other preoccupations of mankind until they
can glimpse a route into spiritual ecstasy.

Which is not a particularly original idea. But it is one that allows
Keats (and Endymion) the opportunity of resolving that other barrier
between humans and gods: the possibility of sexual love. Love is the
gateway between the two worlds, just as, in '*I stood tip-toe*', imagination
acted as the portal between them. In '*I stood tip-toe*' Keats used the
term 'tip-toe' to imply this movement or a condition of being poised
between the two states, an idea which occurs again and again in his
poetry (see also *Endymion*, II.261, where Keats uses it of Diana).

Diana herself alludes obliquely to this concept of transcendence in
Book IV as she and Endymion stand on the threshold of discovery.
Although a god she pronounces on the power of earthly sensuality
above all other delights, and describes how she was knocked over by
'the warm tremble of a devout kiss' (IV.744). For Endymion love is,
until the end at least, a deeply ambiguous concept because having
tasted both earthly love and even 'love immortal' has served only to
deepen his anguish.

At the outset of this discussion I mentioned that the extracted
passage contains a controversial section, and I can hold you in
suspense no longer. The controversy relates to the theme of beauty,
which may seem odd at first since the extract does not contain any
direct references to beauty itself. However, the poem as a whole
frequently touches on this topic and the famous opening line sets a
sort of keynote to the whole,

A thing of beauty is a joy for ever...

(I.1)

This is strange too, perhaps, given that the rest of the poem looks like
a rambling saga of passion and frustration. At least on the surface,
anyway.

Well, one thing is that Endymion's tormented pursuit of Diana is often linked with a bright, beautiful light, implying that his quest too is the search for the 'thing of beauty'. And then, as we noted in Chapter 1, Diana herself is revered as a symbol of chaste beauty, beauty that 'exceedest all things in thy shine' ('*I stood tip-toe*', line 207).

That a thing of beauty is a joy *for ever*, is crucial here in helping us see how beauty as a theme might relate to that of time (together with the 'fragile bar' between the two worlds of gods and humans, the temporal and the timeless, the physical and the spiritual). Moreover, in the narrator's preamble to Book I the theme of beauty is set in opposition to many unsettling reminders of death. The underlying idea is a recurring Keatsian one, that art – the object of beauty – although it is created by mortals can actually transcend this world of flux and decay, of fret and fever, by way of its beauty and partake of the eternal realm of the immortals, still and 'unravished' (for more on this idea see the discussion on 'Ode on a Grecian Urn' in Chapter 4).

For our present analysis the key section is in lines 777 to 781 ('Wherein lies happiness...the clear religion of heaven'). For many critics this section along with others has provided conclusive evidence that Keats intended *Endymion* to be read as an allegory. In other words that the poem should be regarded as less of a simple narrative involving characters, and more in terms of what they and their actions may represent.

An allegorical interpretation of the poem reads it as more than just a romance but also as a symbolic journey for Endymion (and for Keats too), a journey through a series of gradations of happiness leading towards a final spiritual rhapsody. The journey begins at a basic level, of sensual happiness, rooted in everyday human experience, and finally reaches up to a summit of a 'fellowship divine' (I.778). In addition, the journey is paralleled by Endymion's symbolic route through the earth (in Book II), and the sea (III), eventually reaching heaven (IV).

Not all critics see it this way but those who do favour an allegorical reading tend to see such a reading in Platonist terms, reflecting the idealist thinking of the ancient Greek theorist, Plato. This philosophy sees our everyday world of the human senses as in a state of continuous flux and therefore regards it as uncertain and unreliable as a source of truth – in contrast to the realm of heaven where existence and truth are both permanent and absolute. Platonists frequently go even further and often claim that on earth we receive only fleeting glimpses of genuine beauty (a 'snailhorn perception of beauty', as Keats called it) – that the absolute essence of beauty can only be apprehended in heaven itself.

The allegorical reading, then, understands Endymion's tortuous journeying as a movement through ascending grades of beauty (as well as of truth and happiness) towards communion with this ultim- ate, essential form of beauty:

> A fellowship with essence; till we shine,
> Full alchemized, and free of space.
>
> (I.779–80)

In this way, the ultimate form of beauty in all things – in art as well as in nature – is symbolised by the goddess Diana, with whom Endym- ion eventually achieves union. For Keats, however, that communion has two implications: for Keats the ordinary human being, this means apprehending beauty around him, but further, for Keats the creative artist, it means striving to instil in his verse something of the vital radiance of beauty which could thereby give permanent life to his art.

Seen in this way, the quest in the poem is effectively one for Keats himself (through the figure of Endymion), a quest of artistic self- discovery. Through it he attempts to reconcile the senses and the spirit by way of the poem's themes of selfhood, love and beauty. It is therefore the struggle to liberate the poetic imagination to reach its most esoteric possibilities in pursuit of absolute beauty. The struggle is re-enacted later, and more overtly, in *The Fall of Hyperion. A Dream*, with the Poet's agonised ascent towards truth (from line I.108).

So, to return to Endymion's question in line 777, 'Wherein lies happiness?', Keats's allegorical reply is that it lies in the discovery of ideal beauty; that is, starting out in the physical world of artefacts and nature, and arriving finally in the realm of spiritual essence, the new realm of gold. Its beginning lies in the world of the obtrusive ego, which passes through ordeals of increasing sublimation and refine- ment until at last the individual's 'floating spirit' gradually achieves that 'chief intensity' of love and friendship.

Figuratively this is represented in Book IV by Endymion's painful dilemma over choosing between the Indian maid and Diana. In the final climax to the poem he settles on the physical, worldly maid, empirical and immediate. But through her he unexpectedly and ecstatically achieves his long-suffering desire for union with the goddess. He comes through: the physical ordeal of the world and the flesh opens spontaneously and forcefully into the realm of spiritual revelation.

In technical terms the allegorical reading of *Endymion* does have the merit of bolstering and enriching an otherwise turgid, sprawling tale of passion, illusion and whimsy. But is such an interpretation valid? In a letter of 30 January 1818 to his new publisher, Keats refers to lines I.777–81 as acutely important, signifying a 'regular stepping of the Imagination towards a Truth', and as the 'gradations of Happiness even like a kind of Pleasure Thermometer'. In an earlier letter (22 November 1817) he also makes clear his conviction that happiness on earth is only a foretaste of a finer happiness to come in the after-life, 'the reality to come'.

Plainly, these reflections are more or less consistent with the above allegorical interpretation but this does not necessarily mean that Keats intended us to read *Endymion* in this way. One objection is that there is not very much inside the poem to support it. Another is that, up to this point in his career, allegory is not characteristic of Keats's general attitude in poetry (although some critics have seen *Sleep and Poetry* as a parabolic poem). Furthermore, many readers dismiss out of hand the notion that Keats was a Platonist in his thinking, preferring to see the whole tenor of his work as unswervingly empirical, grounded in the physical world of the senses.

And yet perhaps the important thing is not what Keats may have intended in the poem so much as what we see in it: the reader's own response to the words on the page. As I have proposed just now, the allegorical reading goes some way to rescuing (or masking) the poem from some of its obvious weaknesses... but perhaps not the whole way.

As a simple romance starting out in a pastoral idyll *Endymion*'s slender narrative struggles to hold the reader's genuine interest for most of its great length. Its dramatic moments are few and not particularly intense for all that. In fact the motto of the poem points to two of its main problems: '*The stretched metre of an antique song*'. It is over-long and is cloaked in an esoteric mythology which even in Keats's own day was redundant and obscure. He struggles to fill out meaning and, while there are still some remarkably fine passages of the Keatsian sublime, he labours to master the epic form and to assimilate his own poetic talents within it. His own severest critic, Keats was very much alert to the poem's flaws and it disappointed the high hopes he had set upon it. There is evidence too that he himself had grown weary of it even before his effort to complete the first draft of Book IV.

Significantly, once he had completed the poem Keats prepared two separate prefaces for publication. In the rejected preface he conceded that *Endymion* was simply an 'endeavour rather than a thing accomplished' while in the published version he derided the poem as mawkish and inexperienced. Deeply disheartened, but eager to get in print, he soon regretted his failure to postpone publication (as his friends had recommended). Yet, even in dejection, he gave resolute notice that he would attempt another verse epic, to be inspired again by the 'beautiful mythology of Greece' (and five months later, in September 1818, he began work on *Hyperion*).

Endymion was finally published in April 1818 – to almost complete silence in the literary press. Its publishers hoped for some 'stir' to get sluggish sales going but when independent reviews started to appear in the autumn they were quite blistering in their attacks. Probably the most virulent (and notorious) among these was that of J. G. Lockhart in *Blackwood's* magazine who under the nom-de-guerre of 'Z' despatched the poem as the 'spectacle of an able mind reduced to a state of insanity'. So venomous was this attack that it later gave rise to the myth of bringing about Keats's premature death (Shelley actually accused Lockhart of murder). On the other hand, most sober and favourable critics of the poem praised its fine sound and memorable images – though the majority verdict was that on the whole the poem was a flop.

Keats's decision to compose *Endymion* was spurred by two impulses chiefly. One was the urge to write a long narrative poem (which he considered to be the proof of a true poet). As he wrote to his friend Benjamin Bailey, it will be a test, a trial of my Powers of Imagination and chiefly of my invention which is a rare thing indeed – by which I must make 4000 Lines of one bare circumstance and fill them with Poetry.... Besides a long Poem is a test of Invention.

(8 October 1817)

And the second impulse, arising from the first, was a contest struck with the poet Shelley for each to produce a long poem of about 4,000 words. Keats set himself the ambitious target of composing fifty lines a day – and the poem sometimes looks as if it bends more to the demands of arithmetic than to aesthetics.

To develop fully his 'one bare circumstance' in any meaningful way might realistically have meant working it into a truly dramatic narrative. However, at this time Keats's genius lay principally in lyric poetry and he had few genuine skills in the depiction of character or cohesive, sustained story-telling, as *Endymion* proves.

In terms of character, *Endymion* is Keats's first real attempt to dramatise human suffering and to explore the psychology of the emotions (including happiness as well as grief and melancholy). The immortal gods, too, have a metaphorical function in this project (in fact they regularly come over as more intrinsically human than god-like). In their suffering and passions they very much resemble the mortals, suggesting that the 'fragile bar' is not quite impervious to them. Within the important power struggle of the poem they often symbolise chaos, the irrational, human instincts, or the power of fate, thwarting free will. Above all, existing as they do beyond the realm of time, they act as a foil to the evanescent mortality of the earthly humans, emphasising themes of time, death and the frailty of the human imprint.

Keats also presents us with a wide range of female characters here. In general terms they are strikingly active and vigorously so, contrasting with the listless Endymion and other generally passive males. The women tend to emphasise the themes of love (both human and divine) and sexual passion in a variety of guises: wicked siren, elusive object of male desire, seductress, fate, and the chaste virgin. In addition the range of female figures implies some complexity in female sexuality; for example, Circe is a complex picture of a destructive sexuality, representing death in sexual love, a concept which energizes the later verse, especially *Lamia* and *La Belle Dame sans Merci*.

When it was published in April 1818, Byron and other contemporary critics lambasted *Endymion* for what they saw as its sexual impropriety in 'openly' suggesting that women actually experienced erotic desires. The poem breaks new ground in acknowledging that both men and women have strong sex drives, indulging in passionate feelings and even erotic fantasies (and thank goodness we do). Having said this much, however, we should acknowledge that sexuality in *Endymion* comes over as a mainly conceptual element, one for which the people in the poem are merely vehicles – very few of them actually seem real in the normal sense (even if our own personal encounters with beautiful goddesses or brooding shepherd chieftains are rare or fleeting).

However, if the poem falls down in terms of narrative tension and character it does achieve some success in other departments. In general, the poem is more attractive if we look at it less as a whole than as a 'rambling storehouse of pleasures', in the words of one critic. It does contain some very effective or highly promising sections, with beautiful lyrical passages (for example, in set pieces such as the 'Song to Pan', I.232–306; 'the Bower of Adonis', II.387–587; and the 'Cave of Quietude', IV.512–611). Keats does take some positive poetic steps into the tricky psychology of love, dream, pain and joy, while exploring the potential of myth, all of which figure strongly in his mature verse. The richly decorative bowers, labyrinths, seascapes and atmospheres, while pointing forward to later, greater things, do attain a separate kind of success here. Remaining as separate features they also acquire a sort of unity without any real cohesion. Through the poet's ubiquitous voice, Keats himself manages to impose an unsteady sort of order on this universe, but one that is constantly menaced by chaos via the persons of Pan and Diana. For most of the time, too, Endymion's own fragile sanity seems under siege to these elements.

Of course, the eponymous hero works as an agency for unity in the poem, especially given the tendency for other figures to metamorphose or dissolve. And this fluidity of character is naturally enough all one with the dynamism of the whole poem, which often borders on the surreal, destabilising the fragile boundary between reality and illusion (each defining the other). This dynamism is one of

the poem's few saving graces even though it is constantly undermined by the many longueurs. And among the poem's labyrinthine
tangles, bowers, caverns and rivers there are genuine moments of
danger and secrecy.

Yet, however promising these many features are it is actually
Keats's own exquisite verse itself that holds the reader's attention.
Would anyone, frankly, return to the text at all were it not for its
dazzling poetry? In *Endymion* Keats's verse reaches a new tone of
self-confidence while its lyricism blossoms in beautiful musicality. He
has complete and easy mastery of the heroic couplet used here and in
its best moments he produces scintillating mosaics of radiant and
exuberant tones – which in beauty and feeling anticipate the power
and insight of the major odes.

Lamia

The next poem I want to look at, *Lamia*, was begun in 1819 and
completed the following year and is among the last of Keats's
narrative poems. Undaunted by the disappointment of his youthful
efforts he had continued to experiment in the narrative form and by
1820 he believed he had mastered the necessary techniques. Soon
after starting the poem he wrote eagerly to his friend John Reynolds,

> I have great hopes of success, because I make use of my Judgement
> more deliberately than I yet have done.
>
> (11 July 1819)

We shall see if his judgement proved right, but certainly one thing he
did achieve was a greater clarity, beginning in the narration itself.

The story is both simple and enthralling. Striking a deal with Hermes,
the serpent Lamia is transformed once again into a woman and she flies
to Corinth to seduce her beloved but innocent Lycius. After becoming
besotted, the two lovers set up a haven and celebrate their union with a
sumptuous banquet – during which their relationship is devastated by
the intervention of the philosopher Apollonius, Lycius's tutor.

The passage I have chosen for analysis comes from Part II, on the
brink of the climax to the poem:

What wreath for Lamia? What for Lycius?   221
What for the sage, old Apollonius?
Upon her aching forehead be there hung
The leaves of willow and of adder's tongue;
And for the youth, quick, let us strip for him
The thyrsus, that his watching eyes may swim
Into forgetfulness; and, for the sage,
Let spear-grass and the spiteful thistle wage
War on his temples. Do not all charms fly
At the mere touch of cold philosophy?   230
There was an awful rainbow once in heaven:
We know her woof, her texture; she is given
In the dull catalogue of common things.
Philosophy will clip an Angel's wings,
Conquer all mysteries by rule and line,
Empty the haunted air, and gnomed mine –
Unweave a rainbow, as it erewhile made
The tender-personed Lamia melt into a shade.

By her glad Lycius sitting, in chief place,
Scarce saw in all the room another face,   240
Till, checking his love trance, a cup he took
Full brimmed, and opposite sent forth a look
'Cross the broad table, to beseech a glance
From his old teacher's wrinkled countenance,
And pledge him. The bald-head philosopher
Had fixed his eye, without a twinkle or stir
Full on the alarmed beauty of the bride,
Brow-beating her fair form, and troubling her sweet pride.
Lycius then pressed her hand, without devout touch,
As pale it lay upon the rosy couch: 250
'Twas icy, and the cold ran through his veins;
Then sudden it grew hot, and all the pains
Of an unnatural heat shot to his heart.
'Lamia, what means this? Wherefore dost thou start?
Know'st thou that man?' Poor Lamia answered not.

Although the extract I have selected is long it is crucial to the poem. Pausing just before the great dramatic climax, this section holds back the action just long enough to give the feelings one last momentous twist before the swift rush into denouement and disaster as theme and emotion merge together.

Prominent among the themes made explicit here is that of philosophy. With detachment and candour the narrator steps boldly out of the convivial party action (the antithesis of Apollonius's intrusiveness) and confronts the reader with the blunt proposition that,

> Philosophy will clip an Angel's wings,
> Conquer all mysteries by rule and line...
>
> (I.234–5)

First, though, we need to get clear what the narrator means by philosophy. By using the word 'cold' he suggests, of course, that it is devoid of emotion, even deathly (while Lamia's 'icy' hand perhaps implies 'witchlike', line 251). The 'dull catalogue' also reinforces the tone of these ideas and yet its power commands high respect: its 'mere touch' dispels all the charms, beauty and mystery in the world. Its dead hand resolves the party into a catastrophe.

Rationalist philosophy puts great store on reason, thought, detachment and unfeeling objectivity; at least according to Keats here. Its conquering 'rule and line' (235) run counter to the mystery and subjective intensity of a life lived on the pulse, which is the version of Romanticism represented by Lamia and Lycius. Its withering sobriety is in contrast to the banquet with its Bacchic riot of escape and warmth, at its 'meridian height' at this moment of the poem. It is escape from consciousness, and conscience too, as well as from the analytical rationality which would 'unweave a rainbow' (237).

For Romantic poets the rainbow was a symbol of the mystery and primitive beauty inherent in nature (hence its being awe-ful here). It is something to be celebrated in emotion and explored, if at all, through subjectivity. However, science (or 'natural philosophy') destroys the object under the magnifying glass in the very process of analysis:

whether it be the fragile mystique of the rainbow or the delicate faith that sustains the angel. So bleak is the fanaticism of nineteenth-century philosophy's 'rule and line' that it sets out to persuade us only of the cold, rational and measurable certainties of the universe. This hard-nosed form of realism was called positivism, which held that if some-thing cannot be proved or observed then stricly speaking it does not exist. And this is the fate too of the 'haunted air, and gnomed mine' (236).

The chill and austere realm of 'rule and line' here echoes the view in *Sleep and Poetry* where rationalistic eighteenth-century poetics were scorned by Keats, characterised by their

> musty laws lined out with wretched rule
> And compass vile . . .
>
> (*Sleep and Poetry*, lines 195–6)

Here, as there, Keats's point is that rationalism not only undermines our emotional life but it impoverishes the literary life too, by smothering the creative vigour of the artistic imagination, so fundamental to Romanti-cism. It even puts at risk the pre-eminence of Beauty itself.

This analytical predisposition of science and philosophy with its unweaving and demystifying rationalism is depicted in the poem by the sombre, lurking figure of Apollonius. This aged, foreboding presence, 'bald-head philosopher' (245), is rigidly intent on breaking Lycius's 'love trance' and recovering him to the old rule and line. This is so because, like those angels and the rainbow, like passion and the Romantic imagination, the trance presents a dangerous threat to positivist philosophy, anathema to the miserable regulation and constraint imposed by reason (the 'dull catalogue').

This trance of Lycius's is, however, of a different (but related) order from that of the dreams of gods, because as we are told at the outset, 'Real are the dreams of gods' (I.127). As elsewhere in Keats, dreams and gods signify other levels of existence, the Other world. Such dreams are again a form of Neo-Platonist idealism. They are the world beyond the pain and cares of human beings: a world in which Hermes might achieve a perfect love with his nymph (as the poem implies) while Lamia as a mortal woman must now settle for the imperfections of human exist-ence, in which 'Nothing but pain and ugliness were left' (I.164).

Thus, the other realm of dream and trance is repeatedly set against this world of hard human reality, as the above extract suggests, illustrated by the terrifying struggle between Lamia and Apollonius for the soul of Lycius. Moreover, the passage makes clear that the ultimate human reality is death, from which there is no escape whether through trance, drug, drink or dream. And the point is coolly emphasised by the diction – 'wreath' (221), and 'shade' (238), then later 'wreathes' (264) and 'deadly' (266).

The trance in which Lycius luxuriates is clearly a love dream, and love epitomises the ultimate sort of 'mysteries' that philosophy sets out to conquer, its final frontier. Yet, from the very beginning of the poem, love's vital influence has been seen to pervade all, or almost all: Hermes is smitten with a nymph, Lamia with Lycius and Lycius with her, while over everything reigns Aphrodite, goddess of love and the tutelary deity of Corinth. As an expression of Gordian entanglements, love is often linked with the theme of power, and both of these subjects converge through the figure of Apollonius, who is goaded into action as much by his power struggle with Lamia as by love for his young protégé.

As in *Endymion*, there lies at the core of *Lamia* a knotty love complex involving a mortal man and an immortal woman. In both poems, the woman retains her presence of mind while the frail, vulnerable man succumbs to distraction: Lycius, becoming transfixed in his love trance, 'Scarce saw in all the room another face' (240). But unlike Diana, Lamia, as a result of her metamorphosis, has a greater freedom to interact with the mortal world. Consequently she is more actively involved in arranging events, as well as manipulating Lycius through lies, deception, and enchantment (with 'charms' and 'spell', lines 229 and 259). She herself is a dazzling rainbow (see I.153), a feast for the Romantic erotic imagination, a stunning seductive illusion.

However, in our extract, the narrator boldly colludes with Lamia in the idea that an amorous illusion is safer than a truthful recollection of cold reality, 'that his watching eyes may swim/Into forgetfulness' (226–7). It is another version of that oblivion proffered by the convivial wine, or a vision of beauty or the honeyed voice. Such forgetfulness *is* a point of safety, a haven from the ever-present dangers threatening the warp and weft of their tangled love, chief of which is the incisive power of reason (in the figure of Apollonius), a threat which seems to intimidate the poem from the outset.

Lamia's painful return to the mortal world marks a transition into a sphere of warring dualities. Reason is pitted against feeling, pain against bliss, duty against pleasure, and the idea of immutability is set against the stark reality of flux. Naturally, she herself becomes subject to these conflicts – not least in her passionate clinging on to a dream of eternal love with Lycius within a world of fleeting impressions, sensations, and desires.

The narrator's reference to 'unnatural heat' (line 253) is a solemn reminder of human mortality, echoed later in 'passion's passing bell' (II.39), implying the transience of life on earth. Eternally conscious, Lamia is actually the embodiment of the poem's chief conflict: she is 'of sciental brain' yet also of love 'deep learned', a 'graduate' in sexual pleasures (I.190–1). Thus the effect of the gruesome philosopher's 'fixed eye' is the unravelling of these dualities in her, the unravelling of the tensions at the core of the human individual, and this effectively entails her death, in which she is 'from human trammels freed'. Paradoxically she 'dies' into immortality, a point which is implied in those silences in part II between lines 255 and 270, where her human powers have already begun to wane.

The theme of change is eminently manifest in the above extract, reflecting its central importance to the poem as a whole. Note all the references in the poem to movements and to altered states. For example, Lamia is first a serpent, becomes a woman and then departs this brief life as a shade or ghost, while Lycius's humdrum existence is translated by love into one of momentary but intensely passionate sensuality. Only the presence of the stony, implacable Apollonius seems to endure, his intransience as a parallel to his intransigence.

Cheated of a natural ripening of her love, Lamia's fate is to wither under the glare of the philosopher's eye,

> no soft bloom
> Misted the cheek; no passion to illume
> The deep-recessed vision. All was blight;
> Lamia, no longer fair, there sat a deadly white.

(II.273–6)

The word I find most interesting here is 'blight'. There are in the poem numerous suggestions of this idea of blighting as well as of ripening; for instance, through the conventional symbol of the rose, but also in Keats's characteristic play of colours, white and red in particular, and in the opposition of references to 'pale' and 'blush' (and Keats makes a pun on their conjunction, at I.286 and II.65–6).

Having snaked almost imperceptibly throughout the poem, these dualities now climax in the final confrontation. Keats reveals that dull philosophy does not merely clip wings and unweave rainbows, it has the awful power – in its distrust and scepticism – to extinguish even the natural growth towards ripeness, to make all 'blight'. He links the bloom or flush with health and beauty. Both point to the maturing of a deep potentiality, even if in this case that potential is the over-brimmed, morganatic relationship of a witch and a philosophy student. As elsewhere in Keats's verse, the blush has strong sexual connotations (see, for instance, I.185–99) and ripeness, of course, implies a relationship coming to full sexual consummation. At the same time, the theme of ripeness holds poignant and urgent personal implications for Keats himself in his drive to achieve artistic maturity while living under the lethal threat of tuberculosis (his mother and youngest brother died of this disease, which is, incidentally, characterised by its victim's pallor).

This red/white tension running throughout also stresses the narrow margin (another 'fragile bar') that hovers between ripeness and blight. Line 250 tries to fix our attention to it and to the deadly stamp of philosophy, pressed onto Lamia's hand,

> As pale it lay upon the rosy couch...

The icy shock of her hand sends a wave of terror through Lycius (and notice how touch, too, is an important motif in this section). Then a sudden 'unnatural' turn to heat alerts his senses to the imminence of disaster. The outcome is a swift blighting of Lamia's 'soft bloom', her sexual passion becoming withered and dispelled beneath the icy touch of rationalism, spelling out her dying fall: 'no longer fair, there sat a deadly white' (II.276).

Ripeness and its fair bloom are further examples of those 'charms' that fly at the merest touch of philosophy. The development of this dark secret love is infected and undone in the bud like a sick rose – and the poem has many hints of this idea (see I.133 and II.143; also compare I.366–7, the lovers folded or tightly budded in their cloaks). Lycius himself was a budding philosopher at the start of the poem and Lamia a budding woman within her 'serpent prison-house' (I.203), while Hermes' nymph is described as 'self-folding like a flower' (I.138).

The tight intricacy of the enfolded bud is the equivalent here of the entangled bower so frequent in Keats's rural idylls. As we might expect, both features point to vital aspects of Keats's psychology, in particular an acute anxiety about blighting his budding poetic prom-ise, together with a persistent concern about bringing to ripeness his relationship with Fanny Brawne, a young woman he had met in September1818.

However, in the poem itself he invests the ill-starred affair with a large measure of moral ambiguity. Gathering up the many references to 'pale' and 'wither', the philosopher is presented as the embodiment of the lovers' deathly blight (in Keats the word 'pale' is inextricably linked with death). Yet Lycius himself anticipates the doom of both his love and his life by opening up or unbudding their love to public inspection. For her part, Lamia too blights their partnership through her use of deception and illusion. Premonitions, hints of failure and destruction thicken the atmosphere of the poem with growing fear and scepticism – ironically the very philosophical doubts that will clip, 'unweave' and devastate it.

While ripeness remains the ideal, for Keats's mortals the nightmare reality is one of blight and pain. The nightmare contrasts with the dreams of immortals such as Hermes, dreams that are typified by success, ripeness and everlasting bliss.

The extract above concerns a ripening, of course, an artistic climax in which the poem's thematic strands converge just as the main characters themselves converge onto the banquet. The extract brings to the fore the poem's chief moral components, and what it lays open before us (or 'unperplexes') is actually a moral ambiguity at the heart of the narrative. It is an ambiguity which owes its origins to the ambivalent allegorical roles of the three main characters in relation to their individual fates. We can examine each in turn, starting with the uninvited tutor.

Apollonius, 'wrinkled' sage, bald of pate and grey of beard, is the figurehead for Keats's assault on philosophy and the excesses of rationalism. This assault emerges fully into the open in the above extract, following the description of Apollonius's factious wreath in line 228. Guilt-inducing, brow-beating, he clearly stands for 'consequitive reasoning'. At other moments in the poem he is calm, austere and severe (II.157–8), a sophist (II.172 and 299), as well as simply a 'ruthless man' (II.277). Keats repeatedly reminds us of his advanced age, as here, and emphasises his function as a symbol of the old order, the existing status quo, which has become threatened by the vigorous sway of the dazzling Lamia working on youthful Lycius, symbol of the new. Lycius himself has in effect discarded his former tutor, the 'aching ghost' (II.294), who has until now stalked the dark by-ways of his mind, the 'ghost of folly haunting my sweet dreams' (I.377).

Apollonius is thus linked inextricably with the conscience. From his first appearance he exerts a shadowy, persistent and unnerving moral presence. Yet the exact nature of its moral thrust is not very exact: what precisely does he revile in Lamia? On the other hand the force of this moral presence is undeniable and is most evident in the section immediately following our extract, with its cumulative negatives and imagery of sickness and horror,

> the stately music no more breathes;
> The myrtle sickened in a thousand wreathes.
> By faint degrees, voice, lute, and pleasure ceased...
>
> (II.263–5)

For Lycius too, Apollonius becomes a 'horrid presence', a 'foul dream' who himself indulges 'unlawful magic and enticing lies' (II.286). What's more, Apollonius may actually possess the power of prescience (see II.162). More than merely a 'moment's thought', this unlawful magic would, if we are correct, make him a wizard too, alongside and of the same order as Lamia. And interestingly, in line

246 he has, serpent-like, 'fixed his eye' on her, 'Brow-beating her fair
form', so that he leaves us with the firm suspicion that we have not
one but two rival magi, two demon forces, warring for the soul of
poor, helpless Lycius.

And what of Lamia? If Apollonius symbolises old age and the
cold-eyed discipline of reason, as well as the male principle, then how
can we interpret Lamia? On one, simplistic, level she personifies
youthful passion, oozes sensuality and seductive beauty: in short a
siren. Exciting and vital, there can be no doubt that she invests the
poem with intensity and sexual verve. But she is more than this
allegorical element, more than a formulaic *femme fatale*. She is the
prime mover of the poem, catalyst of Lycius's tragic end, and as such
she has to be a complex player. And Keats makes her so.

Catching the moment of her nemesis, the extract describes her as
'tender-personed' (i.e. sensitive, line 238) and 'aching' (223). This is
more of woman than of serpent. To see Lamia here pale, trapped and
paralysed stirs our deeper sympathies especially as we recall her
bright charm and quicksilver vigour, centre of bliss and pain in the
poem, and her passion to take part in human life. Seen alongside the
two flat figures of Lycius and Apollonius, she is ironically and
essentially more human than they are, less than serpent.

Though he presents her as a witch ('Circean', I.115) Keats seems
to underplay this aspect. In balance with her fully developed emotions she is also 'of sciental brain' (I.191) and is therefore a worthy
match for Apollonius, so that while Lycius is overwhelmed by lustful
passion her own wisdom and judgement remain relatively unim-
paired. She is the pivot as well as the central focus for the poem
both in its morality and in its narrative. The most fully rounded
character, she is significantly described by Keats as 'Tip-toe' (I.287),
denoting again a character that has existed in more than one sphere;
Lamia experiences life in the full range, animal, human and supernatural spheres. Her sciental cunning together with her canny haggling
with Hermes at the start demonstrate that she is to be understood in
the tale as more than just an emblem of carnal lusts. On the other
hand, the allure of her voice – 'bubbling honey' – together with her
readiness for shape-shifting reminds us that she is also Keats's
representative of the Romantic poetic imagination.

Among her many other paradoxical nicknames she is a 'penanced lady elf', a 'dreamer's mistress' and the 'demon's self' (I.55–6), a 'virgin' though of 'deep love learned' (I.190), a 'fair creature' (I.200), 'cruel' (I.290), yet 'gentle' (I.334), a 'goddess' (I.336). And she may even have been a prostitute before encountering Lycius (see I.311–14). Of infinite variety and conflicting traits, she remains beautifully elusive to us, a mysteriously charismatic shadow. Her pains and bliss, and her anxiety of both, elicit a strangely similar host of responses from the reader, mixing sympathy and censure in varying ratios.

From the very beginning an air of doom seems to hover over Lamia, signalling the victim. Beginning as a knotted serpent, she is fiercely enmeshed in her own vexed emotions, and then as a woman she is moved by these to deceive and subtly entangle Lycius in her complexity, and she weeps for this. Is it fair to denounce her simply for cruelty? On balance, I think not. In fact it is not possible to attach blame or guilt to Lamia on the normal grounds. She does no evil as such and nor does she invoke death. At worst she falls victim simply to becoming human. That and the fact that she appears to bear death and destruction like a mark or stigma in her glittering train.

If she is to be denounced morally by the outcomes of the poem then this must only be in allegorical terms. As the 'brilliance feminine' (I.92) she is an exquisite foil to philosophy's 'dull catalogue of common things'. Moreover, in spite of the philosopher's 'wrinkled' disdain (his conventional moral attitude) towards her she succeeds in drawing out the reader's sympathy. This comes about because of her suffering, of course, but is also due to her loneliness, as well as her eventual demise. Neither is our admiration slow to stir. She is a single-minded agent of free will, stepping out of line to impose herself on the picture and achieve her heart's desire. Like so many of Keats's heroines she seizes the sexual initiative and does so in face of the obvious risks. Cruel deceiver? Probably. Eloquent enchantress, possessed of the 'delicious tongue' (I.249)? Without any doubt. For Lycius she is youth and magic, excitement, gusto, the quintessence of Romantic imagination. But ultimately and disappointingly, she is ethereal, elusive and, of course, ephemeral. Like the rainbow's blush she too becomes blighted in an instant by that 'mere touch of cold philosophy'. Lamia's quicksilver spirit is formulated beneath Apollonius's sciental pin and she is gone 'with a frightful scream' (II.306).

Finally, how does Lycius fit into this allegorical triangle, between Lamia and Apollonius? Our extract stresses his youthfulness (225). He is 'in chief place' and 'glad', implying a degree of naive conceit. He is, of course, callow as well as gauche, and lacks the guile and experience of the two antagonists. He is biddable by both while his lame attempt to curry his teacher's approval ('to beseech a glance . . . / And pledge him', lines 243–5) exposes his naivety and its despair.

We should not overlook the fact that Lycius himself is a victim. He pays the fullest price and yet he is less a victim of Lamia than of his own unmanageable feelings. If this is true, then in allegorical terms what is the point of his death? Punishment for his selfishness and ruthlessness? Yet this does not ring true since Apollonius too is guilty of these. Or is it that he performs sex with an animal? This is not feasible either, because he is ignorant of this (he doesn't even know her name let alone her species). His will becomes quickly subsumed beneath Lamia's, melting and swooning, until the blundering impulse to publish his love brings him into disastrous conflict with the everyday reality of Corinth and he is damned. In contrast with Endymion, Lycius is ineluctably mortal and since Apollonius ensures that he remains so, his 'deep-recessed vision' of immortal bliss is doomed (II.275). If Lamia represents the far-sighted vision and Apollonius the commonplace reality that will unweave it then Lycius is the inevitable failure to unite the two. This is his tragedy.

In truth, however, while Keats's intrusive narrator continually draws our attention to the possibility of allegorical readings these are never fully settled. Allegorical readings offer us conflicts of age and youth, male versus female, reason and passion, moderation and excess, and so on. But there is no debate. We get the undeniable impression that *Lamia* is a moral tale but what the moral is remains problematic. Is there a hero and, if so, who is the villain? Is this the bowery Garden of Eden or perhaps the purple stews of Sodom and Gomorrah? In spite of Keats's efforts to make the moral more lucid than that of, say, *Endymion* the allegory fails (frustratingly) to reach a tidy ripeness.

At the same time a reading that tries to insist on working out a full allegorical interpretation would be reductive and impoverishing – and probably impossible, anyway. For Keats to have made this a straight-forward parable would have stripped out the beautiful complications of the characters and their overwrought tale. Reduced to a simple philosophy, the poem would be deprived of those tensions between the elusive allegory and its fevered love story: the 'ruddy strife / Of hearts and lips' (I.40–1).

It would also have been an affront to Keats's marvellous poetic skills. He brilliantly judges the teasing suggestiveness of the poem's (and Lamia's) mysteries, leaving the reader in delightful uncertainty, 'without any irritable reaching after fact & reason'. This quotation comes from one of Keats's letters to his brothers (21 December 1817) and explains a readiness to accept the mystery of life. He coined the term 'Negative Capability' to describe the condition of simply accepting or celebrating the mystery of our being in the world. Accept it for what it is, it says, without rationalisation, instead of struggling fretfully for absolute definition – which is what rationalist philosophy would advocate, to 'Conquer all mysteries by rule and line' (II.235). The concept of Negative Capability appears repeatedly in his verse and there are early hints of it in *Sleep and Poetry*, and *'I stood tip-toe'*.

Technically speaking, *Lamia* is very much concerned with the art of judgement. In contrast to the baggy *Endymion*, *Lamia* achieves a beautifully fine tuning of poetic and narrative poise. This is largely due to Keats's application of his own theory of Negative Capability, a measured balancing of the reader's desire to be told against the author's need to reveal. It is very much a matter of Keats's sensitivity as to what to say, what to hint, and what to 'smother'. So the tensions and desires in the poem are largely generated through the fluctuating interaction of these three points; for example, the relationship be-tween the allegorical and narrational aspects, the friction between the three main characters, and the frisson between the substance and the silences. All these areas, desires and conflicts, reach their head in the above extract, where they come to a thrilling denouement.

How then does Keats actually pull it off and so superbly here? The devil is in the detail. Just before the start of the extract, we see

Lycius's sumptuous banquet beginning to get into its bibulous flow, the 'happy wine' freeing every soul from its 'human trammels' (II.210). And then the swelling optimism is brusquely halted by those three menacing questions in lines 221–2: What... What... What? and their ominous references to wreaths. Their effect is to jolt the viewpoint out of the gathering action, cutting and detaching us (like the guests themselves), into the sudden haunting vacuum of that 'deadly silence' in line 266, into which Lycius's desperate cry of 'Lamia' sinks and dies. Apollonius, and Keats too of course, takes abrupt and insistent control now, thrusting into the poem a numbing tone of alarm. From this point, the icy horror unfolds over the following fifty lines or so with all the helplessness of a slow-motion disaster.

The diction plays a crucial part here in creating this intimidating pressure. The studied interplay of sight and touch weaves a fine tangle of danger while lurking beneath it the imagery of intimidation and aggression deepens the menace: 'strip', 'spear', 'spiteful', 'pains', 'terror' and so on. The horror is worked out against a cauldron of sounds which putters, spouts and hisses with gathering venom (for example, listen to lines 226–8 and 265–6).

Nor is this the first time that we have heard the explicit voice of Keats's narrator. It has been there all the way through, unmistakably at our elbow and sometimes ahead, anticipating and controlling our responses. In contrast to that of *Endymion* this is a new type of voice, focused and infused with authority and self-assurance. And there is a new economy of style. The author gets to the heart of the story promptly and runs with it, making events urgent, lucid and with a strong sense of direction – in the story-line at least.

One indication of this mature confidence is Keats's technique of repeatedly foreshadowing the demise of the two lovers even in the moment that they first meet (see, for example, I.260–70, II.7, and II.221). He carries off this objective chiefly through the manipulation of the pale/red colour duality, and his use of dramatic ironies to create an awesome sense of doom for the helpless victims (Keats's success here is achieved by working through the characters, but compare *Isabella; or, The Pot of Basil* where he is much less effective in this). While the price is some loss of suspense, the poet more than compensates by way of his brilliant pictorial effects, the intriguing silences about Lamia and Apollonius, as well as the bristling tension generated between the two of them.

While Keats's voice is ever-present in the poem there is no great sense of intrusiveness about it. His opening and closing remarks frame and contain the narrative, cutting off all escape for its characters (compare *The Eve of St Agnes* where the narrator's voice builds up a similar claustral effect). Equally, it seems to me that Keats holds back his own direct emotions from the story (another lesson learned from *Endymion*) and yet he moves along, close by his characters, commenting on them while repeatedly involving and challenging the reader in the moral discussion (see, for example, lines 229–36 in the above extract and lines II.1–4).

The lyrical beauty that was evident in *Endymion* and the early verse has lost none of its power in the later narratives. There is now, too, an unmistakable versatility in Keats's voice, by turns ironic, feeling, mocking, brisk and frank, balancing a full spectrum of narrative moods and nuance while flighting the tragic arrow on its lethal line. With his new spareness of treatment, Keats's settings are now more convincingly humane, more vividly intense. He replaces the bosky rural idyll of *Endymion* with something approaching a more modern, metropolitan scene and he seems quite at ease with it (for instance, in the atmospheric Corinthian street-scape at the end of Part I). Further, the mythological elements seem less cumbersome, less clogging than those of *Endymion* – it is not necessary to mug up the 'Lamia' myth in order to savour the drama on its various levels.

The lyrical beauty endures and there is no stinting on the rich musicality or heady poetic sensuousness. In the train of its pulsating momentum, the verse now reveals Keats's more expert management of language's resonances. Almost every phrase is packed with deep possibilities of meaning so that words like 'fretted' (II.137) and 'spoil' (II.145) reach into fertile moral and emotional horizons at the same time as they operate on the literal level (in the extract, try exploring the prospects implicit in the words 'aching' and 'haunted' in the way that we have explored 'blighted' in line 275). More than anything, it is this dazzling fluency in allowing words to operate with so many rich possibilities that distinguishes the Keats of 1819 from that of 1817, imbuing the texture of the poem with an almost occult quality.

Keats now has what we might call a more architectural attitude to language. By this I mean the facility to set up contrasting modes of language side by side. For example, he sets up starkly realistic passages (such as the streets of Corinth, the banquet itself, and Apollonius's 'assault') against accounts of magical and supernatural appearances or transformations (such as Lamia's metamorphosis and the fantastic preparations before the banquet).

This dualism is mirrored in the different modes of language used by Keats and also in the other teasing ambivalences of the poem. While representing himself as the reliable narrator of the story he repeatedly induces doubt and ambiguity to 'perplex' the mind of the reader; for example, Lamia is mysteriously both a virgin and sexually experienced (I.189–90). Each character can be understood equivo-cally as both hero and villain and there is the familiar Keatsian paradox of bliss with its 'neighbour pain' as well as of sensation and thought. When we add these in with the ambivalent allegory we may justifiably feel that the apparently lucid text involves a subterfuge – an attempt to induce that very dis-comfort which drives the characters themselves. Even in the ending of the poem we have no real sense of calm or ease.

In spite of these paradoxes, *Lamia* has a distinct feeling of rugged-ness about it. Perhaps this arises from the solidity of the poetic metre in which Keats sets it. *Lamia* marks a return after almost two years to the heroic couplet, the 'stretched metre' as Keats called it, of *Endym-ion*. But now the most noticeable literary influence is John Dryden. Keats had made a detailed and eager study of this seventeenth-century poet during the summer of 1819. The Hermes episode of Part I of *Lamia* is quite typical of Dryden's subject matter and treatment, and the metre of rhyming couplets echoes Dryden's style, especially his penchant for occasional alexandrines (iambic hexameter; for examples, see lines I.75, I.152, II.121 and II.198). And to disrupt the risk of monotony inherent in such a simple rhyme scheme Keats also sporadically inserts triplets here (see I.63, I.150–2, I.206–11 and II.154–6 for examples). For the same reason he deftly manipulates run-over lines, shifting the stress and the pause from the end of the line towards the middle (a feature which was quite controversial for its day). In addition he freely experiments with irregular and sight rhymes, particularly in Part II where the atmosphere becomes increasingly impassioned.

This readiness to experiment (along with his success in it) is one of the bench-marks of Keats's style at this stage in his career and it points to his keen professional interest in the techniques and potentialities of his vocation. Even a cursory glance back at *Endymion* will discover the great advances achieved in *Lamia* with its tremendous grace and sweep, the boldness of stroke. It is a truly dazzling creation, fascinating in its tensions and ambiguities, its dangers and gordian intrigues, as well as in its alternative realities and complexities, not least in its eponymous heroine. And underpinning all of this broad synthesis of delights is the exquisite medium of Keats's music.

Conclusions

In this chapter we have discussed two poems from opposite ends of Keats's writing life. This has enabled us to observe the progress made between them in terms of themes and contexts. We have seen that his own comments on *Lamia* reveal his awareness of the importance of 'Judgement' and this is one of the key underlying differences between the two compositions.

The two poems graphically reveal developments in style, thematic awareness, and artistic attitude but, perhaps above all, the greater clarity of vision by the time he wrote *Lamia*. We can see, too, some easing in those personal tensions which had detracted from Keats's apprentice works: his anxiety to achieve poetic fame, the fury against Neo-Classical attitudes, and his muddled ideas about composing a 'long Poem'.

With less worrying attention to critical reception or personal ambition Keats is free to translate the tensions of his own life into the poetry itself. Accordingly, by the time of *Lamia*, a more relaxed voice achieves some very satisfying dramatic intensities by way of the deployment of dramatic setting and conflict, opposing dualities, and realistic characterisation. In simple terms, a more studied Keats has by now discovered his own clear voice and refined his overall approach.

Comparing the two texts with regard to Keats's thematic interests, some common focuses are equally evident; these include issues of time, the nature of human mortality (especially in the context of the supernatural), the nature and importance of the imagination, and in particular how it bears on the relationship between dream and reality. We have also seen something of how Keats strives to resolve his problematic attitude to women, especially in his ideas on love, inspiration and sexuality.

We can note too the great leap forward in Keats's stylistics, for instance in his exploitation of the perspectives inherent in the heroic couplet - in addition to a greater understanding of narrative techniques (such as characterisation, plot, form, theme, and authorial viewpoint). Furthermore, we see in *Lamia* an elevated capacity to combine metaphysics and narrative in a more natural synthesis. In his concept of Negative Capability too he demonstrates the extent of his intellectual and aesthetic sensitivity as well as his full commitment to the art of poetry. More fundamentally, *Lamia* reveals advances in the subtle manipulation of desire and his exploitation of other worlds and presences – an approach which is clearly manifest in the major odes and in the other mature narratives.

Yet ultimately both poems attest to Keats's steadfast devotion to a rich textural music but a music increasingly employed for structural as well as for pure sensual impact. Though *Lamia* betrays a relaxing of his enmity towards rationalist philosophy it continues to show the poet's delight in the senses, in 'a Life of Sensations rather than of Thoughts', as he recorded in November 1817.

Further Research

To further develop your appreciation of Keats's style in *Lamia* take a close look at the section in Part I in which Lycius and Lamia enter the city of Corinth (I.350–97). Show how Keats creates the atmosphere of the city that night and in particular how he evokes a sense of danger. Why is this passage important to the rest of the narrative?

Some readers argue that Keats should have let the story finish at this point – what is your view, and what reasons would you give to support it? What is the effect of the final four lines of this section?

3

The Two Hyperions: 'a more naked and grecian Manner'

Hyperion. A Fragment

Where in *Lamia* Dryden was foremost among Keats's poetic models, in *Hyperion. A Fragment* he came under the hypnotic spell of one of Dryden's contemporaries, the great poet and republican John Milton (1608–74). But it was a spell which brought uneven blessings.

Having discussed two long love poems I would now like to turn to Keats's two attempts at the story of Hyperion. The first, *Hyperion. A Fragment*, was begun in Autumn 1818, at the start of what is usually regarded as Keats's great creative year. Following a relatively dry period, artistically speaking, Keats got down to try once more the 'beautiful mythology of Greece' as he had promised in his preface to *Endymion*. But its progress was far from smooth and, in particular, two key events intervened to disrupt it.

One of these events was the gradual decline and eventual death in December 1818 of Keats's brother Tom, whom he had tirelessly nursed over his final months. And the other crucial event in Keats's life was his introduction to Fanny Brawne, the woman who quickly came to occupy his emotional life most intensely. After a highly agitated courtship they became engaged and she emerged as the leading inspiration for the character of Mnemosyne in Hyperion (and the force behind almost all of the verse in Keats's later career).

While his original scheme for the first Hyperion was a treatment in twelve books, he later revised this to only four. And then after a harrowing struggle with problems in the verse he eventually, in April 1819, gave it up. The basic plot of *Hyperion* is quite simple and can be summarised in three sentences. The Titans, an ancient order of gods, have been overthrown by their offspring, the Olympians, and only Hyperion himself remains unvanquished by this new order (though he is deeply troubled by premonitions of doom). Enceladus, a humiliated Titan, is moved by Hyperion's tenacity into proposing a counter rebellion, though his speech gets a mixed reception. Book III opens with a magnificent new dawn and the emergence of Apollo, dazzling as the new god of the sun.

The passage I have chosen for discussion is from Oceanus's speech in Book II, lines 190 to 229. Saturn is conscious of the need to respond to the recent rebellion and approaches Oceanus diffidently on account of the latter's composure, 'That severe content / Which comes of thought and musing' (II.165–6; compare this with the description of Oceanus in *Endymion* at III.997, where he goes to 'muse for ever...'). Although Keats describes him as 'Sophist and sage', anyone expecting a weak or vague equivocator will be surprised by the passion shown at the start of his speech (though still 'not a bellows unto ire', II.176).

> Thou art not the beginning nor the end.   190
> From Chaos and parental Darkness came
> Light, the first fruits of that intestine broil,
> That sullen ferment, which for wondrous ends
> Was ripening in itself. The ripe hour came,
> And with it Light, and Light, engendering
> Upon its own producer, forthwith touched
> The whole enormous matter into life.
> Upon that very hour, our parentage,
> The Heavens, and the Earth, were manifest:
> Then thou first born, and we the giant race,   200
> Found ourselves ruling new and beauteous realms.
> Now comes the pain of truth, to whom 'tis pain –
> O folly! for to bear all naked truths,

And to envisage circumstance, all calm,
That is the top of sovereignty. Mark well!
As Heaven and Earth are fairer, fairer far
Than Chaos and blank Darkness, though once chiefs;
And as we show beyond that Heaven and Earth
In form and shape compact and beautiful,
In will, in action free, companionship,   210
And thousand other signs of purer life;
So on our heels a fresh perfection treads,
A power more strong in beauty, born of us
And fated to excel us, as we pass
In glory that old Darkness: nor are we
Thereby more conquered, than by us the rule
Of shapeless Chaos. Say, doth the dull soil
Quarrel with the proud forests it hath fed,
And feedeth still, more comely than itself?
Can it deny the chiefdom of green groves?   220
Or shall the tree be envious of the dove
Because it cooeth, and hath snowy wings
To wander wherewithal and find its joys?
We are such forest-trees, and our fair boughs
Have bred forth, not pale solitary doves,
But eagles golden-feathered, who do tower
Above us in their beauty, and must reign
In right thereof. For 'tis the eternal law
That first in beauty should be first in might.   229

As we might expect, Oceanus's speech works on a number of different levels (one of which is that Oceanus is very much a mouthpiece for Keats's own ideas at this time). We can begin by examining some of the issues it raises, and then move on to consider aspects of style, relating the extract to the rest of the poem.

As a whole, *Hyperion* is very much concerned with two important thematic elements, both of which are touched on here by Oceanus: one is the role of suffering as an essential ordeal in the development of a poet (hinted at in line 202), and the other is the nature of beauty – especially its relationship to truth and might (lines 201, 209 and 229).

To begin at the beginning, Oceanus sets out both a Chaos theory and a Genesis myth (see II.132). In the beginning is Chaos and darkness and out of this primeval, prelapsarian condition comes light at the right, ripe moment. There are, of course, Biblical hints in the language and concepts here but, as we might also expect, Oceanus offers a pagan explanation of the origins of the universe. There is no creator, not even a mind or will behind it all, simply Light coupling with 'its own producer' (i.e. darkness; line 196), triggering off the whole of the material universe. Primeval Chaos is character- ised by darkness, which is amorphous and unformed. However, in time, as light and substance materialise so too does 'form and shape' (209), and then even the Titans themselves, 'The first-born of all shaped and palpable Gods' (II.153).

The notion of shape coming forth from amorphous, pre-temporal night is highly interesting for Keats's concept of the artist and also for the theory of beauty set out here by Oceanus. But first let us explore some preliminary reflections on background themes.

It is paradoxical that Oceanus should be the mouthpiece for ideas about 'form and shape' since of all the gods the god of the sea must be about the most formless, or protean (and the poem as a whole has many references to things taking shape or having no shape at all; see, for instance, line II.79). At first, 'form and shape' is expressed in terms of sequence (line 190) and of time (implicit in the references to ripeness and 'engendering', lines 194–5). Understandably, these points lie at the heart of Oceanus's conciliatory message to the Titans: in other words, rather than feel humiliated by defeat they should view their overthrow as merely an inevitable consequence of evolution. So, as 'first born' (200) they became part of the time-sequence, caught up in events emerging from Chaos and Darkness: since time caused them to become supreme in the first place they should not grumble now they are subject to change and casualties of that process.

As Oceanus points out, Chaos ceased when the moment was ripe, and this characteristic Keatsian theme of ripeness is a familiar facet of his theme of time. The view expressed here is that time itself is a manifestation of order on the wider scale, a means of organising the world and its events, so to speak, chronologically. Evolution, too, typifies this notion of temporal order, though Oceanus does add that the underlying assumption in his theory is that precedence is based on might – itself a function of beauty (229). All of this adds up to the fact that the overthrow of the Titans themselves also reached its moment of ripeness (which is strangely paradoxical given that we would normally regard the gods as living outside the realm of time, and therefore beyond the realm of change and death).

On the other hand, inside Oceanus's doctrine of evolution the fact of precedence is neither disinterested nor completely accidental. The younger generation expels the older simply on the basis of a more fitting, more advanced kind of might and beauty:

> So on our heels a fresh perfection treads...
>
> (II.212)

The keyword here is 'perfection'. It emphasises Oceanus's faith in evolution as progress, as an improvement, a view shared by Keats himself, who believed that the development of mankind obeyed an obscure law of progress (in a letter to his brother George in September 1819 Keats optimistically claimed that mankind was becoming increasingly more enlightened).

With all this in mind, time is thus presented as an element of the natural order. A tenacious vein of time imagery runs throughout the poem and through Oceanus's speech in particular, constantly reminding us of its inevitable elapse. It is linked throughout with the themes of action and free will and, in this context, with the idea of ripeness, which is crucial if we want to understand the vital relationship between Hyperion and Apollo.

In stressing the notion of fate in his theory of evolution, Oceanus makes it clear that progress is less a matter of absolute free will than of ripeness from within: things naturally come to their fruition (and he refers directly to fruit and ripening at the start of the extract). Keats was keenly sensitive to the possibility of his own moment of ripening as a poet and I think this is manifested in the plight of Apollo in Book III. The germ of Apollo's deep-rooted anxiety is an acute awareness that in order to fulfil his radiant promise as the god of the sun he must come to ripeness at this moment... or wither in pain, unregarded beneath the darkness of oblivion. In Book II,

Oceanus's concern with time draws out the whole central thrust of the poem and directs it towards Apollo's climactic moment in Book III, his moment of ripeness and thus of apotheosis.

By paralleling Apollo's position with that of Keats himself we can open up the poem to some interesting allegorical interpretations. For example, the theme of revolution suggests an analogy with the recent French and American Revolutions and at the same time hints at the ousting of eighteenth-century, Neo-Classical literature by the Romantics. Yet more important to Keats is the matter of his own poetic ripeness: the fulfilment of artistic potential, especially in the light of tormenting doubts about his real poetic worth.

Creativity in general is referred to early on in the poem; for example, Saturn moans in exasperation,

> But cannot I create?
> Cannot I form? Cannot I fashion forth...?
>
> (I.141–2)

Deposed, Saturn can be interpreted as a lapsed artist, bereft and impotent. And in the extract above, Oceanus refers to darkness as the 'producer' which, together with light, is essential for converting matter into life. But, most important of all, out of parental darkness comes forth beauty because, in the process of evolution, 'form and shape' are imposed on rough, unformed matter – as the artist too creates meaning and beauty from nothing, sparking 'The whole enormous matter into life' (I.197). It is an idea that occurs early in Keats's work; for instance, in '*I stood tip-toe*', he conceives of the poet as someone 'bringing / Shapes from the invisible world...' (lines 185–6), translating this other world into a coherent beauty.

Oceanus's speech anticipates the advent of Apollo in Book III (as does Clymene in her speech immediately following Oceanus's, prophesying the beautiful and mysterious music of Apollo, who is also god of art). However, the moment of ripeness, of full realisation of the potential, is not to be achieved without some suffering, a point implied in the phrase 'the pain of truth' (202). Apollo will not achieve apotheosis, attain his divinity, without first enduring the pain of worldly experience. In the same way, Keats was convinced that the

new Keats, the true, fully humanised poet, could only supplant the
'old Keats', his old uncertain self, by enduring human pain in the real
world and thus acquiring the authentic poetic voice. Thus the emergence of the new Apollo in Book III represents the genesis of the
new Keats's true poetic soul rising resplendent above the relic of
the old. The new voice is fashioned by knowledge forged in turmoil,
and in the brutal ordeal of witnessing his brother Tom's agonising
death in December 1818.

It must be said, however, that Keats's concept of ripeness also
involves a paradox. Is ripeness a matter of choice and action (that is,
of free will) or is it simply a question of time, of destiny and merely
waiting for the moment to arrive? The poem makes many references to
laws, power, might and freedom, as well as to doom and fate, and
almost all the characters are faced with the problem of action. The
'problem' is partly a question of *how* to act and partly having the *power* to.

In fact at the end of the extract Oceanus describes two of the laws
of the universe: the law of progressive evolution which controls the
course of history, and the law or force which lies behind evolution
itself,

> For 'tis the eternal law
> That first in beauty should be first in might.

> (228–9)

When we first meet Saturn and the Titans, at the start of the poem,
they are paralysed by inertia, 'quiet as a stone / Still as the silence'
(I.4–5), and 'nerveless, listless' (I.18). In Book II they are a disjointed
collection in painful disarray, some tortured in chains, others simply
wandering. Only Hyperion hints at the exercise of free action
(though at home in his palace he is besieged by doubt and angst).
Yet, while Books I and II point to the Fall, Book III deals with the
Call, and Mnemosyne's annunciation, stirring Apollo to assert the will
at the moment of ripeness, breaking free of the determinism which
imprisons the fallen Titans.

Given the beauty–might principle expounded by Oceanus the
basic premise of Apollo's triumph over Hyperion is that he is 'first
in beauty'. But to understand Apollo's elevation more fully as the

central event of the poem we first need to examine more closely what exactly Oceanus means by this.

In Book I, Keats gives us an awesome impression of Hyperion's power over the sun (e.g. I.288–9). At the same time it is clear that the god's power is subservient to the 'season due', that he must therefore obey Nature's order. Even if he wished to 'seize the arrow's barb' (I.344) he does not have the absolute power to do so. What Hyperion stresses is in fact not freedom at all but raw power and a blazing passion, both of which are undermined by his ineradicable anxiety. At the very heart of Hyperion, his anxiety or uncertainty betrays a deficit of truth – and it is this truth which is the integral premise of Oceanus's concept of beauty.

With this in mind we see that the extract exposes the important link between beauty and the artist, and the free will which is essential to both,

> In form and shape compact and beautiful,
> In will, in action free...
>
> (II.209–10)

Each generation deposes the previous one on the basis of might and beauty. For Oceanus/Keats the essence of beauty lies in the word 'shape', the emergence from darkness into light at the moment of fruition, that moment being the point of truth or (as we might say) self-realisation. In other words, beauty is the vital source of assurance when it is also grounded in truth, the truth of one's own genuine nature. To achieve this kind of awareness however, also requires imagination, of course, and this is something the declining Titans are deficient in.

This point is particularly apparent in the case of Apollo. Prompted by Mnemosyne (yet another of Keats's encounters with a mystery woman) he discovers the truth about his own nature, instilling in him a radiant self-assurance, leading him on to deification. Thus, beauty is not simply pulchritude or glory but significantly it has an ethical dimension, entailing a form of self-knowledge, conviction or honesty.

This complex idea is one which buzzed about inside Keats for most of his writing life. As he was completing *Endymion* he drew together some of these threads when he wrote in a letter, 'What the imagination seizes as Beauty must be truth' (22 November 1817), and then later in 'Ode on a Grecian Urn' (1819) he famously proposed that 'Beauty is truth, truth beauty' (line 49). However, in comparison with *Endymion* at least, the poet of *Hyperion* has a much more coherent perception of beauty, which springs from his deepening vision of the human experience, of the complex relationship between suffering and joy. *Hyperion* reveals these new depths and insights, most vividly and maddeningly, in the unfinished portrayal of Apollo.

So far we have tended to follow a philosophical interpretation of the poem. But this does not mean that Keats has reneged on his blast against philosophy in *Sleep and Poetry* and renewed in *Lamia*. It is not difficult to see that Keats invariably links beauty not with knowledge but with feeling, and as we have noted in the above extract, Oceanus/Keats refers explicitly to the 'pain of truth' (202). The object is to endure, to 'bear all naked truths, / And to envisage circumstance, all calm' (203–4), to triumph over anguish and to come through, 'A power more strong in beauty' (213). Paradoxically it is Keats's insistence on suffering and the pain of loss that humanises the fallen gods, lending the poem its deeper psychological appeal. Moreover, in the agonies of Apollo, Keats presents us with the idea that sorrow can actually be creative (see I.35–6) and in this aspect the critic Kenneth Muir identifies Apollo as a Christ-like figure taking upon himself the pain and sorrows of mankind.

We can observe that Apollo does become the end-point for the vein of suffering that runs through this poem. Yet Keats's use of gods, the Titans, to demonstrate this human idea never quite comes off. Either as gods or as people, they are never fully convincing and this may have been one of the reasons why Keats abandoned the poem. In addition, by this point in the text the poem had become too abstract. Still another, more likely reason for dropping it lies in Keats's concept of Negative Capability, which we considered briefly in the previous chapter. In a letter to his brothers he defined this concept as a state in which 'a man is capable of being in uncertainties, Mysteries, doubts, without any irritable reaching after fact & reason' (21 December 1817).

Hyperion has many allusions to uncertainties and mysteries and doubts (see I.277–81 and II.129–31; and Hyperion himself is referred to as 'Son of Mysteries' at I.310). Such mysteries are to Oceanus the equivalent of that 'old darkness' and 'shapeless Chaos' out of which the light of the Titans had emerged. What he tries to alert them to now is the idea that the new generation represents a new light, a new grasp of the truth. The old Titans are obdurately resistant to truth, having fallen from 'sovereignty', but if they would only face up to truth it would become for them the source of healing 'calm'. As he says later in his speech, 'Receive the truth, and let it be your balm' (II.243).

In this context Mnemosyne ('supreme shape') is a key figure because, as the Call, she represents a particular type of enlightenment for Apollo (self-knowledge), and in his own address to her he himself makes frequent references to knowledge, as well as to power and to poetry. It is Mnemosyne who presses him to face up to reality and to discover that through his experience of the world and especially its suffering he will be transformed into a deity. In the triumphant climax to Book III, Apollo's deepening self-awareness and surging pride is mirrored in a glorious exuberant dawn, golden and red, expanding to the moment of ripeness in which light, truth and the new order blaze out from darkness and pain, until at last Apollo proclaims:

> Knowledge enormous makes a god of me.
>
> (III.113)

It is not, however, intellectual knowledge (of 'fact and reason') that brings about the change but experiential knowledge, in the form of suffering – in Keats truth is seldom a propositional statement, but rather a feeling for the inner identity of something, including the self.

To return to Oceanus's speech, as 'Sophist and sage', his speech is of course closely argued and expertly structured: it moves from themes of Chaos and Darkness, through those of time, truth and beauty, to climax in that 'eternal law' in line 229. His restrained dialectic, grounded in reason, contrasts him with the irrascible Enceladus and his knee-jerk appeal to violence and confrontation.

Oceanus functions both as a character and as Keats's mouthpiece in the poem. In both aspects he derives closely from Keats's

intensive reading during this period. Shakespeare's plays are a major
inspiration here (as well as in the rest of Keats's work). The work of
Dante, the great medieval poet of *The Divine Comedy*, was also a very
important influence, now as later, and in particular the *Inferno*
section of that work. But probably the heaviest presence in *Hyperion*
is John Milton's *Paradise Lost*. For Keats's generation Milton casts a
long and powerful shadow. As a model of epic verse, his poetic
style is highly individualised and its rhetoric is infectiously compelling. Inevitably Keats succumbed to its lofty strains, its Latinisms,
rhythms, repetitions and inversions as well as to its exalted imagery
and vocabulary. Yet while Milton's echoes remain loudly audible
in *Hyperion*, Keats gradually came to regard them as an 'alien tongue',
eventually asserting that 'Life to him would be death to me.' At
last, in March 1819 he broke off the project – for the time being,
anyway.

Oddly, the speeches of Oceanus and Apollo incorporate the
least in terms of Miltonic mannerisms (in the above extract the
best example of Miltonic inversion is in line 226, 'eagles golden-
feathered'). As a result these come closest to Keats's own authentic
voice and, accordingly, they add strength to the view that these
two characters most closely represent the poet's own outlook and
feelings.

With its theme of progressive evolution, that outlook is unmistakably positive, optimistic and, in contrast to that of Enceladus, a
balance of reason and feeling. Along with Clymene's speech it acts
as a bower of quietude amid the clout and clamour of the gloomy
Titans (especially of Hyperion and Enceladus). Although it is perhaps
marked by some degree of resignation, the main thrust of the speech
is conciliatory and forward-looking, for example in lines 211, 215–17
and in the Biblical sounding

> Thou art not the beginning nor the end.
>
> (190)

His composure here is but briefly ruffled, punctuated by the exclamations in lines 203 and 205, and the questions in lines 219, 220,
and 223.

The mood of tranquillity produced by Keats here at the heart of Book II also contrasts with those massy crags and thunderous waterfalls towering above the despondent Titans. The beautifully colossal scenery, gleaned by Keats on a walking tour of the North, are the raw and gritty counterweight to the 'abstractions' into which Keats had lately plunged. Their gargantuan angularities are gloomily sympathetic with the stony paralysis of the Titans. On a pictorial level too they are a stunning production, vividly evocative in contrast to the blandly conventional pastoral of *Endymion*, for instance.

But in our extract we have the unruffled composure of Oceanus. The mood and tenor of his voice is reflected in the simple diction and unforced idioms. Typical of Keats's mature style now is the harmony of a clear theme with a naturalistic, lucid and objective verse style, what Keats himself called 'a more naked and grecian Manner'. Through this purer 'grecian Manner' he sought to avoid the more sentimental cast of *Endymion*, even if in the end he came to feel that it was bedevilled by the awkward Miltonisms that led to its being dropped altogether. Written in a more limber style accommodating a wide range of intensities and scales, *Hyperion* is a still more rugged showcase for Keats's supple range of epic skills: from heroic grandeur to intimate reflection, from the despairing sonorities of the diffident Titans to the triumphant euphoria of Apollo's deification.

Oceanus's speech illustrates well this new 'grecian Manner', concerned as it is with 'naked truths' (203). Not surprising, perhaps, is that it should be short on the rich colour and sound which chimes throughout other parts of Keats's work. Its imagery naturally reflects its primary thematic interests – time and ripeness, power, action, and beauty. Yet at the heart of the speech lies the extended metaphor of the 'proud forests' (lines 217 on). Picking up a line from Book I with its 'green robed senators' (I.73), the figure contrasts with most of the rest of the speech in the vivid character and imagination of its conceit. The references to soil, tree and bird (lines 217 and 221) act in two directions. They suggest a sequence in stages of evolution of course, while at the same time indicating three distinct horizons: *in*, *on* and *above* the earth. Moreover, the increasing sense of freedom in this progression ('in action free', line 210) anticipates the freedom shown in Apollo's elevation in Book III. Significantly, this is as eagles 'golden-feathered' (Apollo's personal colour, line 226), not as 'pale doves', in which 'pale' is Keats's familiar shorthand for death (see also Book III, lines 128 and 131, where Apollo exchanges 'pale' for 'golden' in his transformation).

In their verse form, Keats's two Hyperion poems are unusual in that they are the only two narrative poems framed in blank verse: unrhymed iambic pentameter. Not surprisingly this is also the verse form of the models behind these poems, *Paradise Lost* and Dante's *Inferno* in the English translation by H. F. Cary. Although Keats's experiments with the metre and its caesurae set out to de-regulate the rhythm, *Hyperion* as a whole nevertheless comes over as unnaturally confining, 'cramped and screwed' (II.25), perhaps in sympathy with the Titans' own predicament.

Having said this, however, Oceanus's speech is untypical, being relatively free from metrical and rhetorical constraints, once more reinforcing the idea that Keats was determined his own message should come through clearly. Most of the lines in the above extract are irregular in metre and one effect of this is to shift the stress from the second syllable to the start of the line. At the same time Keats is careful in Oceanus's speech to avoid unstressed line endings by putting strong syllables there or just in front of the caesurae (for examples, see lines 194, 198 and 202). The upshot of these refinements is to make Oceanus sound clear and assertive.

As we should expect, a complex impression similarly emerges from the interaction between the sounds of Oceanus's speech. The cunning interplay of soft /s/ and /f/ sounds with more gritty, insistent /k/ and /d/ consonants seeks to agitate his impassive audience. Other key sounds are also used for specific effect; for example, by turns the speech sizzles and purrs in the mix of /z/ and /r/ sounds (see lines 220–5). Given the lenience in the metre the consonants act together to produce a remarkable unity of sound and texture. This, of course, seems to strengthen Oceanus's noble bearing, his decorum contrasted with the choleric Enceladus and the hypersensitive Hyperion.

As regards the vowels of the extract, this is a good point to take a look at what has been called Keats's 'theory of melody'. In October 1848, long after Keats's death, his very close friend Benjamin Bailey recalled that 'one of Keats's favourite topics of conversation was the principle of melody in verse', which involved the careful combining of open and closed vowels,

> He had a theory that vowels could be as skilfully combined and interchanged as differing notes of music, and that all sense of monotony was to be avoided, except when expressive of a specific purpose.

Bailey actually raises this issue with specific reference to *Hyperion* and suggests that by his varying of the vowels in the poem Keats creates an 'exquisite harmony' even in the moment of its variation.

We can see the principle at work here. Taking lines 220 to 223, notice the way in which Keats combines open and closed vowels:

> **To** wander wherewithal and **find** its **joys**
>
> (II.223)

(I have highlighted the open vowels.) Try this exercise on the other lines. Note also just the sheer variety of vowel shapes in these and other lines. However, to consider the full complexity of Keats's acoustic effect here, examine too the pattern of stressed and unstressed syllables working simultaneously with this melody.

With all this going on inside we might well expect the poem to sound quite fragmented. But it does not and the reason is that the effects are so brilliantly marshalled by Keats that they tend to harmonise on a deeper level than, say, the rhyme and rhythm. Just for fun, check the movement through the extract of the short /a/ sound or the long /ee/ sound and notice how their assonantal effects help to harmonise and unify the passage, weaving through its complex internal rhymes. Or try a passage from Book III where Keats reserves his most exquisite music for Apollo's speech.

On the death of his brother Tom, Keats suspended composition of *Hyperion* but briefly took it up again to compose the fragment in Book III. By April 1819 he had discarded it altogether and did not feel stirred again by the myth of Hyperion until he began to redraft it in the late summer of that crowded year.

Like the Parthenon marbles which so enthralled Keats, this fragment of the poem is both stunning in its profound beauties and
insights as well as mortifying in the frustration of its great promise.
While it makes a good many allegorical gestures in terms of contemporary political and aesthetic revolutions its full meaning is not, of
course, manifest. Very probably Keats himself was not fully seized
of the deeper possibilities of his design (he told a close friend that
Apollo's speech 'seemed to come by chance or magic' rather than by
his own intention).

Yet what we do have demonstrates the great strides that Keats has
made in his art. The poem is, among many things, a vision of spiritual
and aesthetic growth, Keats's own of course, and growth in terms not
just of his pictorial and musical lyricism but also of his powers as a
narrator. His contemporaries considered *Hyperion* to be among his
best work, if not actually his best: Byron announced that it was 'proof
of his poetic genius' and Shelley called it 'second to nothing that
was produced by a writer of the same years'. Nineteenth-century
readers such as D. G. Rossetti and Matthew Arnold generally praised
its boldness and saw neither weakness nor lumber in the Miltonisms
which Keats had so lamented. Just as the deification of Apollo
announces the arrival of the mature Keats, so the momentous acclaim
of his contemporaries confirms that he had at last fulfilled the desire
in *Sleep and Poetry* that he might become a 'glorious denizen' of Poesy.

The Fall of Hyperion. A Dream

Soon after he had abandoned the first attempt at the Hyperion
legend Keats's poetic genius reached its full peak. Summer 1819
ran at full tilt with glorious weather, his love for Fanny Brawne
took on a more even complexion, and then there was his crafting
of the major odes, crown of his writing life. On an extended trip to
the south coast of England he began *Lamia* and then took up again
the challenge of Hyperion.

The plot-line of *The Fall of Hyperion* is quite a vivid yarn. Seemingly
in a wood, the Poet/narrator discovers the remains of a banquet and
after swallowing some mysterious 'draught' he swoons unconscious.

He comes round in an ancient temple where a priestess, Moneta, challenges him to ascend the 'immortal steps'. Roused by her challenge yet also tormented by incessant pain the Poet at last persuades her of his worth and is permitted to witness the awful grief of the Titans. In despair at their suffering he pleads for his own death, until finally Moneta leads him to the palace of Hyperion.

The passage I have selected as a starting point for analysis and discussion is the first 18 lines of Canto I:

> Fanatics have their dreams, wherewith they weave
> A paradise for a sect; the savage too
> From forth the loftiest fashion of his sleep
> Guesses at Heaven: pity these have not
> Traced upon vellum or wild Indian leaf   5
> The shadows of melodious utterance.
> But bare of laurel they live, dream, and die;
> For Poesy alone can tell her dreams,
> With the fine spell of words alone can save
> Imagination from the sable charm   10
> And dumb enchantment. Who alive can say,
> 'Thou art no Poet – mayst not tell thy dreams'?
> Since every man whose soul is not a clod
> Hath visions, and would speak, if he had loved,
> And been well nurtured in his mother tongue.   15
> Whether the dream now purposed to rehearse
> Be Poet's or Fanatic's will be known
> When this warm scribe my hand is in the grave.

One of the things that strikes me first about the difference between the above passage and the style of *Hyperion. A Fragment* is that we have here the authorial voice of the poet himself, speaking directly and explicitly to the reader. From the start, Keats places himself firmly inside the poem. Compare this opening with that of the first version of *Hyperion* where Keats adopts a more conventional narrative attitude. The authorial voice of the poet is most important here not only because the poem concerns the actions and events of the Poet/narrator but also because poetry itself is the chief subject.

Thus we hear the authorial voice of Keats himself and he makes some forthright assertions: 'Fanatics have their dreams' (1), 'Poesy alone can tell her dreams' (8), 'every man whose soul is not a clod / Hath visions' (13–14). This opening passage – or 'Induction', as Keats labelled it – is also a self-contained unit set apart from the rest of the poem that it introduces, so it acts as a banner or a guide, or even as a warning to the reader of the poem. On the surface it is a definitive statement of the poet's position; something like: everyone has dreams, including fanatics, savages and poets (though they do not all record them in any lasting way), and everyone is potentially a poet, providing that they fulfil some minimum conditions.

But if we look more deeply we can see that Keats is not quite so definitive or confident of his position (and this condition is shared with the Poet through the rest of the narrative). A great deal of this apparently forthright passage actually refers to uncertainty or related ideas: 'dreams', 'traced', 'sleep', 'shadows', 'spell', 'charm', 'enchant-ment', 'visions', 'paradise', as well as death. And what precisely is a fanatic: a madman, a politician, an intellectual?

The two questions in this passage (in lines 12 and 16–18) also help to create a feeling of unrest. Equally, some of the constructions in it are hardly straightforward; for example, the phrase in lines 4–6 omits the subject, while in line 14 the phrase 'if he had loved' means loved what? other people? or language itself? or merely loved as a vague general sort of affection? Lines 8–11 present another construction which is difficult to follow.

The passage is, however, important because it marks a key point in Keats's career as a writer. Clearly it begs the question of what then is a poet, and at the heart of his (unclear) response is the theme of language itself. Keats is here deliberately drawing attention to the ambiguities, uncertainties, and fluidities inherent in language and especially in verse. Like the dreams of the fanatic and the savage, poetic ideas are ultimately written in sand or water. They may leave a relatively permanent mark, metaphorically 'upon vellum' (5), but the ideas signified are ephemeral, difficult to pin down and a source of deep anxiety.

The poem as a whole, of which this Induction is only a hint, marks a period of upheaval for Keats. Having abandoned the first version of the poem in the spring of 1819, he then went through a period in which his own finances and those of his brother George became critical. As a relatively impoverished writer he was not a very eligible candidate for marriage either – a point which was coming home to him at this time. His private and artistic life had become so hectic that he even contemplated chucking it all in for a career as a ship's surgeon. Troubled by the disappointment of *Endymion* Keats now took stock of his life and reassessed his conception of the 'poet' as well as the value of his own aspirations. All of these anxieties and uncertainties find their way into *The Fall of Hyperion* with its themes of artistic ordeal and alienation – though, for the rest of his life, doubts about his worth as a true poet were never fully extinguished from his mind (see lines I.93 and I.354–7).

Where in *Sleep and Poetry* he had dedicated himself wholly to 'Poesy' (line 47), now, over three years on, he is still not certain if he will be 'among the English Poets'. Both *Sleep and Poetry* (lines 48–9) and *The Fall of Hyperion* (I.2) refer to the idea of an exclusive circle and Moneta, too, taunts him with questions about his 'tribe' (I.198): is he of the true poet tribe or merely a dreamer, an idler or self-deluded waster? But the Poet/narrator, like Keats himself, appears cursed, to be chained eternally to the frustrating uncertainties of poetry, symbolised in the horrendous ordeal of the 'immortal steps' (I.117). He seems to have no choice in the matter and the maddening uncertainty of the poet's quest appears early on, in the closing lines of the Induction,

> Whether the dream now purposed to rehearse
> Be Poet's or Fanatic's will be known
> When this warm scribe my hand is in the grave.

(I.16–18)

He is still unsure of his talents (Poet or mere fanatic?) and wearily concedes that he will never be assured in his own lifetime.

In spite of the references to sleep and dreams, the Induction (and *The Fall of Hyperion* as a whole) points to the turmoil of and suffering inherent in the curse of poetic sensitivity – especially when it is allied to poetic ambition. This aspiration is suggested by the word 'laurel' in the passage (line 7), an aspiration for the sort of renown that is denied to the simple dreamer or the fanatic, with all the pejorative force too that the latter word carries. And Keats is infuriatingly unsure which of the two actually applies to himself.

The Induction deals then with dreams and aspiration. In doing so it looks back, as I have said, to the youthful bristle of *Sleep and Poetry*. But the uncertainty and crisis immanent in Keats's mind in *The Fall* permeates the whole of these eighteen lines. Further, the viewpoint looks beyond the miserable uncertainties of the present ('now', line 16) towards the looming certainties of death – explicitly in lines 7 and 18 but implicitly in the metaphorical, 'sable charm' (10) and 'clod' (13). All three periods – past, present, and future – vividly co-exist in the consciousness of these eighteen lines, pressing and grating against each other, working a deep, unsettling tension into the start of the poem, which almost bursts under the pressure of its feeling.

Placed at the start of *The Fall of Hyperion*, these eighteen lines sound an ominous, doleful tone and one that reverberates sullenly through the Poet's later ordeal. It sets up the keynotes of insecurity and fear, especially fear of failure, that his artistic vision may be lost or simply that he be exposed as a fraud, the fanatic stalking his dreams. He is well and truly caught inside the dream (implied by the word 'weave', in line 1, and 'fine spell' in 9). Escape is not a viable option and the success or failure of his poetic enterprise can be decided only after death, 'When this warm scribe my hand is in the grave' (18). It is with deep irony, then, that he looks to 'Poesy alone' as his salvation:

> the fine spell of words alone can save.
>
> (line 9)

We have noted already in other narrative poems Keats's tendency to address the reader directly from the outset, setting out his themes, the tone or the scenario, taking control. The Induction serves these purposes, of course, but more important here I think is that it places Keats himself at the centre of the poem.

In these eighteen lines he speaks to us as the writer and then following these he takes on the complex persona of a Poet–narrator–

traveller both inside and outside the poem. This is one of the most important shifts in Keats's redrafting of the earlier *Hyperion* material. It is not difficult to see that he lifts whole passages from the first version of the legend but the major development lies in the change of the narrator's point of view. In general terms the use of the first-person narrator ('I') has the advantage of being a quite intimate form of telling. The fact that the narrator is also a character in the story thus implies a more personal and therefore more realistic response to those ordeals described in it, particularly the suffering which he experiences at first hand (compare this aspect here with Coleridge's *The Rime of the Ancient Mariner*, for instance, another kind of death-in-life nightmare – and Keats was very much interested in Coleridge's work at this time).

Naturally, the intimate viewpoint of this narrator – the Poet – cannot dip into the minds of the other characters (as a third-person narrator quite often does). But here this mode has an added advantage in intensifying the emotional pitch of the poem in addition to highlighting the terror and vulnerability of the Poet himself. As a result the poem as a whole is made more compact – at least in the fragment that remains, where the narrow range of characters helps to restrain the scope for action and deepen the claustrophobia of the temple setting in Canto I.

Within this claustrophobic setting Keats indulgently interweaves a complex web of pictorial images, narrative action, oratory and commentary. In *Hyperion* these tended to feel more like separate, uncoordinated features of the narrative. However, here in *The Fall* his subtle exploitation of the Poet and Moneta both as windows on the action and as the responses to that action opens up deeper, more tangled layers of experience and consciousness.

The Induction prepares the way for these complex layers by way of its questions and ambiguities. It does so by directly locating the reader inside the mind of the Poet. Otherwise the opening scene has no particular setting. The title tells us it is a dream, but has the dream already begun? And where are we as readers in relation to it? The Induction, like the title, takes part in the poem as a whole in a strange sort of way, as a separate but at the same time an integral feature.

Keats describes the poem as 'A Dream' and then, immediately, the first line warns us that 'Fanatics have their dreams,' inviting us to judge if this itself is the work of a fanatic (as in lines 16–18). So the title is in its way self-referential, constructing the terms on which some aspects of the poem may be judged. If the writer is not a fanatic then perhaps he is a poet or maybe just a dreamer, since Moneta proposes,

> 'Art thou not of the dreamer tribe?
> The poet and the dreamer are distinct,
> Diverse, sheer opposite, antipodes.'
>
> (I.198–200)

The uncertainty and ambiguity continue, for Keats as for the reader. But, of course, it can be argued that the brilliance of the writing together with the amazing conception behind *The Fall of Hyperion* indicate that this most definitely is not the work of any ordinary dreamer or fanatic, who 'venoms all his day' with self-torment (I.175); unless maybe we accept that a 'poet' is a synthesis of all three!

From the beginning, ambiguity is indigenous to all of Keats's verse. The difference now is that Keats fully acknowledges his own awareness of it and makes a virtue of it. Not surprisingly, Negative Capability is a component and a symptom of this but there is more to it. Keats deliberately omits and blunts his detail – for example, withholding the identity of Moneta until I.226 and confusing Moneta and Mnemosyne at I.331. And in the 'steps' ordeal, what precisely do the steps lead to: immortality? Peace? The ordeal generates lots of intense feeling but also intense confusion. His frequent use of oxymoron, too (e.g. at I.209 and 259), both here and elsewhere graphically reveals his delight in obfuscation.

In this way the reader is manipulated to undergo something of a similar (but, hopefully, less traumatic) experience to that of the Poet. Using the 'I' narrator allows Keats to control naturally the flow of information to the reader and to develop the ambiguities of the text (note also the hesitation in words such as 'methought' and 'seemed'). Through its teasing ambiguities, anonymities, lacunae and silences we suffer a sort of strange beauty of frustration that arises from incomplete knowledge, only half-woven,

> The lofty theme
> At those few words hung vast before my mind,
> With half-unravelled web.

(I.306–8)

At this period of his life Keats's maturing verse style is increasingly more open, ambiguous and provocative. With the skill of an impressionist Keats's delivery becomes more prompting, connotative, swelling. Yet, it is of course a relatively simple matter to incorporate ambiguities into a piece of writing, especially in poetry, which is inherently ambiguous. Even fanatics could manage it. The trick is to generate interest in the text too, stimulating the reader to interrelate with the gaps, ambiguities, silences etc. and to savour them. So how does Keats achieve this . . . if he does?

First, there is a stunning verse style. Again this version of Hyperion is in blank verse but the advances that Keats has made in the three or four months since the first are quite dazzling. We now hear an unmistakable note of self-assurance in his delivery (which may seem ironic given the above) but also a new order of beauty. There are far fewer Miltonisms or archaic poeticisms and Keats seems altogether much less interested in other voices or rhetorical effects for their own sake.

Nowhere is this freshness more evident than in the Induction. These eighteen lines with their confident assertiveness prepare for the supple muscularity of the narrative proper, which is as intense as it is uncompromising. But note here Keats's subtle positioning of the caesurae, his melodic organisation of the vowels, with their echoes and parallel sounds (fanatic/paradise, fashion/heaven, guesses/vellum). These draw us towards more positive ideas (paradise, loftiest, melodious) but then drop us tersely onto colder realities (die, clod and grave). Even as he writes this beautiful verse Keats is vividly aware that the too too solid vellum is potentially a mere tracing upon the leaf (and significantly he chose for the epitaph on his anonymous gravestone, 'Here lies one whose name was writ in water').

There is a calm, an ease about the verse of *The Fall*. This is ironic really in view of the emotional turmoil of the narrative enacted within it. In place of the lofty Miltonic grandeur of the earlier attempt there is now a more dignified progress, measured and grand, yet portentous as a nightmare. Compare too the awful intensities of *The Fall of Hyperion* with the tamer climaxes in *Endymion*.

Before and during the composition of *The Fall of Hyperion* Keats had been reading Cary's translation of Dante's *Inferno* and this had a marked influence on Keats's treatment of the Hyperion story. On a simple level he used Dante's 'Canto' divisions for his own poem but, more profoundly, his hero now takes on a more humanised cast. Moneta too derives in part from Dante since she combines the roles of Virgil and Beatrice, the two guides for Dante's epic journey (though in *The Fall of Hyperion* Keats places more complex demands on the role of Moneta). Most importantly, however, by adopting Dante as his own guide or mentor Keats switches the allegorical focus of *The Fall* away from pain and personal loss resulting from the processes of time and change. Instead, he now presents a view of suffering that operates as a form of profound personal revelation, a form of catharsis and one which holds out the hope of redemption. And with this shift Keats infuses the world of his hero with unmistakable Christian overtones (in spite of the fact, of course, that it has a pagan setting).

Keats's remarkable ability to create new worlds and other consciousnesses has been very much conspicuous from the beginning, with his bowery isles, 'realms of gold' and so on. *The Fall* further develops this Keatsian characteristic with a complex interplay of widely diverse states of mind: including dreams, visions, intoxication, hallucination, sleep, trance, death and resurrection (along with other associated phenomena like charms and veils). For the reader, too, the universe of the poem seems elusive and fleeting, a point that is mirrored in the distinctly hesitant diction; such as seemed, guess, if, might, and may. However, the Induction warns that where previously such altered states could offer escape from current reality, now there is to be none.

Instead, the Keatsian fascination with the 'other', the co-existing alternative, finds its most sophisticated expression in the fascinating role of Moneta, the most substantial and intriguing female character in Keats's verse (and perhaps in Romantic verse as a whole). On the surface she is merely remote, aloof, a forbidding woman, scornful of this feeble, weakling poet/dreamer. The Poet thinks of her as a tyrant (I.119) and trembles in terror of her (I.251) – though strangely she also speaks to him as a mother (I.249–50).

The Poet's encounter with her is a recurring archetype in Keats of meetings with mysterious, often immortal, usually alluring females; examples include the maiden in '*I stood tip-toe*', Diana and the Indian maid in *Endymion*, and Mnemosyne in *Hyperion. A Fragment*. As a sort of demon woman she has also been anticipated in *Lamia* and *La Belle Dame san Merci*. Typically her eye is unveiled, blank, unseeing, insouci-ant, yet spellbinding,

> They held me back, with a benignant light,
> Soft-mitigated by divinest lids
> Half-closed, and visionless entire they seemed
> Of all external things – they saw me not....

(I.265–8)

Again, like Coleridge's nightmare witch she is a death-in-life, her face possessing 'an immortal sickness which kills not' (I.258).

At this time in his life, Keats's thoughts are inevitably never far from the theme of death. Yet his presentation of Moneta is far from simple. Seemingly asexual, she is nevertheless a woman of infinite variety. Her 'benignant light' promises hope even though, like the Poet, she has suffered much and wept (see I.220, 231, 240). As the guardian of Saturn's temple, 'Sole priestess of his desolation' (I.226–7), she seems the very distillate of sorrow. At the same time she exerts a more penetrative presence than that expressed by Saturn's turgid and monotonous 'moon'.

In common with so many of these mysterious Keatsian women, Moneta functions as a catalyst both for the male and for the narra-tive, in a life-changing way. Keats himself seems to have clung to an unerring belief in the great momentousness of such a chance en-counter in real life (he had in fact had such encounters, one with an anonymous woman in Vauxhall Gardens and several with the

mysteriously precocious Isabella Jones). In *The Fall of Hyperion*, however, the Poet is to be no passive recipient of a woman's 'benignant'
counselling: she is to bring about a painful realisation of his deepest
self. However, with suggestions of courtly love again, he must
achieve this through chivalric ordeal and endurance, Moneta as his
judge.

Casting back to the first *Hyperion*, it is easy to see parallels between
Moneta's role and that of Mnemosyne. The Poet himself makes this
more explicit in I.282 when he greets her as 'Shade of Memory!' Like
Mnemosyne she represents 'the Call', in which role she is an unyield-
ing confrontation to the errant knight–poet. In this figure she also
acts to unify most of the poem since her presence looms large
over the whole piece and most of its action functions through
her agency. Further, in uniting Dante's Virgil and Beatrice she
effectively combines within a single person both human reason and
wisdom-in-suffering. The fact that she can speak to gods and to
poets also emphasises another duality, the divine in art, which may in
fact be the mission of the artist. Both of these roles together point to
a further element of her complex role in the poem: her transcenden-
talism. Like Diana, she has the freedom to act equally in human and
immortal worlds. She seems to exist outside of time and, accordingly,
she directs the Poet towards the immortality hinted at in the Induction.

In her role as 'the Call' Moneta is the embodiment of knowledge
or revelation, the object of desire. She is an archetypal Keatsian
woman: dominant, drawing man to knowledge, controlling, initiating,
evading. She is a mediator or translator for the Poet (and for the
reader, too) since without her the wisdom of the gods would be as
incomprehensible to him as the meaning of the wind already is (see
II.5). Symbolically she unveils her face (I.255–6) with 'sacred hand'
and he is permitted a privileged sight of 'what things the hollow brain
/ Behind enwombed' (I.276–7). The Poet is allowed to see into the
fall and purgatorial suffering of the Titans, enacted through the
womb-like mind of Moneta. Thus the coming together of the Poet
and Moneta, via ordeal and judgement, represents the essence of
Romantic creativity; the conclusion of the steps ordeal brings about
the uniting and reconciliation of imagination and reality in beauty.

This brief analysis of the character and narrative functions of Moneta gives some idea of Keats's brilliant inventiveness in this poem – as well as of the advances that he has achieved in redrafting *The Fall of Hyperion*. She is central to Keats's theme of artistic creation. But if we regard Moneta as the essence of creativity then we must extend our analysis to consider other elements of Keats's concept of the Romantic artist. In particular we should examine what he has to say about the roles of suffering, vision and dream in the process of poetic creation.

A reasonable starting point is to look at a letter which Keats wrote in the spring of 1819 to his brother George and his wife after they had settled in America. He wrote of the trials of mankind in its struggle to achieve the impossible, namely happiness during one's lifetime. Keats rejects the idea that life is a vale of tears in which suffering is the moral price of happiness in the after-life: in other words, the Christian concept that mortal life is a period of trial after which we are redeemed by God and promoted to Heaven. Keats offers a significantly alternative doctrine: 'Call the world if you Please "The vale of Soul-making".' By which he means that when a human soul comes to the earth it is only part-formed and it becomes completed through its experiences (chiefly suffering) in this world: 'A Place where the heart must feel and suffer in a thousand diverse ways' (14 February–3 May 1819, 'Letter C').

This theory of 'Soul-making' relates closely to Keats's theme in *The Fall of Hyperion* and gives us a step up to a fuller picture of the role of Moneta in the poem. By referring to the three types of dreaming man (the fanatic, the savage, and the poet) the Induction sets up between all three the conflict and tension that will later invest the fragment with its chief interest and most powerful climax. And it is of course Moneta who controls this and makes the conflict explicit.

The dreamer must undergo a trial, a sort of dying into life and it is to take place on the steps of Saturn's ancient temple. So, from beyond the realm of time itself, Moneta draws the Poet into a trial of his mortality. However, is this crucial moment a moment of ripening or of withering? The Poet's time has arrived but his mood is decidedly that of a withering upon the bough, as if he were about

to be annihilated. And like the dead in Dante's *Inferno* he is made to
feel there is no hope:

> Of nothing, then to eastward, where black gates
> Were shut against the sunrise evermore.
>
> (I.85–6)

At the heart of his trial lies the dilemma set out in the Induction, and
in turn, behind this lies the crisis in Keats's mind about which type of
dreamer he himself might be (and even about the worth of poetry
itself). His self-doubt is first expressed as 'the fine spell of words'
(I.9). But this fails to solve the crisis because fanatics and savages
inhabit the same circle of dreamers – and as Moneta points out later
to the Poet, a dreamer merely 'vexes' the world (I.202), the dreamer
'venoms all his days' (I.175).

She torments him with 'What benefit canst thou do...?' and then
dismisses him merely as a 'dreaming thing,/A fever of thyself'
(I.167–9). However, she simply verbalises his own fear and uncertainty, confronting him with an objectifed, external version of his
own consciousness. His words are made flesh and on those testing
steps of the temple the two figures may be understood as two parts
of the same consciousness, namely Keats himself: Poet and Sceptic.

Nevertheless, the Poet's reply to Moneta's question about his
worth is hopeful. The confrontation here carries the ironic and
cunning effect of actually rousing the Poet's tormented spirit. Poetry,
he pleads, has a social as well as life-giving function,

> sure not all
> Those melodies sung into the world's ear
> Are useless: sure a poet is a sage,
> A humanist, physician to all men.
>
> (I.187–90)

Accordingly Moneta must concede; poetry is after all 'a balm upon
the world' (I.202), recalling a similar sentiment in *Sleep and Poetry*, that
verse may 'soothe the cares, and lift the thoughts of man' (line 247).

In her own way, Moneta as the destabilising spirit of scepticism
eventually brings this enfeebled, dispirited man to knowledge. But it

is not knowledge for its own sake, as philosophy, that is. What she brings him to is a clearer understanding of his own dilemma, a wisdom that will save both him and the sacred imagination from death of the spirit, the 'sable charm' referred to in the Induction. Poesy is to be his own salvation, if only he could realise it, redemption by way of the vale of suffering and soul-making.

Moneta makes this clear to the Poet once he has begun to mount the steps of the way of pain. The higher levels of existence are reserved for visionaries, those of more exalted sensibilities than the altruists, 'slaves to poor humanity' (I.159; and see I.147–9). The latter suffer for the good of mankind but it is the curse of poets to undergo a more intense pain in order to bring about a new vision to the world, ultimately for its benefit.

This idea touches firmly on the issues of the position and duties of a poet in relation to his society. The Induction suggests that while the poet's special consciousness may transcend physical reality, his creative energy exists primarily to fulfil only him/herself; in other words, it is principally egoistic in its direction. But, in his crisis on the steps, the poet suddenly becomes aware that he may not actually belong to the community in which he lives, asking himself,

> What am I then? Thou spakest of my tribe:
> What tribe?
>
> (I.193–4)

The horror strikes him that it is one thing to be deluded as a poet (not yet a 'denizen') but it is even more wretched to be alienated from his native community.

More than anything else these are the twin thorns of his suffering and Moneta holds out no easy soothing balm. She is uncompromising, cruel, but her true purpose is to drive him out of his unreality. With hints of the crucified Christ, he cries out in despair to his tutelary deity, 'Apollo! faded, far-flown Apollo!' (I.204).

At this early stage in the drama Moneta is still veiled, a distant voice, and the anguish of the poet is really self-referential, diverted through his own ego. Yet this anguish does not seem especially egoistic or self-pitying, and the reason for this lies, of course, in

LIBRARY LRS

Keats's idea of this ordeal of soul-making. However, in *The Fall of Hyperion* he does not give a specifically Christian spin on this concept and his reference to the fanatics in the opening line of the poem seems to warn against such a religious interpretation. By so doing, he holds the focus firmly on the process, the 'soul-making' within the poet.

Even though the Poet is granted a brief vision of existence beyond his earthly reality, Keats's proper interest here is less in the abstract than in the actual physical world of the senses: the living world of empirical experience. As he pointed out in another famous letter, to his friend John Reynolds, we can only judge who or what we are through experience even if it is painful, 'for axioms in philosophy are not axioms until they are proved upon our pulses' (3 May 1818).

So in *The Fall of Hyperion* we are more likely to feel closer sympathy with the Poet's suffering than with that of Apollo in *Hyperion. A Fragment*, for the reason that we are given it upon the pulse, the direct 'feel', or as direct as he can make it for us. In spite of the ambiguity of the text, which I mentioned earlier, Keats manages to fasten our minds close onto the harshness and pain, the actual world. Furthermore, the vision achieved by the Poet is never presented as a form of escape from this, as it might be elsewhere (for example, in *Endymion*) and it may even be available to those fanatics and savages mentioned in the Induction (even trees apparently have their dreams; see I.374).

At the core of Keats's idea of this vision is his view of the imagination. The Induction points to the Poet's theory of the imagination in which Poesy interprets and gives meaning to a visionary insight of the world. This is an insight which is made real and valid through the process of suffering, again felt on the pulse. Keats too needed to convince himself of the validity of what he was doing as a poet. Thus the gods in *The Fall of Hyperion* act as the objective symbol of Keats's own pain (unlike those in the first *Hyperion* whose suffering is simply the growing pains of evolutionary progress, though no less painful for that).

The Fall of Hyperion hints strongly at this resolution of the vision. It contains a theory of imagination that also takes account of intuitive sources of truth, those deriving through anguish, to be expressed in art. The Poet offers a defence of poets as beneficial to all of mankind and affirms his duty to that defence. Although Moneta has acted as the devil's advocate she accepts his account and is satisfied at his proof of the axioms. She unveils, both literally and figuratively, and then proceeds to grant him insight:

> The sacrifice is done, but not the less
> Will I be kind to thee for thy goodwill.
> My power, which to me is still a curse,
> Shall be to thee a wonder....

(I.241–4)

In a letter of 21 September 1819, Keats claimed that he had given up *The Fall*, this 'very abstract Poem', because there were 'too many Miltonic inversions in it'. He was convinced that these invested it with a 'false beauty'. While this is a fair comment on *Hyperion. A Fragment*, I think it is less true of *The Fall*, where Milton's influence is much less obvious. In fact, the most likely reason for Keats's giving it up is a structural one, since by the close of Canto I the poem has already achieved its thematic climax – it would have been highly impracticable to try to extend it beyond this section.

By the end of the first Canto Keats has achieved his artistic aim: to set up a melting pot in which to assimilate and eventually crystallise his ideas about the nature of poetry as well as of the responsibility of the poet. Keats proposes that in essence it is this responsibility and that vision characterised by the 'fine spell of words' which defines his nature, in contrast to the mad superstitions of the fanatic and the wild hauntings of the savage. Yet in order to express this he develops his own quasi-religious order of poetry which manages to be at the same time both intensely subjective and severely impersonal. Any attempt to build out beyond this climax would merely have plunged it into diffusion and frustration.

Conclusions

The two abandoned versions of the Hyperion story constitute Keats's further refinements in the 'beautiful mythology of Greece'.

Though unfinished, neither can be considered a failure, particularly in the light of their beautiful music and what they reveal of Keats's brilliance in transposing ancient myth into the substance of modern allegory.

We have noted Keats's increasing professional interest in exploring the theoretical foundations of the art of poetry. Symptomatic of this are the concept of Negative Capability and his theory of melody, both of which are evident in these poems. Equally we can see Keats here striving to define the status and position of the poet, especially in relation to his society, and this forms the hub of his allegorical endeavour, particularly in *The Fall of Hyperion*.

The two poems also embody new sophistications in the role of the narrator, chiefly in his relationship to the reader. The fruits of these experiments find their most momentous treatment in the major odes, which are discussed in the next chapter.

Although Keats attributed the impasse in the poems to the obstinate influence of Milton it is clear that his verse benefits immeasurably from the assimilation of his literary research, underpinning theme and plot and opening up diverse allegorical and metaphysical possibilities. As an adjunct to this we also observe here a mature Keats addressing the deeper thematic and metaphysical implications of his raw materials and reading. Indeed his personal credo has by now reached such elegance that in *The Fall of Hyperion* he strongly hints that metaphysical speculation is no longer the province of the Sage but of the Poet.

Further Research

Re-read the following passages in *Hyperion. A Fragment* and try to assess the *methods* which Keats uses in them to evoke the characters of Hyperion and Apollo:

Book I, lines 213–50;
Book III, lines 76–120.

4

The Major Odes

In 1819 between his two faltering attempts at Hyperion, Keats worked on what are usually considered to be his greatest achievements in lyric poetry, the six major odes. The year 1819 marked a period of new realism in Keats's private life as well as a fresh surge in creative ambition. Illness persisted and he was still haunted by financial difficulties. However, his relationship with Fanny Brawne was now on a more congenial understanding and he was formulating a project with his friend Charles Brown to make big money as a dramatist, or so he hoped. Even the weather that spring was exceptionally agreeable.

The ode form had a special appeal for Keats as the supreme test of his poetical skills, in spite of the fact that narrative verse was regarded as more serious and ambitious. Keats was especially careful in his use of the term 'ode' in the titles of his poems since he had in mind a particular kind of verse: namely, a highly formal lyric of intricate stanza structure, elevated in tone, expressing personal reflections on profound themes.

The origins of the ode extend back to Greek and Roman models and the form has been explored by most major British poets, including Dryden, Gray, Wordsworth and Shelley. Keats himself seems to have been most deeply influenced here by the work of Edmund Spenser and William Collins. He had already made some tentative experiments in the ode before 1819; for example, in the fragment Ode to May (1818) and in *Endymion*, which contains two ode-like songs ('Song to Pan' in Book I and 'Song to Sorrow' in Book IV). But now he made a dedicated effort to master the form and turn it to his own requirements.

Effectively Keats invents his own kind of ode, usually one containing a stanza of ten lines adapted from key elements of the sonnet form. He takes the opening quartet of a Shakespearean sonnet (rhyme scheme ABAB) and clips onto it the sestet of a Petrarchan sonnet (rhyme scheme CDE CDE), using iambic pentameter as the starting point. In Keats's hands this new type of ode, his transfigured sonnet, also undergoes many minor and individual variations though all of them conform to the strict disciplines of the traditional form (for instance, 'Ode to a Nightingale' has a short eighth line and 'To Autumn' has an extra line in each stanza).

In general terms, Keats explored a stanza form that was long enough to allow the internal development of thought and feeling yet offered a complexity which could sustain the necessary tone for an ode, dignified and exalted. On the other hand, limiting the stanza to no more than ten lines reduces the risk of making each stanza feel like a separate poem – as, say, fourteen lines could easily do. The Keatsian ode permits both the full scope of a poetic paragraph and the challenging constraints of an intricate rhyme structure.

In this chapter I have decided to limit the discussion to four of Keats's most celebrated odes and to take them in the probable order in which they were composed: 'Ode to a Nightingale', 'Ode on a Grecian Urn', 'Ode on Melancholy' and 'To Autumn'. Each of these was constructed as an individual piece yet because they all spring more or less from a core of shared themes and concerns they also constitute a highly coherent sequence. While sharing this range of common interests each poem, however, does represent a distinctive and stand-alone treatment of them. Broadly speaking the sequence of the major odes is unified by its discussion of points including beauty, time, physical reality, art and the artist, knowledge and uncertainty, love, pain, sorrow and joy. For instance, 'Nightingale' and 'Grecian Urn' are concerned with (among many things) art and the imagination, mortality and time, and 'Melancholy' considers artistic sensitivity and mortality, while 'To Autumn' is a highly sophisticated treatment of the themes of beauty and time. Though separate, each poem complements the rest in terms of theme, mood, images, and perspective. (The two major odes not analysed here are 'Ode to Psyche' and 'Ode on Indolence' – but see 'Further Research' at the end of this chapter.)

'Ode to a Nightingale'

'Ode to a Nightingale' was written at the start of one of the happiest periods in Keats's life, a detail which comes out eloquently in this magnificent poem. In the middle of an exceptionally warm spell in spring 1819, he composed a jubilant letter to his sister Fanny,

> O there is nothing like fine weather, and health, and Books, and a fine country, and a contented Mind . . . and, please heaven, a little claret-wine cool out of a cellar a mile deep . . .
>
> (1 May 1819)

But the weather was only partly responsible for Keats's happiness now. That glorious spring a nightingale had built a nest close to his house in Hampstead and its sublimely beautiful song had sent Keats into a trance of ecstasy, a 'drowsy numbness'. Nightingales were also on his mind when he bumped into the poet Samuel Coleridge one night on Hampstead Heath and the two of them discussed the bird (among a great variety of other subjects) and both of them composed verse to it, stirred by their dialogue that night.

However, the bird itself is only the starting point and the Hampstead garden merely a going forth. The largely unseen garden quickly dissolves into a more literary scene, and rural images merge into mythological (for example, 'Flora', line 13) or Biblical figures ('Ruth', 66) – with evocations quite remote from those of a Romantic English landscape poem. Even so, all the various inspirational elements come rapturously together. A 'beaker full of the warm south' (the very inspiration of the Hippocrene fountain) plus the still dark moment draw the mind into a profound creative trance. This brilliant poem stands as the climax to Keats's early poetry yet also represents a watershed. 'Nightingale' gathers up thematic threads, moods and tones from earlier verse and re-shapes them into this new mature form through a new voice, the fresh perspective of Keats the mature poet. The 'Ode to a Nightingale' has an extraordinary compression of effect, an intense refinement of ideas, feelings and tones that has been murmuring away in Keats's poetic psyche, now gathered up in a new measure.

We have much to cover here so I would like to examine the poem by focusing on the final two stanzas

VII
Thou wast not born for death, immortal Bird!
    No hungry generations tread thee down;
The voice I hear this passing night was heard
    In ancient days by emperor and clown:
Perhaps the self-same song that found a path   65
    Through the sad heart of Ruth, when, sick for home,
        She stood in tears amid the alien corn;
            The same that oft-times hath
    Charmed magic casements, opening on the foam
        Of perilous seas, in faery lands forlorn.   70

VIII
Forlorn! the very word is like a bell
    To toll me back from thee to my sole self!
Adieu! the fancy cannot cheat so well
    As she is famed to do, deceiving elf.
Adieu! adieu! thy plaintive anthem fades   75
    Past the near meadows, over the still stream,
        Up the hill-side; and now 'tis buried deep
            In the next valley-glades:
    Was it a vision, or a waking dream?
        Fled is that music – Do I wake or sleep?   80

After the strangely voluptuous ache which opens Stanza I, the poet's voice unravels the poem's subtle complexity of movements and moods. His mind drifts in and out of different levels of consciousness. The poem is an almost amorphous sinew of interwoven currents. Here, in Stanza VII, the voice attends again to the 'immortal Bird' after a brief flirtation with the idea of 'easeful death', personified as a sort of succubus. Keats has toyed – or at least half-toyed – with the seductive call of escape through suicide. His own mortality is in the foreground of his themes here.

However, the chill reality of the present intrudes upon the poet's reverie, disrupting the feint prospect of release. The first line of Stanza VII proclaims against this temptation, recalling the force of that outburst which opens IV. We witness a mind repeatedly slipping away from life and then snapping back to try to keep awake and alive. The poem vacillates continually between the two conditions: release from, and then recall to, mortal reality. The fact of his addressing the bird in this abrupt manner seems to be what shakes him out of torpor into a drainless shower of sobriety, to confront mortality once again.

This is especially so if in line 61 we stress the first word 'Thou', to distinguish the bird from himself and mortal human-kind. However, some critics have objected to line 61 on the grounds of contradiction: how can something which is born avoid the actuality and inevitability of death? The bird is 'born' to mortality and yet, as Stanza III suggests, it has not known the 'weariness, the fever and the fret' (23), which are features of human life, at least. Furthermore, how can it be an 'immortal Bird' when earlier in the poem it has represented Keats's desire to fade away into death and oblivion?

To the first objection – the charge of contradiction – the rest of Stanza VII supplies quite a strong reply: namely, that nightingales as a species have sung for centuries, their song being heard in 'ancient days' (64). In other words, the bird is immortal in the sense of countless generations achieving a kind of seamless permanence. The concept of generations of the same bird transcends the narrow transient mortality of a single life (which is Keats's very dilemma here; so the reply also points up his own sharp awareness of mortality).

The second objection – that the bird is coerced into symbolising both the mortal and the immortal – is more easy to resolve. On one level the song of the nightingale represents the mortal human senses – chiefly the voice or hearing of course. But it does stand for more than this, more than just a beautiful noise. Keats interprets the song of the nightingale as a metaphor of beauty-in-poetry. As the invisible 'viewless wings of Poesy' (33) its music moves via a loftier horizon than that of the physical senses and comes to symbolise poetry itself and even art as a whole. So, as well as being a real, physical animal (though not actually visible), the bird stands for something timeless in art and beauty, and the word 'ancient' points to this existence in another order of time apart from the human realm: that of eternity.

John Barnard describes Keats's experience at this point as one of those 'rare ecstatic moments when consciousness loses its sense of self, and the ego is overwhelmed by visionary being, freed from clock time'. As a moment of stillness at the heart of a mortal world of 'the fever, and the fret', the eternal birdsong hints at a brief glimpse into eternity. Ironically, the divine moment permits a vision of timeless-ness, a charmed other realm, a waking dream of sorts (in his own verse William Wordsworth labelled such moments as 'spots of time'). Even though both Keats and the nightingale are 'born for death' the sublime song, like the essential beauty of poetry, offers the slight savour of something eternal within human life. It offers a moment of stillness in the everyday mortal world. That Keats prized these rare moments is witnessed by their frequent occurrence in his poetry.

The fact of such moments is also the cause of Keats rejecting the wiles of 'easeful Death'. No matter what release or escape death may hold out to his troubled spirit it would also preclude the experience of beauty (in art as well as in nature): 'To thy high requiem become a sod' (60). Accordingly, in another of the poem's many turns, the opening to Stanza VII, with its strident note of adulation, marks a determined reversion from the smothering thoughts of self-destruction.

The themes of time and mortality are among the key threads uniting the major odes. More so than the narrative poems, the odes focus on the effects of time on mankind (where *Endymion*, *Lamia* and the two *Hyperion* poems are more concerned with the implications of space and the pictorial imagination). 'Ode to a Nightingale' begins and ends in the present moment of human aches and pains and the theme of time is insisted upon throughout by its imagery: 'One minute past' (4), 'vintage' (11), 'a long age' (12), the 'passing night' (63), 'ancient days' (64), and the sombre tolling of the bell suggested in the final stanza. It is a fluid, dynamic poem of changing move-ments, fading and merging consciousnesses, opening and closing viewpoints. So we should not be surprised at the complex shifts in time: in and out of real time; jumps between present, past, and future;

to the 'sole self' and the 'waking' present. Time, for Keats, here is a highly protean entity, slithering and evading, but always controlling the attention.

As we might expect too, Keats is much concerned with ideas of ripening and withering as adjuncts to these themes of mortality and time. For instance, in Stanza V he talks of the 'coming musk-rose, full of dewy wine' (49) and of the 'Fast-fading violets' (47), and in VII the reference to 'corn' (67) hints at ripening. Elsewhere, there are significant references to ripe fullness (lines 10, 15, 16, 27, 49), while the idea of withering is implicit in the repeated mention of 'fade' (lines 20, 21, 47, 75). There are, of course, numerous glances at 'death'. These themes are also mirrored in the play of colours – green and blushful, against grey, pale and white.

In Stanza VII, however, time is vividly present in a wide range of natures and experiences. The nightingale is oblivious to the revolutions of 'hungry generations', has sung to all classes, ruler and ruled, its song transcending class as it overmasters time. With a hint of profanity it even triumphs over the ancient Biblical time implied by the image of the despondent Ruth (whose appearance amid the alien corn recalls the sorrowful, exiled Indian maid in *Endymion*, IV).

'Nightingale' is linked temperamentally too with *Endymion*. Once again, mortality is characterised by human sensibility: our sensitivity to the pleasures and emotions of everyday existence as well as to its pains and horrors, the melancholy of feeling and the sting of memory. Memory is the function of time passing and as such is the poet's storehouse of life's fevers and frets, in addition to its joys and gusto. It lies at the very heart of the vale of soul-making. So hand in hand with the defiant optimism of line 61 (the idea that the nightingale eludes death and the pangs of human mortality) comes the reality of the 'sad heart' of Ruth, personifying sorrow. The nightingale thus assimilates symbolically both the peak of human ecstasy and the pit of human despair.

Keats reaffirms his characteristic theme that to become fully human is the consequence of a complex yet vulnerable sensitivity to the world. The complexity of this belief is implied in the paradox in line 6 of 'Nightingale', the notion of being 'too happy' (a prospect that reappears in 'Ode on Melancholy'), and elsewhere Keats frequently communicates this type of intensity by use of an oxymoron: in '*I stood tip-toe*', for instance, he talks of 'sweet desolation – balmy pain' (line 162; a poem which, like 'Nightingale', is set in deeply wooded seclusion). Here, however, the 'pain' arises from the distance between the ecstasy of hearing the birdsong and the 'weariness' (26) of mundane life in the mortal world. The actual, physical world becomes more commonplace after the brief glimpse of release rendered by the divine song of the nightingale. As always in Keats the sublime vision is invariably rooted in a firm knowledge of human reality.

To say that the song of the nightingale is the vehicle for these complex psychological effects is to state only half the case. In the intricate workings of this process the imagination too plays a decisive role and so we should spend a little time examining this role.

The song of the nightingale is as a gateway, a magic window on alternative worlds, the Other realm,

> Charmed magic casements, opening on the foam
> Of perilous seas, in faery lands forlorn.
>
> (69–70)

As a symbol of poetry (and of art in general) the birdsong acts first through the senses and then through the mysterious agency of the imagination working to seduce and manipulate the minds of emperors and clowns (as well as of poets!). Even though Keats claims that the 'fancy cannot cheat so well' (73) it does seem to have done a pretty fair job here. (In a letter of 22 November 1817, referred to in Chapter 3, Keats famously proclaimed 'What the imagination seizes as Beauty must be truth' – and see the conclusion to 'Ode on a Grecian Urn'.)

We should not forget, of course, that this statement is embedded in a work of the imagination – the poem itself. The poem was not written spontaneously at about the same time as the events described in it. It is a highly structured imaginative re-creation, fusing together recollection, invention, imported images, allegorical and thematic word-play and numerous other creative elements.

In addition to performing as a character in the poem the nightingale also functions as a compound imaginative symbol – standing for, among other things, poetry and poetic inspiration, beauty, mortal life and, connecting them all, the imagination itself. There is the historical or mythological dimension too; through the ancient story of Philomel, a Thracian princess who was raped and mutilated, the nightingale has come to symbolise grief as well as beauty. In the same way that the song of the bird becomes a sort of disembodied, insubstantial entity for Keats, so as a symbol it takes flight through the imagination to embark on a life of its own beyond the confines of the text.

As the symbol of poetry, the nightingale thus exemplifies the supreme power in art, ideal beauty (see *Sleep and Poetry*, line 236). As well as representing a seductive illusion ('deceiving elf', line 74), the bird stands for the perfection of artistic expression, higher even than thought itself. Like the Grecian urn, the song signifies the ideal work of the Romantic imagination, a voice so exquisite it is almost supernatural, in contrast with human fumblings (which are suggested in the poem's imagery of numbness, dull, pale, dull brain, sad, sick, forlorn). In spite of this the song is a perennial goad or challenge, a 'fever' to the poet (denoted in lines 61–4 and 79–80) – and there is the correspondent 'fret', the anxiety that the finished poem may fall short of the ideal. Given this notion of the goad, the poem implies that Keats is driven by his own artistic sensibility to compose, trapped in a 'drowsy numbness' of reflex creativity.

Yet, just when the fancy is beginning to cheat so well, drawing him through magic casements to fantasy worlds, the word 'forlorn' draws him solemnly back to his present lot. The fancy is not so good as an escape here because being so agile it can just as readily turn the mind back to bleak reality as to escape from it – as it does here, returning Keats to face his own malaise. It makes the reader too realise that the fancy is less free or capricious than it was in, say, *Endymion*. Now Keats's mind seems constrained by the narrowing straits of anxiety, a point borne out by the fact that once the nightingale's song has faded, the imagination deserts him and he is returned to the 'aches' and 'pains' of everyday reality. His solid flesh has neither dissolved (21) nor taken flight with the bird (31) but he is tolled back 'from thee to my sole self' (72), back to the existential uncertainty indicated in the final two lines.

As a foil to the tricksy imagination, this earthly mortality is (iron-ically) also the source and seat of the emotions that play so vigorous a part in this ode. The coarse body, its senses, is actually the starting point for the working of the imagination. Keats hears the rhapsodic song and the fancy does the rest. From the pain of sense at the start to the fled music at the end, the body's receptivity to sensation acts as Keats's interface between his own mind and the world at large.

The body's senses are the casement of the imagination and the pathway for desire. Imagination and its workings stimulate the poet's desire to experience the other world, beyond the physical, to become like the sylvan warbler itself, a quintessence of mind or spirit in 'full-throated ease'. This spiritual or creative refining, not merely demise itself, is what I think Keats desires when he talks of being half in love with 'easeful death': to progress from body and sense to a higher plane, to a world of mind and ideas by the action of the imagination. He would 'leave the world unseen' and co-exist with the spirit world, those 'shadows numberless'.

I would like to return later to this theme of mortality, but first let us look closer at what Keats means by reality, not only reality *per se* but also, and more precisely, what he means by knowledge of that reality. In exploring beyond the actual, physical world of the senses Keats is delving once more into the realm of Platonist philosophy (as he does in *The Fall of Hyperion* and *Endymion*). Under this ancient theory, truth or reality is discovered through a form of intuition rather than through direct experience of the world via the senses. Keats alludes obliquely to this in Stanza IV when he says,

> But here there is no light,
> Save what from heaven is with breezes blown.

> (38–9)

In other words, our sure and certain knowledge comes about by a mysterious process of spiritual intervention, imparting sudden insights.

The poem refers to several sources of knowledge on earth (includ-ing mythology) but, in spite of this, Keats remains 'embalmed in darkness' (43). Ironically, the source that appears more insistently in the poem is the subjective imagination, which Keats equates with the fancy and even with intuition. It cannot cheat and so reveals truths that come about by a non-physical route: because the senses have been numbed (1–2), the imagination is set free to explore dream-like ideals (and as *Lamia* suggests, 'Real are the dreams of Gods').

The poem repeatedly sets up a fluctuating movement between the real world of sorrow and dis-ease (Ruth's domain) and the contrasting other world of 'ease' and 'faery lands' (almost always in Keats's verse there lurks the other world or other person). The channel between the two is the operation of desire, which also makes the reader invitingly aware of the gap between the two. Human desire, continually striving, is one more aspect of 'the fever and the fret' (23) and it is this which pursues (in the imagination at least) the fading song of the nightingale in the final stanza 'Past... over... Up... In' (76–8). For a brief moment (which in the imagination also becomes eternal), he has held private communion with the ideal, the purest distillation of art – as symbolised in the song of the bird.

As I have mentioned, this song is for Keats the pre-eminent object of creative desire, the perfection of beauty in art, especially in poetry. It is the object of his highest aspiration, and the fever. Yet desire for Keats here is also the quest for truth, for certain knowledge (whereas, by contrast, in his earlier verse desire was the yearning to be recognised as a poet, a 'glorious denizen').

After a relatively lucid opening, the perspectives of the poem modulates, repeatedly dissolving and jolting back into some new order of reality, until the senses become forlorn and uncertain. 'Ode to a Nightingale' lucidly expresses a momentary doubting of his former trust in empiricism. This indeterminacy which he feels is of course the state of Negative Capability (being in 'uncertainties, mysteries, doubts') and is signified by the questions in line 79. However, this offers his mind no hope of stasis – it is not blissful uncertainty, static, without the reaching after. Rather, the final line of the poem re-starts the fever and the reader is returned to the opening line, back to the ache and numbness which began it.

It is thus a brilliant finale. The finely judged ambiguities are epitomised in the unresolved uncertainties of the final stanza. The diction alone points us to ideas of insecurity: vision, waking, dream, wake, sleep. Yet these words are merely the culmination of a slender thread of uncertainty that is laced through the whole piece, a manifestation of the poem's dichotomy of truth and deception (for example, consider the ambiguities in lines 19 and 59). Keats himself has been 'winking at the brim', cheating and perplexing the reader with ambiguities, puns, oxymoron and evasion. 'Nightingale' superbly achieves a sort of ending (though not a conclusion) which manages to accommodate contradictory states of awareness in the reader. In other words we are left with a feeing that we have followed Keats's mind towards certainty, yet along the way this has simply made us aware of how ignorant we probably are.

We do not resolve our world into clarity but we might resolve the consciousness. If so, then we may be able briefly to cope with if not resolve the poem's multiple dualisms: namely, body/spirit, youth/age, myth/truth, sleeping/waking, fancy/reality, and life/death. They can ultimately force us to question the very foundations of our sanity. It is Keats's own sharp and receptive intelligence that lies at the hub of this turning poem. As one of the many currents of the poem, Keats's inquiry about the integrity of his 'self' traces an inwardly spiralling pathway 'to toll me back to my sole self!' (72), along mazy, labyrinthine paths, the 'winding mossy ways' (40). And perhaps this circularity is what in the end really denies the poet any convincing feeling of relief, or 'ease'. He has stirred in luxurious pain for the bird, evening's minion, only to be galled finally by confusion.

Much of this great poem's great appeal lies precisely in this marvellous emotional complexity. Keats compresses an astonishing range of sensation, belief, mood, sound and perspective, and all in the space of a mere 80 lines. The ode seems to be in a state of continual flux, a turmoil of voluptuous tensions which repeatedly threaten to overturn and escape until a sudden new turn urges the movement forward, remorselessly deferring the coveted release. It is these changing emotions, with their variations in pitch and intensity, that govern the structure and rhythm of the composition.

The poem's incessant movement offers no respite, or 'ease', even by the final line. Keats was, of course, too much of a realist to entertain the possibility of a get-out clause. The real world repeatedly disrupts his ideals with its smotherings and even the most intense joy is transmuted into confusion, beckoning to oblivion. Such beckonings bring to mind the tormenting figure of Moneta in *The Fall of Hyperion* (summoning likewise from a 'veiled shadow'; I.141) and even hint at the fatal charms of *La Belle Dame sans Merci*, which seduce the knight and detain him in haggard thrall (where in fact 'no birds sing').

'Ode to a Nightingale' is Keats's longest and the most personal of the 1819 odes. In the dazzling richness of its images and music it is surpassed perhaps only by 'To Autumn'. But it outshines all the odes in the brilliant daring of its silences, negatives and omissions, its latent world of ripening potentialities (see lines 5, 19, 32–3, 41, 73). Above all, these silences, unheard melodies, together with the poem's lavish actualities gather to suggest the true evasiveness of the nightingale's ephemeral song, the poem's central artistic metaphor, and symbol of art. In the next of the 1819 odes, 'Ode on a Grecian Urn', this symbol becomes more explicit and more distinct along with the possibilities inherent in it.

'Ode on a Grecian Urn'

'Ode on a Grecian Urn' was probably written in the same month, May 1819, as 'Ode to a Nightingale' and springs from a similar state of mind. Although the precise order of composition of these odes is only conjectural, 'Grecian Urn' was probably written soon after 'Nightingale' since it covers similar themes and sensibilities. I have decided to look in detail at the final stanza.

> O Attic shape! Fair attitude! with brede
>   Of marble men and maidens overwrought,
> With forest branches and the trodden weed;
>   Thou, silent form, dost tease us out of thought
> As doth eternity: Cold Pastoral!   45
>   When old age shall this generation waste,
>   Thou shalt remain, in midst of other woe
> Than ours, a friend to man, to whom thou say'st,
>   Beauty is truth, truth beauty, – that is all
>   Ye know on earth, and all ye need to know.   50

In marking the thematic climax to the poem, this stanza plays a vital and elaborate role in the structure of the whole. The exclamations of the opening lines here rouse the reader as well as the poet from the melancholy thoughts in the previous stanza, for a brief moment at least (and thus have a similar function to that of line 31 in 'Ode to a Nightingale'). The poem now stands back from examining those images which were the succeeding subjects in Stanzas II, III and IV, to regard once again the urn itself. 'O Attic shape!' draws attention to the vase as a whole thing, and introduces its eerie silences and stasis. Its shape seems to be hovering motionless in time and space. Or it might be more accurate to say 'out of time' as it has survived unbroken, 'still unravished', over the generations since it was fashioned – and 'shalt remain' after Keats's generation too has passed into history.

The opening apostrophes to the urn here signal a marked break from the preceding stanzas. Yet we can also see how this final section gathers up and resolves the themes that the earlier stanzas have set up: art (41 and 44), time (45–7), beauty and the imagination (49), the possibility of escape (47), plus truth and knowledge (49–50). There are other connections too: 'silent' (44) mirrors line 39 but also hints at 'still' in lines 1 and 26; 'Cold Pastoral' (45) takes up again the melancholy tone in 'desolate' at the end of Stanza IV (and so performs a similar function to the word 'forlorn' in 'Nightingale'); while 'marble men and maidens' (42) rounds off the ritual procession in the previous stanza. After the joyful conviviality of that happy throng (recalling the festive sacrifice to Pan in *Endymion*, I), Keats's thoughts take on a more sombre tone with the chill associations in 'tease', 'waste', 'old age', 'woe', and 'overwrought' (this last word describes the frieze on the urn as well as suggesting anxiety). The phrase 'teasing us out of thought' is itself teasing in its fuller possibilities but all at once it implies a leading out from that morose brooding induced by contemplation (cf. in 'Nightingale', 'but to think is to be full of sorrow').

To emphasise the return to the viewpoint of Stanza I the rhyme scheme now returns to that of the opening stanza (namely ABAB CDE CDE; the three other stanzas have variations in the sestet). However, with regard to sound, the final stanza is unique. This stanza could just about have stood alone, self- contained, though of course it does play a key role in drawing together the different facets of the whole poem. At the same time, its tightly knit composure of theme, sound and rhythm marks off this stanza as an outlier. For example, we can note the ribbons of Keatsian internal rhyme at work, in the intricate repetition of the vowels /or/, /o/ and /oo/, with the alliteration of /m/ in line 42 and /r/ in 43. And then there are those echoic words Attic/attitude, Cold/old, and to/Beauty/truth.

After the wilder ecstasies of Stanzas III and IV, with their 'ever panting' of passion and procession, the final stanza strives to reassert decorum and control. This it achieves primarily through its pauses. Almost every line has a strong caesura acting as a brake on the thrust generated in the middle sections of the poem. The iambic pentameter has become quite irregular by now while the tongue-twisting /th/ sound also helps to reduce the momentum in readiness for the grand sonority of the famous epigram in the final two lines – the great rhetorical effect of which is to make them too stand beyond or above the rest of the poem.

In this final section of 'Grecian Urn' the poem's three major themes are dynamically marshalled, assimilated and then brought to a fine climactic stillness ready for these two lines. At the same time the movement remains clear and uncluttered. And yet, to appreciate Keats's brilliant handling here we need to examine in detail the full significance of each of these themes in turn. They are art, beauty, and lastly time and mortality.

As I have already noted, the two exclamations at the start of the final stanza announce a change in the point of view. They also take hold of the poem's brisk progress in order to step back from the urn to regard it as a single artwork again. Keats breaks off from examining the three separate scenes to bring the object into wholeness and harmony through the workings of the poet's spatial imagination. At the same time the reference to 'Attic' here recalls Keats's speculations in the opening stanza, the Greek settings of 'Tempe or the dales of Arcady' (7).

Throughout the middle stanzas Keats has explored the images adorning the vase in close detail. They have fired up his seminal imagination, filling out scenes, making connections, filling up the silences. And yet something at the heart of the vase eludes. This is implied again most momentously in lines 44–5:

> Thou, silent form, dost tease us out of thought
> As doth eternity . . .

A niggling statement in itself, this opens up a whole range of possibilities. The word 'tease' implies to 'trick' or 'seduce', as well as to 'draw us on'. The urn's being 'silent' points us to its inscrutability, refusing definitive answers or easy solutions, in spite of Keats's careful inspection of those pictures. It provides no explanation of its own existence, merely proposes some delicate scenes, a few curious Greek figures. However, whilst its fertile silence may inspire us to visionary interpretations, that very silence ('still unravished') seems to imply that its ultimate meaning is too profound for modest human thought to penetrate – like trying to grasp the concept of 'eternity'.

On the other hand, the word 'tease' could actually imply this very idea: that the urn has the power to raise us from the realm of human thought onto a more exalted plane of perception. In that case Keats might then be arguing that we experience both sensations and thoughts in response to art but that art has an even greater potency: the capacity to elevate us from these two states onto a third, a more sanctified plane of consciousness.

The urn itself, though, is as much concerned with time as with art: it has survived the centuries intact or 'unravished' – and one of its effects is to give insight on ancient life. It therefore exists both within time and yet beyond it. It serves as a mysterious loophole in time, providing subtle revelation, on tip-toe between two dimensions of time: human time (fixed, temporal) and the sacred (or eternal). Under this interpretation the urn as the quintessential work of art transcends time, goes beyond itself as a symbol to speak to us in a quasi-religious or philosophical mode (as indeed it does in the final two lines).

If the urn is capable of doing this, of transporting us into some metaphysical domain beyond the here and now, then it has the power to reach beyond mortal cares and frustration (as the nightingale's song could reach beyond the 'fever, and the fret'). In other words, in the process of teasing us *into* the sacred it also teases us *out* of the mundane, fretful world (characterised in Stanza III by 'burning', 'parching', 'high-sorrowful'). In a fairly simplistic reduction then, art in the form of the urn can be a perfect therapy for our 'other woe' (47).

Keats pays high spiritual tribute to the urn as artwork, setting great store by its profound effect upon him as both a man and an artist. It is clearly a considerable inspiration (even if his emotions are more restrained than in 'Nightingale') – a conundrum to him, a balm for the mind, a pivot for the wild surmise, kindling that same exhilaration he felt previously for Chapman's *Homer*. Symbolically the art of the urn is understandably an ideal paradigm for Keats. It is an incarnation of perfect form and order, a foil to the messy imperfections of life itself. Yet, in spite of (or even because of) this it displays a cool indifference, an insouciance which is more than slightly frigid. Despite its enticing offers of escape ('What struggle to escape?' line 9) from the bonds of mortality, the fret and woe, this 'silent form' projects a trio of snapshots of life, paralysed in action. Although its arrested reality promises an end to mortal woe, its people never actually stir alive in the way that Keats's imagination strives to make them. The musicians cannot bring their melodies to full tip nor the lovers consummate their 'wild ecstasy'. Not surprising then that it is a 'Cold Pastoral!' As John Barnard has pointed out, the people figured on the urn 'belong to an ominous world of coldness and fixity'.

It is, of course, Keats's intense imagination that invests the urn and its figures with life and narrative. The viewer of visual art, like the reader of poetry too, creates his or her own impressions, filling gaps and imposing meaning. The urn is essentially passive ('still') before Keats's nimble eye, which flies beyond the immediate object into a realm of subjective possibilities. Unmistakably it is Keats himself who imbues a commonplace Greek pot with the spark of profounder reality and sees in it the ground for metaphysics. He converts the fact or *truth* of the pot into poetic beauty. Truth becomes beauty, while the beauty of the urn inspires the poet to higher truths still.

And this is the matter of the final two lines of the poem, probably the most hotly debated of all Keats's lines:

> Beauty is truth, truth beauty, – that is all
> Ye know on earth, and all ye need to know.
>
> (49–50)

The final two lines of 'Grecian Urn' have been edited in a variety of styles since the poem's first appearance in a journal in January 1820. Keats himself generally took little interest in printers' punctuation of his verse and since no manuscript copy in his own fair hand exists there is no definitive version of these lines. I have opted for the above format because it retains the idea that the epigram (Beauty is truth, truth beauty) is 'spoken' by the urn while keeping open other possible interpretations. It also comes closest to transcriptions of the poem made by friends of Keats at that time.

What can we make of these highly enigmatic lines? How may something which is true necessarily embody beauty? How can beauty guarantee truth? We can start with two ideas which Keats probably did not intend. The first is that art should exist for the sake only of art itself (i.e. without reference to truth, real life), and the other, that art or beauty should be exploited for narrow practical or ulterior purposes (for example, for moral or political crusades). These represent two extreme positions and there is scope for many others between them.

The poem itself is, of course, a work of art discussing another work of art, the Grecian urn (though in lines 3 and 4 Keats modestly proposes that poetry is less eloquent than visual art). On a quite simple level, the urn does exist realistically, at least for Keats: its existence as an object of beauty is a sort of truth, a fact. Keats makes us believe in the reality of the urn, which was at one time before him. In itself it is a thing of beauty both in its form and in the images marked upon it, which the poet brings alive in his fancy. But in what sense can the beauty of the urn be its truth?

In taking the Grecian urn as his subject, Keats is using it as an exemplum, a metaphor of all artistic objects, and his 'theory' seeks to embrace all forms of art, visual or literary, ancient or contemporary. Equally he does not set out with any preconceived notions of what abstract qualities a work must exhibit in order to qualify as art. So by arguing that *Beauty is truth, truth beauty*, Keats may be affirming that these are not two separate entities but a single concept viewed from two different points.

The urn is held up by Keats as the ideal work, a timeless work, demonstrating as it does such a keen harmony between its chaste form and the sensuality of its pictures. So fine is the balance between its own beauty and realism (or truth) that it emanates an almost palpable stillness, a timeless radiant stasis ('for ever new', line 24). Keats clearly implies this in his choice of diction, referring to 'silence', 'ever silent form', and the keynote word 'still'. The urn is timeless in the sense that it has miraculously survived the centuries unbroken, but also in the sense that it has endured the whims and vicissitudes of artistic fashion over those years, a 'friend to man', and a joy for ever. Aloof and disinterested it adsorbs Keats's rapturous adulation, the wild surmise which momentarily threatens its cool propriety.

My reading so far has advanced a Platonist view of beauty and truth. In other words, the urn symbolises a perfect and distant model for art that is only imagined – 'unheard melodies' (11). Such beauty is apprehended through the process of the imagination, which Keats believes may reach beyond worldly sensual experience into an eso- teric realm of artistic truth,

> therefore, ye soft pipes, play on;
> Not to the sensual ear, but, more endeared,
> Pipe to the spirit ditties of no tone...
>
> (12–14)

However, we have seen already that the Platonist view of art and life does not square easily with Keats's more familiar empiricism, his trust in the senses and immediate physical experience. Another view of the poem's closing epigram and one more in keeping with his empiricism would be that beauty is very much a matter of one's subjective response to a work of art, especially a response working through the emotions rather than through reason or philosophy. Beauty would then be a source of truth which sprang from the close interaction between the work of art and the intense engagement of the reader (or viewer, listener etc.). This view would also be consistent with Keats's conception of the role of the imagination which he outlined in the letter of 22 November 1817, which we have referred to previously:

> I am certain of nothing but of the holiness of the Heart's affections and the truth of the Imagination – What the imagination seizes as Beauty must be truth.

The imagination actively beholds or even creates truth but, in addition, the emotions (or 'intensity') also play a vital role as a pathway for truth. Keats makes this point clearer in another letter to his brothers, written a month later, about a painting that had failed to move him,

> The excellence of every art is its intensity, capable of making all disagreeables evaporate, from their being in close relationship with Beauty and Truth.
>
> (21 December 1817)

Let us pause to take some stock of where we have reached in this empirical view of beauty and truth. According to this view the beauty of the urn acts directly on the senses of the observer, stimulating his or her emotions as well as the imagination. This process can thereby discover subjective truths about the urn and even about the observer. In the poem itself the pronounced impact of the urn on Keats is fully demonstrated by the frenzied questions at the end of the first stanza and by the romanticised narratives in Stanzas II, III and IV, conjured up through Keats's imagination.

Beauty is truth or furnishes truth, and yet the epigram of the poem insists that art be rooted in truth, that is should imitate reality. An example of this is that Keats regarded the Parthenon frieze (or 'Elgin Marbles') as a paragon of beauty because its figures were such an accurate reproduction of life. Art should therefore be true to life (including life as psychological or other truths as well as simple physical replication) – if it is to partake of beauty.

Beauty is truth, truth beauty: I have proposed two radically different interpretations of this intriguing line and of course there are other possibilities. At the same time, we should ask how this epigram works within the conclusion of the poem: Is it Keats himself or the urn which speaks at the end? And is this really all we know on earth or, indeed, all that we need to know?

Whoever it is that utters the final and slightly pompous aphorism, in structural terms it marks a pulling away of the voice from the rest of the ode. The focus turns away from the urn itself and outwards onto the readers (the word 'Ye' in the final line is of course plural). The final clause leaves behind it the tensions and uncertainties of the ode and leaves them still, immanent in the abrupt silence at the close. The dramatic effect, if not the meaning, is supreme. With a twist in the tail, we are left with a bold, apparently axiomatic statement, generalising about mankind (in June 1819 Keats wrote to a female acquaintance, 'I hope I am a little more of a Philosopher than I was...'). The famous clause seeks to look beyond the ode with an air of some certainty but in effect it sets the reader off, grasping for meaning. The final line thus deconstructs itself by evading certainty, setting up further questions for the reader. Again he teases us out of thought, spurring us first into a disruptive perplexity and then back into the poem once more, conscious that the 'bride of quietness' and 'foster-child of silence' is not going to come up with anything like a straight answer.

At the end, the urn refuses to unperplex. At best it offers only a starting point (significantly, Keats elsewhere associates urns with enigmatic silence; see *Endymion*, III.32 and 'To Sleep', line 14). It continues to be a shrewdly equivocal historian, confounding definitiveness, as inscrutable for the reader as the nightingale was for the poet. Where Keats's narrative verse is the journey towards order out of chaos, these two great odes reverse the direction: beginning in apparent order, in stillness and clarity, they voyage into a wide expanse of deepening chaos and into Keats's uncertainty principle, Negative Capability. Yet Keats deftly and wilfully provokes in us that irritable reaching after of solutions and the wild surmise that renders line 48 tersely ironic.

While Negative Capability is among the prime movers of the 'Ode on a Grecian Urn', ripeness and time are among its chief themes:

> When old age shall this generation waste,
> Thou shalt remain...

(46–7)

Significantly, almost every word here refers to the theme of time and in the poem as a whole practically every line makes some reference to it. In lines 46 and 47 the word 'generation' stands out partly because of its ambivalence (suggesting 'creativity' as well as 'human eras') but also because it connects with a similar reference in 'Ode to a Nightingale' (line 62). Here Keats implies that the urn exists outside of the limitations of human mortality and of time itself – and we have already noted the urn's special capacity to transcend its own current time and sphere as well as ours.

References to 'waste' and then to 'woe' (47) recall the 'fever, and the fret' of 'Nightingale'. As ever, Keats grounds his reflections in reality but here they also face up to the actuality of temporal human life as it was for Keats – in contrast to the idealised and timeless world of the humans pictured on the side of the urn. The switch to future tense in line 46 points the reader to a time beyond the poem, even to beyond the lifetime of the poet himself, where human life will continue to be haunted by sorrow, but relieved perhaps by the perfection which the urn holds out as a consolation, a 'friend to man'. Moreover these lines take up those references to 'ever' in lines 20 and 26, and the idea of life persisting long after Keats and his generation have passed away. On the other hand, unlike the voice in 'Nightingale' he seems here less convinced of the solace that such persistence may hold out (a point highlighted by his choice of the doleful verb 'waste', conspicuous at the end of line 46).

Consequently, the prospect of escape is much less convincing, less genuine here. Keats's tone is a fusion of delight in the teasing beauty of the immortal urn and melancholy at the reality of his own mortality. Its promises of release – immortal beauty, 'wild ecstasy' and visions of perfect love – remain simply a frustrating literary fiction, unconvincing despite the rich and passionate joys they arouse. In its role as 'Sylvan historian' the urn is a chill reminder ('Cold Pastoral!') that we are firmly rooted in the heavy clays of time and decay. The only feasible relief suggested is through the bowers of the creative imagination.

On the other hand Keats's own seminal imagination generates an abundance of human delights: love (above all), but also art, religion, music, poetry, and the life of collective elation. Typically – and ominously – these are presented as snapshots, imagistic moments in time, paradoxically separate yet an integral part of a sequence. A whole range of moments come together in Keats's urn: the moment of the urn's creation, the classical tableaux, the occasion of Keats's inspection of it, plus many others compressed into the poem's own instant or moment of being as a cheating, fragile glimpse into reality.

Such moments remind us of our mortality. A good illustration of this can be seen in Stanza IV where the ritual procession of the sacrificial heifer points allegorically to the death of Youth as well as to the fading of Keats's dream of a happy golden age in pastoral idyll (cf. the 'Song of Pan' episode in *Endymion*, I). As a religious snapshot this picture calls to mind the 'men and gods' inquiry in line 8. The urn is thus one more example of Keats's 'tip-toe' motifs, communing with both the human world and that of the gods. Moreover, it encapsulates the duality of the tomb and the womb, as a container of funeral ashes as well as a primitive symbol of generation (tying in with the poem's many hints of copulation, such as in the opening line).

'Grecian Urn' has many opposites: mortal/immortal, pain/bliss, death/life, eternity/waste, negative/positive, and so on. They suggest a finely judged equilibrium while at the same time spinning a highly agreeable air of tension, being 'overwrought', a tension that is physically personified in the silent figures captured on the urn. The urn arrests and fixes the moment of plumping ripeness, pregnant with possibilities, containing its imminent release in the eternal moment once more; a moment that 'cannot fade' (19). But there is a dilemma. Is the love scene depicted here a climactic instant of ecstasy, gloriously prolonged for all eternity ('For ever warm', line 26) or is it merely a failed, unconsummated passion paralysed before its fulfilment ('That leaves a heart high-sorrowful', line 29)?

Consummation of this love would quite naturally entail the completion of sexual intercourse, implying 'generation' and 'brede', which would also bring with it change and decline. Stanza II brilliantly crystallises the fixed eternity of a moment in time: balanced erotically between acquiescence and denial, 'ever...never, never...ever' (16–20). My own view is that this balance signifies the failure of desire. The 'wild ecstasy' of the yearned-for intercourse ('still unravished') finally becomes a withered 'Cold Pastoral'. The lovers fail to consummate their love and their frustration is doomed to be exposed for ever in freeze frame, locked together eternally in the room of unresolved possibilities.

'Ode on a Grecian Urn' is without doubt a bravura performance, the performance of a poet in complete mastery of his art. The troubled ego of 'Nightingale' looms less large here, freeing Keats to sing with full-throated ease, striking a clarity to match the superb symbolism at the heart of this poem. At the same time, it has to be said that in spite of its clarity, its brilliant linguistic virtuosity, and the intensity of its metaphysics it does not quite attain the gusto and emotional range of 'Nightingale'. The emotional eruption in Stanza III does not quite convince and the poem's limited sensations are less near, less consoling in answer to the sober realities of which the poem makes us so trenchantly aware.

'Ode on Melancholy'

Written in the same spring spell as 'Nightingale' and 'Grecian Urn', 'Ode on Melancholy' is the shortest of the major odes both in its physical length and in the scope of its vision. It is a strangely singular, even eerie, poem whose surprises hinge on its plasticity of language and drama. For example, the dramatic impact of Stanza I comes about chiefly because of Keats's having discarded his original, more macabre opening stanza; the four negative words in the first line wrong- foot the poem in terms of its overall tone – which is generally optimistic; and the poem as a whole has an unexpected unity of sound, being orchestrated through an intricate web of echoes and harmonics.

I have chosen the third stanza for textual analysis but it will be useful to see the whole of this short poem:

I

No, no, go not to Lethe, neither twist
    Wolf's-bane, tight-rooted, for its poisonous wine:
Nor suffer thy pale forehead to be kissed
    By nightshade, ruby grape of Proserpine;
Make not your rosary of yew-berries,   5
      Nor let the beetle, nor the death-moth be
        Your mournful Psyche, nor the downy owl
A partner in your sorrow's mysteries;
      For shade to shade will come too drowsily,
        And drown the wakeful anguish of the soul.   10

II

But when the melancholy fit shall fall
    Sudden from heaven like a weeping cloud,
That fosters the droop-headed flowers all,
    And hides the green hill in an April shroud;
Then glut thy sorrow on a morning rose,   15
      Or on the rainbow of the salt sand-wave,
        Or on the wealth of globed peonies;
Or if thy mistress some rich anger shows,
      Emprison her soft hand, and let her rave,
        And feed deep, deep upon her peerless eyes.   20

III

She dwells with Beauty – Beauty that must die;
    And Joy, whose hand is ever at his lips
Bidding adieu; and aching Pleasure nigh,
    Turning to poison while the bee-mouth sips:
Ay, in the very temple of Delight   25
      Veiled Melancholy has her sovran shrine,
        Though seen of none save him whose strenuous tongue
Can burst Joy's grape against his palate fine;
His soul shall taste the sadness of her might,
        And be among her cloudy trophies hung.   30

The swift sensual tumble of Stanza II, with its lucid scintillating images, is brought to a brief halt by the repetition of the word 'deep' in line 20 and in that brief pause the poem re-adjusts its focus and tempo in preparation for the final section. The pronoun 'She' in the opening to Stanza III emphasises this adjustment, changing the point of view here from second person to third. This is another of the poem's surprises since it is only in line 26 that the mistress is after all revealed to be 'Veiled Melancholy'.

The third stanza now takes up some of those darker hues which coloured Stanza I, as well as 'Ode to a Nightingale' (for example, die, poison, mouth, grape) and fuses them in the 'aching Pleasure' more characteristic of Stanza II (that is, Joy, sips, Delight, taste). In drawing together these two paradoxical elements of the poem, the final stanza creates a wholly new voice among the odes, one that is genuinely assertive and assured. The pain of melancholy is to some extent cheated by exploiting it for art's sake and for the sake of a fuller experience of the world, informed by human realities. The final two lines, with their mysterious fateful flourish, hint at a submission to some strange cult of Melancholy.

Keats here uses the word 'melancholy' in at least two different and possibly confusing ways. In his first use of the word in Stanza III, melancholy is linked with Beauty, Joy and Pleasure (21–6), but melancholy has a more 'sovran shrine', a more permanent state through which the sensitive/sensate individual may come to savour even pain and sorrow. Under this first use of the word, Keats employs 'melancholy' in the more conventional sense: a generalised form of sadness which reduces human action to a deep, pensive contemplation. This is not a specific mental pain, like grief say, nor is it the nausea of boredom. It is more like the generalised 'drowsy numbness' that pains the sense in 'Nightingale', a lethargy that in Keats's own words 'does not take away the pain of existence'. One might think here of Hamlet's lassitude as well as of Keats's own occasional bouts of depression. During the spring of 1819 he had been reading from the seventeenth-century treatise *An Anatomy of Melancholy*, in which the writer Robert Burton encourages his readers to make use of this condition, to exploit it, as Keats urges in Stanza II:

Then glut thy sorrow on a morning rose...

(15)

At the same time Keats has another, more limited sense of the word here: to mean a highly specialised artistic faculty, a refined creative sensitivity which galvanises the writer to respond to his experiences and to convert these into poetry and other forms of literature. We need to spend some time on this second, slightly more problematic meaning.

The opening stanza of the ode warns us against regarding melancholy as a mood akin to despair, defeatism or horror, from which suicide might offer an escape route. The middle stanza proposes other means by which to rigorously divert the melancholy frame of mind, chiefly through pleasurable sensations. And then the final stanza invites the anguished soul to indulge life to its fullest, savour all experience, even that which involves deep torment. Keats himself had, of course, suffered many such occasions in his brief life and it must have demanded deep emotional resources even to entertain this as a plausible option. A mere eye-skip across the poem's imagery should be enough to convince the reader of the heavy scars of pain that run through it: bane, poisonous, pale, nightshade, cloud, die, suffer, anguish, weeping, anger, death-moth, shade, shroud, aching. Moreover, the discursive 'Ay' in line 25 implies that it is genuine personal experience which informs the emotions of the poem – and it also implies some inevitability in its persistence.

As a whole, the poem represents a brief sketch, a stab at the psychology of melancholy as Keats had experienced it. He energises his sketch by revealing how this condition relates to other mental conditions such as delight and pain, and to themes of love, beauty and life's transience:

She dwells with Beauty – Beauty that must die...

(21)

However, unlike 'Nightingale', which does capture something vivid of such pain, 'Melancholy' remains by and large a detached analysis or statement of it.

By contrasting melancholy in this stanza with more transient features such as Beauty, Joy, Pleasure and Delight, Keats underlines his point that melancholy is a background syndrome (and not a mood either) across which these other features traverse: like a 'weeping cloud' (12) or the 'rainbow of the salt sand-wave' (16). Thus the second stanza significantly begins with 'But when...', urgently capturing that tone of inevitability I mentioned earlier. Furthermore, this tone of fatalism coils through the middle and final stanzas to the doom and enthralment at the conclusion, to be 'among her cloudy trophies hung' (30).

We have been here before or hereabouts. As early as '*I stood tip-toe*' Keats had formulated the essence of this figure as 'Full of sweet desolation – balmy pain' (162), and in his 'Pleasure Thermometer' letter (30 January 1818) he characterises Drama as the 'playing of different Natures with Joy and Sorrow'. His use of oxymoron to adumbrate this complex condition has already been noted and there are hints of this trope in 'Melancholy' too: references to oblivion and glory begin and close the poem, there is 'aching Pleasure' (23), 'poison' and sweetness (24), ideal beauty and worldly sensuality (21–2). As before, pain originates in many delightful sources: Beauty (21), Joy (22), and sex (25) are the usual suspects. And line 25 reminds us that quite typically for Keats, sorrow begins in 'being too happy' in his happy lot ('Nightingale', line 6); in other words, in the highest moment of ripest joy the grape may burst, leaving the sorrowful after-taste of melancholy. As the Victorian critic Florence Owen first observed, the saddest images of this ode are not those of Stanza I but those in II and the start of III. Keats is now resigned to the impossibility of ever unperplexing 'bliss from its neighbour pain' (*Lamia*, I.192).

More than anything, melancholy is proposed not as a deficit but actually as a condition of the mind in which feelings and responses become re-formed and exalted. It is one more precision instrument at the disposal of the writer and Keats's analysis of this instrument here and elsewhere also highlights the key role played by the ego, the soul as the seat of sensitivity (see 'Melancholy', lines 10 and 29). As always with the Romantics the poetic soul, the filtering ego, is the 'sovran shrine' of the imagination and the gauge of reality. As always with Keats himself, reality is very much a matter of time, ripeness and mortality.

As said before, 'Ode on Melancholy' presents us with analysis rather than direct experience of its subject matter, and consistent with this, the poem delivers an open discussion of these temporal themes. In Stanza III Keats confronts the persistent empirical fact of human mortality, most bluntly in line 30 with 'Beauty that must die'. Where the previous two odes held out some relief or consolation for this fact (in the nightingale's charming song or the constancy of the urn), this poem faces up to the reality without respite. Unlike sylvan warblers and their sylvan historians, human beings *are* 'born for death'. Equally, human emotions are rigorously transient; joy, pleasure, delight as well sadness and anguish are, naturally, forever 'Bidding adieu' (23). As we might expect, this transience is mirrored in Keats's choice of imagery here: the frailty of passing nature, animals, weather, plants. All fairly conventional too, until that is we reach that most striking image of Joy's grape, in Stanza III:

> Though seen of none save him whose strenuous tongue
> Can burst Joy's grape against his palate fine.
>
> (27–8)

Taking up the earlier reference to 'ruby grape of Proserpine' and her deathly associations (4), 'Joy's grape' thus draws into the poem Keats's characteristic antithesis of ripeness and withering, while at the same time transcending it with thoughts of pleasure and indulgence. The full plump image of the grape superbly epitomises the theme of ripeness (compare 'To Autumn' on this too), as well as of the thing untested, untasted, pregnant in time's waiting capsule. The grape collects up other references in the poem to oral sensuality: kissing (3), sipping (24), and tasting (29; and even the sand has a salty taste, in line 16). Beyond this poem, too, the grape connects with other vines and wines, of pleasure and escape in 'Nightingale' and 'Grecian Urn', as well as in *Endymion* and *Lamia*.

As an emblem of human mortality the grape is a complex phenomenon. Coaxing out its double aspect as both poison (2) and sweetness (24), Keats in essence characterises it in terms of the evanescence of its joy, made all the greater by its brevity and variety. The ruby grape untasted remains untried, mere potential, yet the moment of its realisation, of fruition, as we bite into the berry is also its ending in joyous bursting. Keats further deepens this insight onto delight through the balancing of his adjectives, in '*strenuous* tongue' (27) and '*palate* fine' (28) (both of which touch faintly on the theme of time). But, at the root, their effect is to keep our attention fastened firm on the actuality of human mortality.

Keats's point is that though we cannot make time stand still we can perhaps get the most out of the mortal delights that experience offers us. All the way through the poem, Keats foregrounds the reality of human transience, a point underlined by his assertive tone, especially in the continual use of negatives together with strategic imperatives; for example, 'will' (9), 'must' (21), 'shall' (29). He does entertain the possibility of alternatives – the other world and other lives – but, as the opening stanza makes plain, they are subordinated here to the reality of this life, good or bad. There are no anodynes (compare 'Ode on Indolence') and little escape. Only the individual self and its journey. Where in other poems there might be relief through dream, art, drink, drugs, sex, oblivion, music or friends, Keats now disdains it to confront the reality of the human moment head on.

What then are these mortal delights? In his 'vale of Soul-making' letter to his brother George, Keats hinted at 'Melancholy's central theme

> This is the world – thus we cannot expect to give way many hours to pleasure...while we are laughing the seed of some trouble is put into the wide arable land of events – while we are laughing it sprouts [it] grows and suddenly bears a poison fruit which we must pluck.

Again Keats sees life in terms of the ripening of fruit, which we are obliged to pluck. Our pleasures are brief and pass across a vale of sorrow. Yet, typically, he recognises that these relatively fleeting moments have the power of great intensity, made more so by their very brevity The key figure of this poem is of course the wryly erotic image of the bursting grape in line 28. As the focal point of the many references to fluids and the body, as well as to touching and mouthing, this vividly gathers up the poem's sensuality in a terse orgasmic release at its climax. The sexuality of this moment is underpinned by Keats's perception of the body as the 'very temple of Delight', a pleasure dome, the subtle membrane of sensation and of voluptuous satisfaction. Thus even melancholy contains the potential for exquisite delight, the location of a mysterious and blissful anguish.

Joy is represented as a male figure (22) while melancholy is clearly female (26), a dominating secretive mistress, 'seen of none' (27). As in previous poems Keats indulges this erotic fantasy and merges it with hints of sado-masochism and the pains of love (compare *La Belle Dame sans Merci*). Stanza I hints at flirtations with death, which gradually become translated into the complex 'wakeful anguish' in line 10, and then Stanza II draws the implicit sexuality of the poem to the surface in those softly erogenous hints of lines 19 and 20 (which have echoes too of Lycius's cruel embrace of Lamia):

> Emprison her soft hand, and let her rave,
> And feed deep, deep upon her peerless eyes.

However, at last, Keats insists that sex must fade, a 'Beauty that must die', even at the moment of its indulgence, 'while the bee-mouth sips'. After this deflowering, Joy and Pleasure yield to sadness, dying away in a cadence of sexual fulfilment. Even so, by the time we reach the final lines, Keats's earlier note of defiant realism makes a return – even if obscurely.

Like the explorer in 'Chapman's Homer', we have now travelled much and far from the conventional concept of 'melancholy'. In opening it up to include this more specialised sense, of a heightened artistic sensitivity with strong sexual associations, the poem has boldly explored the more obscure and complex psychological implications of the syndrome. For the ordinary person, such a probing self-exploration might be highly risky if not utterly self-destructive. Yet Keats appears to say here – as elsewhere – that for the artist there is really no choice in the matter: what makes the artist/writer what he or she is is the combination of a heightened innate sensitivity and an equally innate obedience to it.

For the Romantic poets, artistic sensitivity is also bound up inevitably with the theme of beauty. This correspondence is made clear at the start of the final stanza, in 'She dwells with Beauty' (21). This line suggests too that Keats now has in mind human beauty in particular – after exploring the beauty of natural objects in 'Nightingale' and artistic objects in 'Grecian Urn'. 'Pleasure' and 'Joy', 'Delight' and 'sadness' are all part of the package of human beauty and the sexuality that is all one with it. But he now takes this analysis a stage further by relating the worship of beauty to the joys and pains of artistic sensitivity, especially as it reveals knowledge about oneself. In other words, the appreciation of beauty is important in itself but equally important in what it reveals about myself as a poet.

Some critics have recoiled from Keats's interest in this relationship between the self and the theme of beauty. F. R. Leavis, for one, deplored it as perverse, a decadent posture leading to aestheticism, or 'art-for-art's-sake' (for more on Leavis, see Chapter 8). However, this seems to me too severe a judgement, especially as Stanza I of 'Melancholy' dismisses any hints of self-indulgent posturings, and the poem as a whole presses for a strong awareness of reality. Nowhere does Keats imply that melancholy is to be self-induced (see line 11 on this) and the imagery of this ode also stresses action over swooning passivity (for example, 'glut', 'Emprison', 'feed', 'burst', 'taste', are all active).

While 'Ode on Melancholy' did inspire later Victorian poets in their pursuit of art for art's sake, Keats himself was never very seriously interested in this venture. The opening line of *Endymion* and the epigram of 'Grecian Urn' were also rallying cries for the aestheticist movement but Keats's own verse is too vitally grounded in everyday reality to be drawn that way. Rather, 'Melancholy' should be seen as an interrogation of human psychology, another response to the imperative 'know thyself'. Keats regards this interrogation as highly significant for the artist and especially in respect of his 'Soul-making' theory of human development: life as a series of limitations and ordeals which refine and define the fundamental nature of the artist as a unique individual. This project, paramount in Keats's philosophy at this time, is also one of the prevailing ideas behind *The Fall of Hyperion*, and as we have seen it is fearfully personified in the figure of Moneta, antithesis of 'mournful Psyche' (and look too at the 'Cave of Quietude' passage in *Endymion*, IV).

This reading of the poem has tried to resolve Keats's radical and problematic thesis of melancholy as something not wholly unpleasant to the 'palate fine'. In spite of an air of uncertainty in this thesis the poem closes on a strong tone of defiant conviction. Elsewhere in the poem, too, Keats stiffens up this tone with a poetic style that simply exudes maturity and authority; for example, in his bold use of pauses and caesurae for control, and note the rhetorical effect of those repetitions in lines 6, 16–18, 20 and 21. At the same time, this brief compact performance is rooted in a highly coherent structure bolstered by strings of internal rhymes; for example, 'peonies...poison'; 'mysteries...mistress...strenuous'; 'Lethe...let...palate'.

Turning to prosody, Keats again makes use of iambic pentameter. The final two lines of the poem are its most regular (compare line 27, its most irregular) and this reinforces the air of conviction at the close. In a confident voice of increasing maturity, Keats makes free with the poetic metre and this in turn lends to it an overall feeling of intimacy and thence also that honesty, which is integral to his thesis; for example, his readiness to drop in trochaic units of sound, as in Psyche, Beauty, Bidding, Pleasure, palate, sadness. The change once more wrong-foots the rhythm, creating a more informal register, investing it too with a mysterious haunting cadence, dropping away.

Yet in spite of the air of conclusiveness and technical assurance in the 'Ode on Melancholy' there lurks throughout an impression of incertitude. This suspicion is fostered by the recurring sound of hesitation in the /er/ and /or/ syllables as well as in the literal uncertainties which punctuate the surface. At the start of Stanza III the pronoun 'She' is ambiguous, as is 'mistress' in line 18. There are other reservations too; does 'glut' (15) mean 'satiate' or simply 'feed'? What exactly is a 'salt-sand wave' (16)? And why are melancholy's trophies 'cloudy'? (Note too the curious puns in 'nightshade' [4], 'peerless' [20], 'morning' [15] and 'berries' [5].)

Strictly speaking, however, these ambivalences never actually threaten the integrity of the poem. While its ambiguities and indeterminacies deepen the tensions of the work, they are also symptomatic of Keats's efforts to break new ground through this radical enterprise. The bold task he set himself was to deconstruct and distance himself from the conventional Romantic view of melancholy, that is melancholy as a dark languorous sorrow, a morose brooding on death. In its place he strove to situate a vision of melancholy as the artistic enterprise and an encounter with life in its full range of contending realities and intensities. These are the terms on which this experiment should be assessed.

Taking the longer view, 'Ode on Melancholy' with its more restricted focus and its demanding thesis is the least successful of the three odes so far considered. Keats himself does not appear to have been all that convinced by its argument, while its earthly compensations are scant and small beer after the lavish glories and metaphysical elegances of 'Nightingale' and 'Grecian Urn'. The poem offers little in the way of direction and at the same time he struggles hard to persuade us that melancholy can actually be somehow gratifying. For a happier integration of theme, fresh feeling and poetic zest we should turn now to a truly superlative production, 'To Autumn', the quintessence of Keats's sensual and imaginative powers .

'To Autumn'

Although 'To Autumn' was not composed until September 1819 it covers much of the same thematic ground as the great spring odes of that year (though it stands apart from them in spirit and mood). Still a very popular poem, it has often been acclaimed as Keats's finest achievement in the lyric, and critics have described it variously as 'flawless', 'a poetic *tour de force*', and the 'summit of Keats's sensual art'.

'To Autumn' is a valediction, a poem of partings – of the day, of the season (and the swallows with it), and behind all this, a parting from life itself. Yet none of this makes it in anyway gloomy. The poem shows a clear and open development of thought and moment over its three stanzas: from maturing fruitfulness to harvesting, and then, with night about to fall, its attention drifts towards the close of this season and beyond. It is not an end either, for the poem argues that these things have no end but only change, that the very idea of 'season' is open to question.

I have chosen Stanza I for close analysis and as the start of a discussion of the poem as a whole.

I

Season of mists and mellow fruitfulness,
　Close bosom-friend of the maturing sun,
Conspiring with him how to load and bless
　With fruit the vines that round the thatch-eves run;
To bend with apples the mossed cottage-trees,　　　　　5
　And fill all fruit with ripeness to the core;
　　To swell the gourd, and plump the hazel shells
With a sweet kernel; to set budding more,
　And still more, later flowers for the bees,
　Until they think warm days will never cease,　　　　　10
　　For Summer has o'er-brimmed their clammy cells.

II

Who hath not seen thee oft amid thy store?
　Sometimes whoever seeks abroad may find
Thee sitting careless on a granary floor,
　Thy hair soft-lifted by the winnowing wind　　　　　15
Or on a half-reaped furrow sound asleep,
　Drowsed with the fume of poppies, while thy hook
　　Spares the next swath and all its twined flowers;
And sometimes like a gleaner thou dost keep
　Steady thy laden head across a brook;　　　　　20
　Or by a cider-press, with patient look,
　　Thou watchest the last oozings hours by hours.

III

Where are the songs of Spring? Ay, where are they?
　Think not of them, thou hast thy music too –
While barred clouds bloom the soft-dying day,　　　　　25
　And touch the stubble-plains with rosy hue:
Then in a wailful choir the small gnats mourn
　Among the river sallows, borne aloft
　　Or sinking as the light wind lives or dies;
And full-grown lambs loud bleat from hilly bourn;　　　　　30
　Hedge-crickets sing; and now with treble soft
　The red-breast whistles from a garden-croft;
　　And gathering swallows twitter in the skies.

From the start of the poem to its close the theme of time is
insistent. It begins with the time word, 'Season', and as my brief
paraphrase of the poem indicates, the three Stanzas treat a progress
through three different (though not discrete) time zones of autumn.
Time references permeate the whole poem and within Stanza I we
can trace allusions to the time-cycle of plant life: flowers (9), fruit (4),
and the seed (7–8). Ripeness itself is demonstrated as the inevitable
natural outcome of time's movement (though by focusing closely on
autumn Keats actually gives the impression that the flowers have
somehow materialised spontaneously).

The abundant imagery of plenty, roundness and fullness is almost
palpable: fruitfulness, bosom, load, round, full, ripeness, swell, plump,
and o'er-brimmed. And as an adjunct of this swelling theme, note too
the many references here to action, movement and change: maturing,
conspiring, load, bless, action, run, bend, full, swell, set, and 'never
cease'. Manifest beneath a scene of homely warmth and sweetness are
dynamic, continuous, fluid transformations, rising, swelling, bursting.
Autumn here is both a symbol of time's advancement, acting through
nature and its processes, as well as its very reality.

Each stanza furnishes a moving picture of time, each image poised
at a crucial turning point in the season. Likewise, each embodies a
tension between the process of time's movement and the impulse to
retard it, to savour the moment (implied later in the word 'spares';
line 18). In Stanza I this dynamic, inexorable process is represented in
the untiring industry of the bees and in the conspiracy working
beneath the cosy mellow picture. And the desire to hold on to the
picture is signified in Keats's exhilarating imagery playing around the
fixed, faintly paternalistic figure of the ancient cottage.

Stanza I does not so much set up the movement as peer out across
a process already begun. We are *in medias res* of the continuous cycle
of growth, inevitably so, and the key features of the cycle are
ripeness, mortality and renewal. But even within this great process
of time Keats sets different points of ageing: the 'mossed cottage
trees' seem ancient in endurance, and offer a back-drop against which
the year, the season, the day and the moment play out their periods
(Stanza I is quickening, then II slows to an oozing, and III picks up
the pace once more).

Stanza I introduces us to autumn as a time of fulfilment, as much a season of glorious celebration as spring was, spring being the more conventional subject of poetry or 'songs'. Ripeness is everything, a positive and happy goal – fill, swell, plump – and Stanzas II and III extend that ripeness into the harvesting and transformation of its products, their enjoyment, before we hear portents of beginnings (Spring, lambs, river) and rebirth. In this fascinating tripartite sequence, Stanza II stands out as a sort of *ricorso*, another of Keats's timeless moments in time, moments of reflection and recharging before the movement accelerates (compare time's 'still unravished bride' in 'Grecian Urn' and the timeless moment of the nightingale's song).

By late 1819 Keats was now dramatically aware of his own mortality. There were increasing signs that he had contracted tuberculosis, probably as a result of nursing his brother Tom. However, there is not the slightest hint of gloom here – in contrast to the more stoical 'Ode on Melancholy'. By now, ripeness for Keats is a rich storehouse of life and of artistic experiences garnered under his own 'maturing sun'.

Ripeness also connects all four of the odes under consideration in this chapter. As the last in Keats's ode sequence, 'To Autumn' offers a most satisfying resolution to the troubling issues of time, ageing, human mortality, and death, in the most English of his settings. Clearly death has a place here – it is hinted at in the instinctive productiveness of the bees and then manifested in the brilliant double perspective of line 10:

Until they think warm days will never cease.

Death has its place in the process of time, yet as Stanza I explains, it nowhere diminishes the beauty of nature; moreover, death actually gives to it definition and the sense of order within.

On the subject of death, the bees mistakenly assume that these 'warm days will never *cease*', while Stanza II finishes on the '*last* oozings', and Stanza III has the 'soft-*dying* day' with swallows gathering to leave the landscape to dormancy. Each stanza carries the consciousness of death as a reality. The transience of the human time-span too is suggested by the poem's great feeling of poise. This poise is first hinted at in Stanza I with its strong threat of an imminent bursting out of control ('more, / And still more...'), then through the 'steady' head in II, and on to the mourning gnats borne on the river breeze, and the gathering swallows – all hint at a sort of tremulous balance in nature.

Thoughts of death or sadness detain neither nature itself nor the poem's transit. Above all no melancholy is allowed to intrude on this double scene of expanding ripeness and transient mortality, even if 'conspiring' might make the process appear subversive. Instead, Keats exalts the fact of ripening as fully natural, as something to feed and glut upon, even if in the very enjoyment or bursting of the grape again we use it up. In this way, to 'fill all fruit with ripeness to the core' (6) perfectly reveals the completeness of the poet's own commitment to life in its full rounded splendour. Thus the images and ideas that flow into Stanza II, of exploitation and harvesting (echoing the bees of Stanza I), also engage with life in its fullest until we too reach a heady 'fume' of consciousness where we might even forget our mortality, if only briefly. Only at that point, at the climax of self-fulfilment can we consider our potential to become 'full grown'.

'To Autumn' gathers up and resolves two distinct attitudes to time: the natural maturing of one's potential either as an individual or as artist and the equally natural transition of human life. It does this by showing that these are actually two aspects of the same phenomenon. Without autumn there would be no spring. Without the passage of time there would be no bringing to fruition or pleasuring in ripeness. This is because of the fact that human life is necessarily tied to a pattern of change but, as such, this also brings about renewal. The point of death is also the point, the function, of life.

Keats wrote 'To Autumn' during a trip to Winchester in autumn 1819. He had sought seclusion in order to reorganise his Hyperion poem and to research the background to *Lamia*. After an evening walk across fields of reaped corn he recorded his great joy in a letter to his friend John Reynolds.

> How beautiful the season is now – How fine the air. A temperate sharpness about it. Really, without joking, chaste weather – Dian skies – I never lik'd stubble fields so much as now – Aye better than the

chilly green of Spring. Somehow a stubble-plain looks warm – in the same way that some pictures look warm – This struck me so much in my Sunday's walk that I composed upon it.

(21 September 1819)

The scene and his mood harmonise in a triumphant chord and the elation is clear and forceful. However, 'To Autumn' is not another conventional nature poem stock full of agreeable scenery and colour. As much as, say, Van Gogh, Keats fills the frame with himself, with gusto and verve, with the energy that he found on that Sunday walk and within himself and moving through the whole world that day.

For instance, note how Stanza I evokes the many mysterious bubbling energies that impel the life of autumn, filling, loading, bending and so on. The stanza opens in a mood of relative tranquillity (with 'mellow' and 'friend') and yet this is soon ousted by all these thrusting forces and secret pressures promising chaos ('more, / And still more...'), for republican summer has threatened to continue for ever, to take over the whole year. And then this insurgency is overtaken and quelled by the narcotic dissolution of Stanza II, in which natural forces become transmuted via man's bee-like harvest, metamorphosed into sensual, semi-erotic oozings. Like the reaper, thwarted by the conspiracy of the interlaced flowers, the process is effectively arrested by its own moment(um).

These strange operations are the chief manifestation of nature's wildness here, because although timeless in its effect this English rural idyll ironically feels both contained and organised. It is exploited by man and bees in Stanza I, reaped in II, and is the place of animal husbandry in III. Yet 'Close bosom-friend' and 'Conspiring' both hint at nature's inner power and superior might: mankind would be as deluded as the bees if he ever thought he had tamed these natural forces.

Instead, Keats presents a picture of man's processes in convivial but obedient harmony with those of nature. Each stanza has its own human presences: in Stanza I, though just out of view, mankind lingers in references to 'friends', 'him', and 'cottage'; Stanza II has four intriguing labourers, real or symbolic; and the final stanza presents an image of man and animals in collective accord, tamed or part-tamed: lambs, robins and swallows.

From the fruitfulness of Stanza I through the harvest and oozings of II (which is the pivotal stanza) to the wailing and moving of III, with its reference to spring and lambs, Keats infuses together human joy and melancholy in the continuous life of nature. It is nature continually renewing itself in its plants, insects, animals and birds, so that although the poem ends on a downbeat note Keats has done more than enough to convince us of the return of these delights.

We also come to know something other than the immediate reality: autumn is over now – or very nearly – but in the future, life will inevitably return. This poem, as with so many of Keats's, is much to do with different realities and with the ways of knowing them. We have already considered how line 10 injects an idea of a higher realism and this faint hint develops into the dawning realisation of 'last oozings' (22), to fill out into the sombre awareness of dying, mourning and wailful choirs in the final section. Such knowledge and the reality it bears helps to define and balance the ode's emotions. More than any of the poems we have so far discussed, 'To Autumn' superbly counterpoises the fullest expression of feelings against the reality of reason and truth. The poem's inescapable truth is that the essential beauty of life lies in its very transience: life acquires its meaning in the act of engaging in and consuming it.

Keats holds the two principal realities, of beauty and life, in tense concord, the familiar blissful pain of life's consummation now fully dramatised. As in 'Ode on Melancholy' there is a brisk refusal to submit to the allure of oblivion, making the rich ripe foison of autumn a match at the very least for the fertile promises of spring. However, again as in 'Ode on Melancholy', it is Keats's receptiveness which makes possible the joy and pain of both seasons and this is the root of the poem's realism.

The pictorial elements are indispensable of course. If we compare these scenes in 'To Autumn' with those in 'Nightingale' and 'Grecian Urn' its world never appears as unreal, the work of the fancy. Each time it comes over as a palpable entity, with physical setting and season, a word-painting growing out of personal experience. This also helps to make the rich positive tone more convincing as real. Similarly, Keats never feels the need here to transcend the drama of the scene into some idealistic realm in order to discover its essence and significance: truth and beauty are open manifestly before us.

Moreover, this happy realism naturally precludes any desire for escape. The fusion of truth and beauty means there is no genuine idea of evasion or flight, and the pleasures depicted are an integral feature of the movements in nature's cycle. The conspiracy of Stanza I and the spectral labourers in II, as much as the sensational context, make up the truth which is inherent in the scene's beauty; and beauty ('first in beauty') is the elemental force driving the green fuse now beginning to mellow.

It is for this reason that I think the poem so richly conveys Keats's concept of Negative Capability, the poet at one with the mysteries of nature (personified by the figures in Stanzas I and II). In seeking to celebrate rather than explain these mysterious metaphysical presences ('Season of *mists*') Keats also personifies autumn as the force of nature in a particular season – a pantheistic spirit working through all things (Wordsworth and Coleridge too had variations on this idea). What is more, this quasi-religious concept might also serve to explain why Keats chose the word 'bless' in line 3 – the natural extension of summer, ripening and making real the fertile pledge of spring.

By the same token, because ripening is such an integral feature of the natural life process, Keats's theism here must also accept death as an intrinsic event in that process. Once more, line 10 offers the first hint of this in the word 'cease', which is then taken up by more hints in II: 'reaped', 'gleaner', 'last oozings', and eventually we hear the more explicit references in 'dying', 'mourn', and 'dies' in Stanza III. 'To Autumn' acknowledges the profound grandeur of nature's supernal reality, the mysterious forces or agencies working through this and the other seasons. The combining of this acknowledgement with Keats's graphic imagination marks the pinnacle of his lyrical and metaphysical powers in what we might call the apotheosis of poetic wisdom.

At the heart of Keats's lyricism is, of course, a highly committed empiricism. Even a cursory reading of Stanza I reveals its close attention to observed actualities. We are placed right in the midst of its heaving and jostling sensual materialism, its actions and swelling juices, plump and brimful. We are made to feel the softness and the fullness of the season too, along with the lusty masculinities of it. This is true not only of the pictures that Keats gives us but also of the rich melodic sounds of the poem, where the sensual materialism bursts through.

Keats is now piping 'to the sensual ear'. In Stanza I, autumn's pulsating determination to full ripeness is paralleled in a series of rounded open vowels: 'how to load', 'gourd, and plump', 'more... still more... warm' (to fully appreciate the poem's rich melody it must be read aloud, sung from a tall building or the top of a bus – try it). The sounds begin to take over. Couplets echo each other in a dizzying chime; these are some examples: 'Close bosom, that... thatch, mossed cottage, later flowers'. Or sometimes they run in threads: 'core... gourd... more... o'er'; and 'fill... swell... kernel ... still... until... will... cells'.

After the lively expansive energies of the opening stanza with its extended catalogue of infinitives, the syntax and the focus of Stanza II suddenly loosen, logic drowses, realities becomes soft and fuzzy. Yet in spite of the dreamy, fumy atmosphere of this still moment Keats continues to prod the physical presences into the foreground. Stanza III on the other hand returns the focus fully onto those concrete realities characteristic of Stanza I, now given a harder edge through its skinny mimetic sounds ('wailful... mourn... sallows... wind... bleat... swallows twitter') and plangent diction ('soft-dying', 'wailful', 'mourn', 'sinking', 'dies', and the doleful bleat of the 'full-grown lambs'). The tightly organised system of vowels used by Keats in I and II is now perturbed by fluttering consonants (especially the repetition of /l/; see line 30).

Yet, at the close, even this sombreness is somewhat lifted by hints of affirmation: the repudiation of the past ('Where are the songs of Spring?') and that strangely conspicuous word 'barred' (25), both of which imply an idea of no going back: the future is the only way. Spring lies ahead as well as behind. It is the 'other' season and it exerts its unremitting presence even on the poet's consciousness of autumn.

As I mentioned earlier, this idea of 'otherness' is a recurring characteristic of Keats's verse: the other person, the other form, world or domain. In relating to the fact of desire these 'others' frequently stand for the aspirational or for the optimistic ('still more'). In other poems, they may represent the lost brother or simply offer escape from current reality. In 'To Autumn' one simple example of this is the four ghostly presences of Stanza II but there are many others lurking: the other seasons (winter and spring in III), unseen humans (suggested by 'cottage', 'whoever', 'reaper' etc., 'head', 'garden', and references to the body). The other land is implied by the 'gathering swallows'. There are other songs too and the alternative existence of winter/death with the overtones in mortality at line 10 as well as the explicit references to dying in Stanza III (lines 25 and 29).

Nevertheless, there is no doubting that the sensitivity at the heart of 'To Autumn' is that of Keats the poet. We do not have a direct statement of his feelings, such as in 'Nightingale' ('My heart aches') or the effusive ecstasy of Stanza III of 'Grecian Urn', but his imprint on the poem is indelible. There is no doubt that Keats's exuberance oozes out in the surfeit of finely observed detail, the incessant movements, and unpausing celebration. The poem projects the profound conviction from a first-hand response to experience, dense and full-rounded, yet precisely weighted in all that bursting exuberance. Where 'Melancholy' delivered objective description and argument, Keats now bursts the grape and drinks the whole beaker, brimful of winking bubbles and sunburnt mirth.

The whole poem is infused with a ripeness of detailed feeling. Keats's letter of 21 September 1819 (quoted above) envisages the autumn scene as a felt response to its pictorial details, 'in the same way that some pictures look warm'. Unlike the other major odes, the meaning of 'To Autumn' begins in its detailed word pictures and sound, rather than from a prior interpretation. John Watson has justly pointed out that the poem makes its point so well that there is no need for Keats to introduce an explicit moral. At the same time, though, we might view the poem as arising from some of those very issues which motivated *Lamia* and *The Fall of Hyperion* (both contemporary with 'To Autumn'), especially the themes of time, mortality and inner truth.

Conclusions

In terms of lyric verse at least, the odes of 1819 mark a triumphant
climax for Keats's skills both literary and metaphysical. More than
in the *Hyperion* poems even, Keats here fully dramatises his
themes, giving us some impressive and influential symbols at their
core.

In his readiness to discuss metaphysics we now see a poet less
reticent towards the clipping blades of philosophy and more directly
engaged in the psychology of human nature. As the mature exercise
of 'Judgement', the odes also reveal Keats's subtle mastery of the
formal aspects of the ode, tailored to suit his specific purposes. We
hear a new voice, or at least an older voice in a new assured mode
of expression, confident in the depth and relevance of his themes,
mining deep his personal experience to load each line with more
and still more richly sensual ore. Decisive too is a shrewd and
delicate management of silence. Important features recorded in
this chapter include Keats's experiments in prosody in 'Ode to a
Nightingale' and 'Grecian Urn', his deconstruction of received
ideas in 'Melancholy', and his extraordinary skill in evoking and
managing the mysterious layers of existence and time in 'To
Autumn'.

We have followed Keats's further probings into the fundamental
nature of the poet along with some profound theoretical
issues relating to art and beauty in particular. Although Keats
himself did not classify 'To Autumn' as an 'ode' we are
justified in treating it as such by virtue of its form, themes and
style. Thus it represents the very incarnation of the 1819 odes
sequence by condensing into its unified and dramatic vision the
full value and significance of truth and beauty as matters of empirical fact.

In spite of occasional flirtations with easeful diversions, the odes
focus sharply on what it is to be a poet, but above all they focus
unanimously on what it is to be human. Keats is the mature poet
speaking for mankind, a most finished artist, his identity refined
almost out of existence, yet lambent on all the many surfaces of
these odes.

Further Research

'Ode on Indolence' was also written in May 1819, probably just after 'Ode on a Grecian Urn'. Read (or re-read) it and note its points of contact with the themes of the other major odes. How does Keats's attitude and treatment of 'Indolence' differ from the other poems in this chapter, especially 'Grecian Urn'? Select one of its stanzas and trace Keats's familiar stylistic effects in it; for instance you may wish to examine the role of the stanza form here, or poetic metre, the narrator's point of view, or perhaps Keats's choice and deployment of features of sound.

5

Three Medieval Love Stories

During the latter years of the eighteenth century a fashionable craze developed for literature with medieval subjects, contexts or idiom. This followed on the heels of the amazing commercial success of Horace Walpole's *The Castle of Otranto*, a gothic horror story set in thirteenth-century Italy. For inspiration and subject matter Romantic writers looked to the Middle Ages and in particular to Chaucer and Italian authors such as Giovanni Boccaccio. Imitations of medieval style and atmosphere proliferated (see Keats's *The Eve of St Mark* for an example) and there were even forgeries of 'lost' documents. It was in this atmosphere that Keats wrote the first of the three poems analysed here, *Isabella*, begun in 1818.

For this chapter I have chosen a triptych of 'medieval' poems: in addition to *Isabella* we will cover *La Belle Dame sans Merci* and *The Eve of St Agnes*. Although they were written at different periods in Keats's life they do share some common themes and settings as well as springing from his passion for things medieval.

Isabella; or, the Pot of Basil

On 27 April 1818, Keats announced to his friend John Reynolds that he had completed his 'Pot of Basil'. He had been prompted to write *Isabella; or, the Pot of Basil* by the essayist William Hazlitt, who had claimed that poetic translations of tales by Boccaccio would be a great commercial success. Accordingly Keats and Reynolds set out to prepare a volume of verse adaptations. However, by the autumn, while Reynolds had completed two translations Keats had managed only one – *Isabella* – before he became completely disenchanted with the enterprise. Over a year after completing it he was still unhappy with the poem and told another friend, Richard Woodhouse, that it was 'mawkish'.

> I will give you a few reasons why I shall persist in not publishing The Pot of Basil – It is too smokeable.... There is too much inexperience of [life] and simplicity of knowledge in it...
>
> (21 September 1819)
>
> [*'smokeable'* = *vulnerable to attack by critics*]

His two main objections were that it lacked experience and that it was simply mawkish. To remedy the former Keats agreed to accompany another close friend on a walking tour of the north of England and Scotland, setting off in June 1818 to 'enlarge my vision', as he phrased it. But, as regards the latter point, when the poem was finally published in 1820 critics were actually less hostile and the poem less 'smokeable' than he had anticipated.

The passage I have chosen to examine consists of Stanzas XXXIX and XL. Here the ghost, 'pale shadow', of Lorenzo visits Isabella grieving for her lover, whom her brothers had reported to be abroad on business. It is an important passage because it stirs her from 'drowsy ignorance' by the revelation of truth and it also offers a new form of consciousness in the poem – the spiritual – as well as presenting a direct expression of Lorenzo's feeling for Isabella, albeit in death. It touches on some of the poem's most interesting issues such as love, the nature of woman, time and reality.

XXXIX
'I am a shadow now, alas! alas!   305
   Upon the skirts of human-nature dwelling
Alone. I chant alone the holy mass,
   While little sounds of life are round me knelling,
And glossy bees at noon do fieldward pass,
   And many a chapel bell the hour is telling,   310

Paining me through: those sounds grow strange to me,
And thou art distant in humanity.

XL
'I know what was, I feel full well what is,
   And I should rage, if spirits could go mad;
Though I forget the taste of earthly bliss,   315
   That paleness warms my grave, as though I had
A seraph chosen from the bright abyss
   To be my spouse: thy paleness makes me glad;
Thy beauty grows upon me, and I feel
A greater love through all my essence steal.'   320

The poem as a whole opens directly into the gentle love between 'poor simple Isabel!' and Lorenzo, 'a young palmer in Love's eye!' The lovers are set vividly before us in a strange, apparently timeless context which seizes the reader's attention. At the start of the poem two exclamations emphasise the lovers' joy and also the simple pathos of their love. On the other hand the two exclamations at the start of our extract emphasise different feelings altogether, such as despair and resignation, while the echoing repetition of 'alas' tolls like a death knell, the sense of which is taken up again in lines 308 and 310. This tolling sound is half heard too in the sombre repetition of 'alone' in line 307.

At first Lorenzo's appearance and his words 'I feel / A greater love through all my essence steal' (319–20) look ominously like Isabella's illusion or dream, an extension of her increasingly desperate state of mind after the disappearance of her lover. The word 'Selfishness' (241) lends some support to this idea at first: bereft of her beloved Lorenzo, her deranged mind compensates and protects itself by conjuring the very image of the loved one. But Lorenzo's ghost comes to perform a number of functions, which include revealing the site of his burial (and in so doing, pointing to the injustice committed by the brothers), but above all to express the persistence or triumph of this 'greater love'. In doing this Keats reinforces the motto that formed the tablature to Boccaccio's original tale – 'that love cannot be rooted uppe, by any humane power or providence; aspecially in such soule, where it hath bene really apprehended'.

So Lorenzo's appearance is effectively to confirm or prove that their love was truly 'apprehended'. The poem portrays two forms of love: spiritual and carnal. We do not hear much about the carnal aspects of love because, naturally, under the intimidating shadow of the brothers any type of love becomes extremely dangerous. But there are hints of it. As part of this reality, there are throughout the poem teasing references to marriage (for example, 'spouse', as in line 318 in the extract) and to motherhood (lines 35, and 470). There is more than a hint in Stanza XI that Isabella and Lorenzo do consummate their love. A crude variation of this worldly 'love' is the sort envisaged by the brothers in their ambitious plans to marry off Isabella to some rich noble 'and his olive trees' (168). The antithesis of it is the idealised, courtly romance that characterises the secretive relationship between Isabella and Lorenzo in the early part of the poem.

This 'purer' form of love has its literary origins in early medieval tales especially of the troubadours of southern France. Among its many features which are found in this poem are that the lovers' affection for each other is distant, unspoken and secretive, and while they fail to break the silence they pine away in sickness and loneliness (see Stanzas III and V). As well as the barriers imposed by their own anguished inaction they are held apart by several other obstacles: their morganatic relationship entails a social barrier and the proposed arranged marriage of Isabella points to the constraint exercised by her brothers and to the idea that she is a commodity with no effective free will of her own. By now, Stanza XXXIX, death represents the final barrier between them, of course, at least for the time being. All of these obstacles can be traced back to the opening stanza and its repeated phrase 'They could not...' (lines 3, 5 and 7).

Whether real or ideal these obstacles, inherent in their love, inject into their feelings a frisson of danger and also a dramatic tension. The eventful course of their simple love begins in ignorance but moves rapidly through courtly gestures and on even to eventual madness, a final point which is hinted at in the above passage, in line 314. Their love is characterised at different times by 'blindness', innocence, clumsiness, purity, secrecy, the balmy pain of 'love and misery' (50) and intense passion, but perhaps above all by commitment and involvement.

Keats does not tell us much about their courtship (unlike *Endymion*, which is concerned with little else). The urgency of his tale draws him onward too swiftly; and he is too absorbed in the kernel of the poem and its romantic effects. Lorenzo lacks the nerve to declare his feelings until Isabella makes something like a first move and then there follows a tender luxurious swooning into a dream state. This idealised dream-love anticipates Lorenzo as a shadow of course, and everything in it is potent, perfect and safe. Like the love between Lamia and Lycius, it is safe so long as its passion remains clandestine: a love in a bower. But once the secret is out, by announcement or, as here, by detection, it becomes explicit, impotent and finished (as Isabella's removing the head symbolises). By contrast, in *Endymion* and *The Eve of St Agnes*, the lovers preserve their secret and in so doing safeguard their love, in-turned and confined. So, significantly, when the brothers begin to sniff out the love affair, Keats uses the word 'unconfines' (163) to indicate 'revelation', with its suggestions of 'exposure' and jeopardy.

Yet just as the poem shows that love does not end at the first obstacle encountered, it also illustrates that love cannot be destroyed even by the greatest of obstacles: death.

Death is both a hazard and a spur to Isabella's feelings. Her feelings, liberated by love for Lorenzo, become transmuted into a blind, single-minded passion, and Keats seems to imply an uncon-scious fear of the powers of the libido. While on the one hand Lorenzo is symbolically paralysed, on the other Isabella is driven first to fretful distraction and then deflected into fetishism over his glove and then his head (with mild hints of necrophilia). The ultimate destination of this movement however, is Isabella's frenzy and the awful pathos that accompanies it.

At length, following the brothers' callous exhumation of the head from the basil pot (LX), Isabella's frail sanity falls victim to the poem's ungainly nihilism. The fact that her love becomes venerated in a Florentine folk song (as well as in Boccaccio and Keats) signals that it has achieved immortality, this time in art, reminiscent of that celebrated on the Grecian urn, another type of pot. Lorenzo's words in the final line of the above passage bring out this similarity by implying the purity of a 'greater love', an 'essence': as passion dies with the murder of Lorenzo, what remains is what began, the assurance of chaste feeling.

This is conventionally moral, a dull agenda to a most unconventional tale. Dull too are the principal male figures. Lorenzo, frequently linked with moisture (see Stanzas XXIII and XXXV), performs his passive functions as the lover and the victim. As the above passage shows, he actually comes over as more fully rounded and realised once he is dead and become a spectre. The shadowy brothers operate efficiently as the embodiment of grasping capitalism with their sweatshops and their exploitation of children, animals and colonial lands (as well as of their sister). These cruel, ruthless 'ledger men' and 'money bags' (in effect one character) also usefully symbolise the social aspirations of the *nouveau riche* and serve to represent cold, brutal realism. Their insensitive materialism establishes a foil against the alternative worlds of the spirit, feeling and art (Isabella herself is often linked with music).

The eponymous heroine is the only figure of the poem given any credence as a rounded character. She also embodies thematic significance and as 'woman' she plays an active role, making real the love of Lorenzo in the whisper of his name. Like other Keatsian heroines, including Diana, Lamia, Moneta and Mnemosyne, Isabella is practical, sensitive, discerning, and Keats implicitly acknowledges the full authenticity of her sexuality and its expression. In contrast to her domineering brothers with their cold constraining rationalism ('paled in and vineyarded', line 132), Isabella personifies freedom and natural growth; though finally and perversely this gets translated in the poem as loneliness.

When Lorenzo acknowledges that her presence makes a 'greater love' alive inside him he is referring obliquely to this idea of natural growth. There are many hints too of Isabella as a figure of regeneration – from the simple idea of her flourishing basil plant (426) to the references that link her with motherhood (e.g. 35, 374, 462; Stanza LIX implies she mothers the basil pot). Where Lorenzo is associated with moisture, Isabella's motifs are softness and light (see line 196; the brothers' motifs are darkness and constraint). However, the regenerative elements tend to be overwhelmed by the increasing surge towards destruction.

Her time with Lorenzo before his murder is usually filled with light (see lines 80 and 177–8) except where darkness expresses the secretiveness of their love (as at line 206: 'amorous dark'). The word 'fair' crops up several times in this period too (e.g. 1, 41, 105, 138) though following Lorenzo's death, 'light' and 'fair' change significantly to 'pale' – as in lines 316 and 318 in the extract. But, here, Lorenzo finds even her 'paleness' alluring. Isabella is also associated with music, especially singing. By linking her with music and thus with art in general, Keats encourages another symbolic contrast with her brothers: as commerce they represent its hard-nosed materialism, cruelty, and exploitation, while art is characterised by transience, joy, creativity and humanity.

As a ghost, Lorenzo's words too have a regenerative effect on Isabella since they waken her from 'snowy shroud'. The narrator in XXXIV tells us she would have died but for the effect of this 'vision' and Lorenzo's words spark her into action, revealing a wholly new side to Isabella, Keats's archetypal active woman. With the fortitude of Sophocles' Antigone, she strives to recover Lorenzo and defiantly confronts the stark reality of death through his corpse and its gruesome decapitation. The poem's only fully rounded character, she is shown to exist on two levels of consciousness, standing as it were on tip-toe between the two worlds, which is Keats's view of complete being.

In his letter of 21 September 1819 (cited above) Keats claimed that 'in his dramatic capacity' he entered 'fully into the feeling' of his subjects. This entering into the being or reality of a character, or even of an object, lies at the very core of Keats's poetic realism: to understand and therefore to depict the subject required him to enter it wholly and to identify its 'essence'. While this poem is not truly dramatic (in the sense that *Lamia* is), in its most powerful passages it does thrust the reader to the heart of the heroine's feelings. The most moving of these are the passages dealing with Isabella's desperate search for the grave – from stanza XLIII on. Equipping her only with a dagger is a neat dramatic touch because as well as stressing the intense ferment of her emotions, the dagger links her with Lorenzo's murderers (line 333) as well as implying a new awareness of the real world (at line 269 'lance' is used to indicate this idea of awakening). However, the fact that it is such an inappropriate tool for excavating a grave (as well as hacking off a head – 'duller steel'; line 393) also points up her frailty and incipient madness. Moreover, to highlight this, Keats lingers long on the details of the exhumation.

The course of Isabella's career is one of increasing instability and the loss of Lorenzo leads eventually to madness. After all, digging up and taking home a boyfriend's head is not what a nice girl does, as a general rule. Burying it in a pot of herbs is fetishism of the worst kind, even for Gothic. But in themselves these are not actually the problem. Given the parameters of the original story and the constraints on the heroine's scope for action, madness seems the only viable course for the narrative. But the fact is that the madness seems to be undeniably sexual in origin and neither Keats's narrator nor the poem's symbols (head, daggers, pot etc.) project this possibility sufficiently to convince us or hold our interest. And we are left with an ending which merely limps away into silence.

In the letter quoted at the start of this discussion, Keats claims that among the main weaknesses of his poem, 'there is too much inexperience of [life]' and 'simplicity of knowledge'. In other words he was worried that what was essentially a love poem would not convince in terms of the reality of people's lives. Lorenzo hints at the kernel of the problem in the extract,

> 'I know what was, I feel full well what is'
>
> (line 313)

That is, striking the balance between 'know' and 'feel' which together make up the theme of reality.

Keats thought that feeling in the poem dominated too much, hence his verdicts that it was 'mawkish' and 'weak- sided'. Through his entering fully into the *feeling*, he feared that the reality or 'know' of the poem was not sufficiently developed. Therefore, to try and even out 'know' and 'feel', Keats gradually subordinates the romance of the story in favour of realism, but a sort of realism that is laid uncomfortably on top of the narrative in the form of Gothic severity. Indicative of this are the hostile description of the brothers and the decapitation of Lorenzo (plus the many references to soil and clay, and to decay, paleness and sickness). By contrast, the love of Lorenzo and Isabella, threatened though it is, takes place in a cosy bower of 'feel' and blissful harmony in which looks and intuition are important. It is shattered by the invasive reality of the brothers, cutting to the heart like that 'cruel pierce' of the lance which awakens Isabella from 'drowsy ignorance' (Stanza XXXIV).

This awakening points us towards truth (in the form of death or knowledge) as one of the decisive themes of the poem. Moreover, many forms of knowing are touched on here: including intuition (17), business acumen (136), and spying (137 and 465). Knowledge itself is a key motivation; for instance, at the start both Isabella and Lorenzo are uncertain of the other's love, the brothers are ignorant of the relationship, Isabella is ignorant of Lorenzo's fate, and the brothers too are beguiled by the great head-in-the-pot mystery. There are countless references to 'seeing', most of which refer to knowing (e.g. spy, glance, gaze, vision).

Time too is an important aspect of the topic of reality especially as it refers to mortality, along with the familiar Keatsian double theme of ripeness and withering. The poem has countless references to time and in some sections time is mentioned in almost every line. The above extract has many instances of temporal or related imagery: 'now', 'while', 'at noon', 'the hour', 'was', 'is', and 'to be', 'forget', and 'grave'. In the first section of the poem, especially during the early days of the romance, Keats is eager to stress the passage of time as Lorenzo and Isabella each hesitate in showing their love. The delay contrasts with the brothers' swift action in the murder of Lorenzo, revealing again Keats's interest in the convergence of themes of love, time and death. An extension of this interest is the poem's dual concern with decay and regeneration; although Lorenzo's body is now decomposing, as 'a shadow now, alas' (305), his love for Isabella is regenerated and he sees her sorrowful paleness as accentuating her beauty – 'Thy beauty grows upon me' (319). At the same time however, her paleness is a function of her withering sorrow, the inverse of the basil plant, which flourishes, its growth nourished by her 'thin tears' (425).

In narrative terms the appearance of Lorenzo's ghost is interesting both in aiding the figurative return of the man and in providing the fillip to Isabella's action. Like the ghost of Hamlet's father, Lorenzo returns to expose injustice. This clearly bears on the theme of knowledge as an extension to that of reality; in addition the ghost reveals the fact of his death, the whereabouts of his grave, and leads Isabella to guess the murderers. Above all, perhaps, is that in the twin climaxes to the poem (the first here in the extract and the second at the exhumation of Lorenzo's body) Isabella learns most about herself, she experiences an epiphany: 'Sweet Spirit, thou hast schooled my infancy' (334). She discovers her brothers' deception and the folly of her own 'poor simple' trust, and for a brief spell she achieves the balance of know and feel. Isabella discovers too, that paradoxically, the vision or ghost is more in touch with truth and earthly realities than her own mortal mind has been (see Stanza XXXIV for confirmation of this – 'And she had died').

Even so it is not clear how the appearance of the ghost is justified within the world of the tale, except perhaps as a conventional roaming sort of spirit which has the power to penetrate the mind of the living. Obviously Isabella's state of mind has much to do with it. Stanzas XLV and XLVI suggest that Isabella, tip-toe, sees beyond this world of appearances and cognitive knowledge to a realm of immortal and, therefore, perfect truths (and Stanza XXXV implies that the mechanism for achieving this is the imagination). This immortal realm beyond earthly woes of fever and fret, of ripeness and decay, uncertainty, pain and even pleasure, is once again that of Platonic truth. Accordingly it comes as no surprise that Isabella eventually achieves a Platonic love with Lorenzo, the macabre affection projected by her onto his decaying remains.

That Isabella returns to an 'ideal' Platonic love, paralleling the lovers' early relationship, is ironic but also apt since it echoes Boccaccio's original motto:

> Love never dies, but lives, immortal Lord.
>
> (397)

Then, after the second brotherly atrocity, she slips irrevocably toward oblivion, recoiling from the appalling empirical truths of the world: 'She had no knowledge when the day was done' (421). By this stage, however,

Platonic love offers no genuine sense of satisfaction or consolation to Isabella. Incomplete, her love has failed to reach ripeness in the natural order of time and she withers uneasily away in paleness.

One of the reasons why the theme of knowledge is accorded such prominence is Keats's anxiety that his poetry was relying too much on sensations and feel. In a letter of 3 May 1818 he wrote on the need to balance sensations with knowledge, revealing that he had amended his famous maxim of only five months earlier ('O for a life of sensations rather than of Thoughts!'). And Lorenzo's statement in line 313 reflects this reappraisal. It is indicative of Keats's efforts to reduce the poem's 'smokeability', bolstering its wild macabre emotions with an ineffectual attempt at order.

One manifestation of Keats's attempts in this direction is the poem's form. But the poem has a strange form, with twin climaxes appearing approximately midway through the narrative, while the weird, gruesome content repeatedly threatens to overthrow it. There are also numerous allusions to madness, wildness, and turmoil and the feelings of the lovers are themselves a threat to the rigid control and constraints of the powerful brothers. On the other hand, order is implicit in a variety of ways: in the decorum of courtly love early on, in the brothers' entrepreneurial dealings, the strongly patterned verse form and the firm control exercised by the poem's narrator (of which more shortly). But one area in which we might have expected order to appear – and it does not – is that of moral justice. We get no genuine sense of justice in the poem and no ultimate power or figure for justice and good. Instead, the universe of the poem frequently finds itself teetering on the brink of chaos and the sort of nihilism we find in *King Lear* – ironically Keats's favourite Shakespearean tragedy.

The main impetus for order is, however, the almost ever-present voice of the narrator and we need to say a little more about this and about the poem's stylistic elements. An unusual feature of our extract is that it is one of the rare occasions when a character speaks directly, when we actually hear the words as spoken. As can be seen from the passage, direct speech places Lorenzo directly before the reader, investing him with presence and credibility, making his emotions seem real and urgent, unmediated by the narrator.

Yet the vast bulk of the poem is related by a detached narrator placing himself between us, the readers, and the bits we are normally most interested in, the characters and events. These are, by and large, told rather than shown. Keats – or his narrator – is our moral guide at every step and the emotions too are described off hand rather than shared, (contrast lines 305 and 315–20, which do have a touching authenticity). As the reader's moral guide the narrator steps back from the action, casting an overview, commenting morally on the action or a character or interpolating his own emotional response (for examples, see Stanzas XVI, XLIX, LVI). On the whole, though, it has to be said that these elements are much better handled here than in *Endymion*.

At the same time, Keats's version of the poem does bring great depth and variety of feeling to Boccaccio's original story. They help to bring it alive, particularly in terms of love and sorrow. Yet a weakness common to both versions is the histrionic air of fatalism about the narration. In Keats's version the narrator is continually anticipating later events – see, for instance, lines 87–8, 209, 446–7. At its best this 'device' does impart to the poem some macabre foreboding, an awareness of doom. A similar effect can be experienced in *The Eve of St Agnes* where it intensifies the danger, and in both poems the text is suffused with a mythic quality by setting the narrative firmly in the past. But in *Isabella* the narrator relentlessly diminishes the emotional impact of the big moments by letting the cat out of the bag (the only occasion when the narrator is at all successful is in the brilliant doom-laden epithet for Lorenzo when he rides away with the brothers, described as 'their murdered man'; line 209).

The dominance of the narrator's voice has one other important consequence for the poem. Through its continual presence, the narrator's voice draws attention to the literariness of the story; in other words, that it is a work of art, not an actual lived experience. I have mentioned already that the poem has the 'feel' of a folk myth or fable (though one without any clear moral) and Keats explicitly refers to literature in lines 94, 153, 260 and in Stanza XLIX, keeping the idea in our attention. It is as though Keats were striving to make something grandiose, tragic or perhaps even something parabolic out of a modest, over-stretched circumstance. It remains at core a simple sad tale of a universe of sorrow and increasingly nihilistic fate.

This impression of the poem's simplicity is supported by its verse form. It is written in *ottava rima*, eight lines of iambic pentameter with the rhyme scheme ABABABCC – and Keats generally reflects the 6:2 structure in his syntax. The fact that this form is Italian in origin probably appealed to Keats but it demands virtuosity of a poet, in its narrow range of rhymes but also in the fact that each stanza should function as a separate unit, a sort of intensified paragraph. However, Keats proves he is up to the task and demonstrates his resourcefulness and imagination in the variety of rhymes, at the same time obviating potential repetitiveness.

One of his tactics lies in contrasting the *lengths* of the terminal vowels; for example, in the above extract the A and B rhymes are short while the C rhymes are long. Another is varying the position of the caesura in a line. So, in line 305, a caesura is placed after the sixth syllable; in line 307 there is one after the second and another after the sixth syllable; in line 309, after the fourth and the sixth syllables ... and so on. This variation is important here because the verse itself is quite regular in order to create a lightness of effect consistent with the mood at this moment. Only lines 310 and 311 break the regular metre – and 310 is an alexandrine, having twelve syllables. Lorenzo's speech has intricate vowel play (see especially lines 311 and 313, the latter with its beautiful symmetry) and points the style towards the complex melodic tapestries in *Lamia* and *Hyperion* and the major odes, as well as *The Eve of St Agnes*. Less rich than in later writing, the verse here feels underfed, poorer even than *Endymion* and with fewer memorable lines. It is used less as a centre for Keats's beautiful sensual music than as simply a vehicle for translating a story – though we might add that the relative spareness of the verse does seem to accord with the horror and deficit of humanity.

Many readers (including Keats himself) regard Isabella as marking the end of Keats's apprenticeship period. If we compare it with *Endymion* we can see how much he has learned during the apprenticeship. But a chief fault of both works, and one common among young writers in general, is that Keats really tells us too much. He is at his strongest when he does not tell us enough (consider here his concept of Negative Capability).

With this in mind we can now turn to examine *La Belle Dame sans Merci*, a poem of enticing silences.

La Belle Dame sans Merci: A Ballad

At the centre of *La Belle Dame sans Merci* we can readily recognise three of Keats's familiar interests – mystery, sex and death. But, in fact, this poem marks a great shift in Keats's poetic attitude. Dashed off spontaneously, nonchalantly even, in April 1819 and practically in a single night, *La Belle Dame* follows hard on the heels of his brother Tom's death, and his despairing abandonment of *Hyperion*. Astonishingly it springs from the same prolific period as the great odes, yet is eerily different.

What is this puzzling literary ballad all about? To begin to answer this question is to begin to see just how uncertain and even evasive the poem is. It may help to read it in three parts. Stanzas I to III seem to be the questions and comments raised by a questioner/narrator on encountering the mysterious knight-at-arms, 'Alone and palely loitering'; in the second part, Stanzas IV to XI, the haggard knight describes a meeting with a beautiful lady in the meadows – they ride his horse and she takes him to her 'elfin grot' where, lulled to sleep by her, he has a terrifying nightmare; then in the final part the knight refers to the 'present' and why he sojourns here on the 'cold hill's side'.

Such a tentative and skeletal account of the poem does scant credit to this hauntingly uncanny poem, in which Keats's silences seem to say more than the actual words given on the page. One way to appreciate the unfathomable depths of the poem is to try to say a few things about a part of it. Accordingly, I have chosen three stanzas from the knight's account:

> VII
> She found me roots of relish sweet,
> And honey wild, and manna-dew,

And sure in language strange she said –
  'I love thee true'.   28

VIII
She took me to her elfin grot,
  And there she wept and sighed full sore,
And there I shut her wild wild eyes
  With kisses four.   32

IX
And there she lulled me asleep
  And there I dreamed – Ah! woe betide! –
The latest dream I ever dreamt
  On the cold hill side.   36

One of the difficulties I have with this brilliant poem is that the
details of it very rarely seem odd or uncertain but, taken as a whole,
they usually appear extremely strange and even absurd. So we can
read the poem without much problem until we attempt to rationalise
it. For instance, what are 'roots of relish sweet' and the 'manna-dew'
in Stanza VII? Knowledge is our problem.

They seem alright until we want to *know* or know more. Roots
suggest magic, perhaps, and manna something religious in ritual or
effect while, taken together with 'honey wild' and the 'language
strange', it points unmistakably to an aphrodisiac or some other drug
at least. These are a magic or heavenly food to feed a mortal. But what is
this strange language in which she appears to affirm her love? Is it really
a strange tongue or is the knight succumbing to drugs or the allure of
the lady (who is also, oddly, a 'child'; line 14)? And how does she lull him
to sleep? In VI she sings a 'faery song', and she has 'wild wild eyes', she
moans, weeps and sighs before he slips into the unconscious.

These are only a few of the poem's many mysteries. Then the
setting: does the meeting with the narrator take place by the lake or
on a hillside, or perhaps both? The withered sedge and absence of
birdsong could be part of the real setting and season here but perhaps
are metaphors for starvation and wasteland or to suggest a psychological effect. Who is the questioner–narrator? We, the reader? And

how has he met this wretched knight? Is the reader then to be the next in the sequence of 'victims' as in the dream (Stanzas X and XI)? Keats's language deliberately exasperates the reader. 'And no birds sing' as a negative denies the song but at the same time reminds us that birdsong is the natural, the expected norm. The poem begins with a question, which the knight does not in fact answer. How exactly do you 'loiter palely'? What is a 'latest dream'? And in line 19 the word 'as' is ambiguous (it could mean 'because' but also 'as if', which stresses the uncertainty of the lady's love again). Keats is also deliberately ambiguous in his use of 'I' at the start of Stanzas III and IV, aiming to confuse, disarm and lull the reader. It leaves us with another 'wild surmise'.

Keats provokes us to analyse the poem, to probe the strange universe of withered sedge, silence, song and shifting consciousness but the poem resists analysis. By desiring to know, we become victims ourselves, drawn into this universe by curiosity, where we undergo an experience but cannot make full sense of it. We make some sense of parts of it, seek its pleasures and dissolve its mysteries but we gradually end up in its thrall, its own 'strange language'. Applying his own concept of Negative Capability ('when a man is capable of being in uncertainties, mysteries, doubts...'), Keats knows full well that by nature, even by definition, readers seek certainty and reason here, and he plays on this. We will strive to make sense of and relate this universe to our *gestalt*, our need for coherence. We have enough clues to know that something is awry, but what?

Another cause of the difficulties we might encounter here is to do with the imagination. Keats encourages the reader's inner world of the imagination to entwine and fuse with the outer, physical world so the two become indistinguishable – in the same way that he himself stands on tip-toe over both. In Stanzas X and XI the knight says 'I saw' but he is really referring to events in his dream – though they were so vividly awful as to seem real (as real as the dreams of gods perhaps; compare *Endymion*, I.572–8). By encouraging the psychic elements of the poem to work on our imaginations. Keats once more puts us in something like the position of the knight so we enter 'fully' into the feeling.

In Keats's poetry, imagination can refer to any of three aspects. It can be Keats's or a character's vision of what ought to be, an ideal or special form of truth, especially the antithesis of pain or falsehood (e.g. *Sleep and Poetry*). It can refer to an invented or fantasy realm, a made-up setting (e.g. the world of the Titans in *Hyperion. A Fragment* or *Isabella*). And it may be the faculty of poetic creativity itself, the arena in the poet's mind where art originates and takes shape. All three are present in this poem, and the third is represented symbolically here by the 'elfin grot' (29), where, inspired by mysterious beauty, love and experience, the knight's dream is created and enacted.

Woman here is for Keats a figure of the cruel curse of art and creative inspiration, but this is only a part of the story, of course. One of the many remarkable things about the poem is the way in which it draws in and re-shapes a great amount of material from Keats's own experiences and reading as well as his own previous writings, from the starkest of realities (such as the death of his brother four months earlier) to the most conceptual or ephemeral of his dreams (such as the recurring Adam's dream about Eve). From all these various sources the poem importantly draws together Keats's complex ideas on the nature of woman in terms of love, death and art.

Let Stanza VIII be our starting point on this theme. This stanza forms one of the poem's two climaxes (the other, more intense one is in Stanzas X and XI). Apparently moved by her tears, the knight shuts her 'wild eyes' with kisses. The sexual connotations in 'elfin grot' and in 'wild wild' (as well as the aphrodisiacal suggestions in the strange food she feeds him) imply that they consummate their 'love' here, while the sleep following this looks like a post-coital nap. Briefly, the knight is the active element and his moment of passion contrasts with elements of chivalric or courtly love elsewhere (such as the errant knight, sick, starving, but fanatically in thrall to his lady in spite of her apparent indifference and for whom he undergoes horrid ordeals; compare *Calidore. A Fragment*, lines 142–51). First he subdues her and then *she* reduces him to sleep. But unlike the sleep of erotic luxury elsewhere in Keats (for example, in the love sonnet 'Bright Star'), this is a nightmare terror confronting love as death.

In the 'Bright Star' sonnet too (probably written October 1820), Keats associates love with death but it is a less overt connection than here in *La Belle Dame*. The link was an extremely poignant one for Keats since his brother Tom had received some hoax love-letters from a fictitious admirer, named Amena, during the latter stages of his fatal illness. It is likely that it was from these 'Amena' letters that Keats got something of the idea of a man dying out of love for an elusive seductress. The poem appears to make a direct connection between their love-making and a sort of death-in-life which the knight goes through in the dream/imagination. He then suffers in the void of a palely loitering life in the wasteland.

Central to this theme of love and to *La Belle Dame* as a whole is Keats's conception of woman. We have seen already some common threads or archetypes in his portrayal of woman. In *Endymion*, *Lamia* and *The Fall of Hyperion* as well as here the key women set out to disarm and detain the principal male characters. In all of these, too, the woman as lover is the active partner, and seducer, but perhaps *Lamia* above all gives us a reasonable clue as to what Keats is thinking of in *La Belle Dame*. Lamia ensnares her man, Lycius, in a 'mesh' and he too falls into a trance (I.295–6); the narrator calls her a 'cruel lady' (I.290). Keats's letters reveal that he was given to idealize women romantically and in one letter he reflected, 'When I was a Schoolboy I thought a fair Woman a pure Goddess.' In another he confessed to a passionate infatuation with Jane Cox after a single, chance meeting. And as we have seen in his poems (e.g. '*I stood tip-toe*' and *Endymion*), he had a sort of fascination with the idea of chance romantic meetings with a precociously worldly woman (based probably on his own experience with the darkly mysterious Isabella Jones whom he first encountered by chance in Hastings).

All of these facets – the goddess, the experienced forceful seducer and the vampire – converge on this poem. Stanza IV describes her as 'Full beautiful', suggesting her sensuous charms, a woman yet also a faery child, indicating her dual nature as mortal and supernatural, vamp and virgin. But significantly the final word there, taken up again in Stanza VII, is 'wild' denoting her passionate character, and they appear to meet full on, in full sexual commitment, implied in the horse ride together. 'Sweet' and 'wild', she is both demure and passionate, an enticing conundrum for this errant knight, described throughout in terms of her strangeness. Is she now even a real woman? (recall that Lamia was actually a serpent.) A 'faery child', she may perhaps be a changeling of sorts, or merely a figment of his fantasy. Yet for a brief spell she gives his wandering life a meaning and an intensity before he falls beneath her thrall.

Although she moans and speaks in a strange language of her love for him, singing a 'faery song' (24), she remains distant, hazy, and evasive to our scrutiny (we 'see' her only at second remove). She seems like an enchantress or even a witch, with resemblances to Coleridge's cruel nightmare life in death (*The Rime of the Ancient Mariner*, line 193) and to the cunning Morgan Le Fay of Arthurian legend. The title description 'sans Merci' carries with it a double strand of a woman lacking in both pity and gracious kindness (she evades the conventional stereotype of a lady). Yet we cannot be certain that the knight blindly falls to a destructive siren entrapment (like the siren–witch Circe in *Endymion* – see lines 413 and 427); perhaps he is the fully active, willing participant which is hinted at in 'I shut her wild wild eyes'. The knight's dream is a warning against the loss of existential freedom, perhaps through passionate and excessive feeling (though, ironically, the gifts which the knight bestows – garland, bracelet, zone – all have encircling, emprisoning intentions). While a moral tone murmurs across the wasteland, Keats makes no explicit judgements.

The knight has 'burst Joy's grape' and now tastes her sadness, having become 'among her cloudy trophies hung' as 'Ode on Melancholy' suggests (lines 28–30). 'Ode on Melancholy' concerns someone taking a full opportunity, full commitment even in the throes of melancholy, and the knight, too, seems in thrall to the prolonged 'melancholy fit', unable to sustain the vision that had inspired his encounter ('the latest dream I ever dreamt', line 35). In the same way that lines 7 and 8 suggest the idea that the summer of joy is now spent, the haggard and woebegone knight himself appears all in and finished, a spent force,

> The squirrel's granary is full,
> And the harvest's done.

She has aroused and drawn his power through intercourse. But unlike 'To Autumn', the feeling is now less of achievement than of decay. It is a wild decay in which 'easeful earth' is cruelly denied, since the knight is condemned to wander the earth alone and pale in a kind of limbo (as Circe denies death to Glaucus in *Endymion*; see III.579). Intercourse with the 'Belle Dame' is both the consummation of desire and fulfilment of himself, come to ripeness, leaving the knight to wither away in paleness, which is Keats's symbolic colour of decline.

It is as though the knight has suffered possibly the worst of horrors: taken beyond life to witness the suffering of others who had experienced his fate, but he himself is denied death, the chivalric *coup de grace*. This idea also connects the poem with *The Fall of Hyperion*, in which Moneta reminds the Poet that he has been permitted to apprehend death before his 'fated hour', a sort of forbidden knowledge (see *The Fall of Hyperion*, I.141–3).

His extraordinary supernatural experiences set the knight apart from the natural processes of human life and regeneration. However, if he has transgressed then Keats does not reveal his sin, which only serves to heighten the sense of vindictive torment he suffers. Furthermore, while the knight is haggard and alone, palely sick, we can only guess at his exact feelings about what has befallen him. Metaphors of the wasteland in which he abides are potentially revealing but, perhaps consistent with a chivalric code, he remains stoic, resigned. The 'cold hill side' (36) on which he wakes after his adventures and phantasm carries more than a hint that he is now a chill realist, bereft of illusions, a wiser if sadder man.

Although we cannot say for certain that the roots of the poem lie in the 'Amena' letters its situation does bear some resemblance to the way Keats responded to them, particularly in regard to his attitude to women, art, and family loyalties. If we identify the knight with Keats's dying brother then the knight may again represent the ghostly 'other', the other self which appears to haunt many of Keats's verses, serving to define the other characters in them. In which case we have in *La Belle Dame* not one but at least two ghostly figures before us – both the pale knight and the succubus, vampire woman.

Keats's own letters show how much he felt a conflict of loyalties between his great interests – women, poetry, family. He sometimes feared that complete commitment to a woman would distract him from his great commitment to literature and from devotion to his brothers (either of which would represent a moral, or living death). His fear of such commitment left him romantically 'palely loitering' on the edge of the dream, and it is probably for this reason that in his verse the woman's first move is so significant; (for example, in the actions of Isabella, Lamia and Mnemosyne).

The 'Belle Dame' lulls the knight to sleep, 'And there I dreamed.' As a privileged view into her timeless world of faery or immortality, the 'latest dream' would constitute, of course, forbidden knowledge for the Christian knight. The punishment for such a vision is death, and the sere and vacant landscape beckons. He has seen into the still moment, the instant made eternal, the moment in which love and death, here as in *Isabella*, become one. The ripening ends, but ends weirdly, his future never being referred to explicitly. Amid the metaphors of time (e.g. lines 7–8, 11, 14, 22), the tenses of the verb all concern the past or the constant present. As part of his living death the knight is paralysed in the oozings of the fixed moment, with nothing ahead, and the past closed off – caught in the gap between 'manna' (26) and 'thrall' (40), the perplexity of bliss and its neighbour pain.

Keats took the title of the poem from a fifteenth-century poem by Alain Chartier (he refers to it in *The Eve of St Agnes*, line 292). Many critics have traced influences on the poem such as Chaucer, Spenser, and Cary's translation of Dante. But it is a brilliant tribute to Keats's own originality – there is nothing like it. Deeply imbued with medieval lore and resonant atmosphere, and the techniques of medieval ballad, Keats evokes much of the setting, character and values of the Gothic romance but he does not simply retail these features. Instead he exploits their values to intensify the poem's themes and his wider interests; for example, he reverses the usual Gothic touch of the knight rescuing the damsel in distress in order to focus on his particular conception of man–woman relations and the metaphysics of knowledge, death and regeneration. He adopted the contemporary taste for the medieval ballad but turned it over to explore the sexuality and murky psychological substrata lurking beneath.

Surprisingly, Keats himself does not seem to have thought much of this poem and excluded it from his 1820 volume, believing it to be sentimental. Yet if anything, this is an anti-Romantic production in which Keats's highly taut perspectives and techniques baulk against the likelihood of 'smokeability'.

It is a deceptively simple composition and must be re-read with care to catch its many sensitive nuances. It is a delicately stylised ideogram in which its stylisations heighten the haunting atmosphere wreathing about its 'action': musical repetitions, reversals, poeticisms, ellipses and lacunae, as well as the deliberate equivocations already noted. The poem smartly demonstrates Keats's extraordinary skill in matching and balancing strong thematic curiosity with a richly suggestive poetic language.

Probably his most deftly original touch here is the strange stanza form. The short fourth line in each quartet and an unusual rhyme scheme (ABCB), together with the poem's repetitions and silences, lend it a curious dissonance which chimes well with the subject matter. By cutting each final line to half its expected length the reader is repeatedly taken by surprise, leaving him or her with a sudden metrical void echoing some spiritual vacancy. At the same time the heavy stressing in the 'half-line' (for instance, lines 4 and 36) results in a continually repetitive cadence, a strangely mystical refrain and a ghostly epigram,

La Belle Dame is a lyric gem, finely crafted so that it is ultimately elusive of paraphrase or definitive analysis. It leaves us, momentarily at least, with a haunting impression of hypnotic paradoxes, an uneasy tension of silence and feeling, and a 'language strange'... spare, condensed, flawless.

The Eve of St Agnes

If we think of these three poems as forming a triptych of romances each concerned with people overwhelmed by great feelings of love, then the central panel of the triptych is occupied by *The Eve of St Agnes*. In many ways it derives much of its force from its relationship with the other two 'medieval' poems; for example, compare the fates of Isabella and the Knight with those of Madeline and Porphyro.

The story of *The Eve of St Agnes* is in essence a quite simple one: on a bitterly cold winter night Porphyro enters a grim forbidding fortress

to persuade Madeline into eloping with him. Aided by Madeline's old
nurse, Angela, he evades the hostile guards, reaches his love's bed-
chamber, and the two eventually escape into the freezing night. First
and foremost, it is of course a love story, and was written by Keats in
a creative burst at the beginning of 1819 while on holiday in Chichester. The subject of the narrative was suggested by his mysterious
friend Isabella Jones (and she and Keats may be the lovers of the
poem), while its striking interiors were modelled on those of medieval buildings studied by Keats in Hampshire, and which invest the
poem with its vivid, almost tangible context.

In literary terms the poem is again an imitation of medieval
romance but this time one in Spenserian nine-line stanzas (see
below). A variation on the *Romeo and Juliet*, or 'forbidden love'
theme it also has hints of the Adam and Eve myth. The passage I
have chosen as the drawbridge by which to enter the poem is Stanzas
XIV to XV, which appear after Porphyro has begged Angela to guide
him to Madeline's chamber.

XIV
'St Agnes? Ah! it is St Agnes' Eve –
Yet men will murder upon holy days:
Thou must hold water in a witch's sieve,   120
And be liege-lord of all the Elves and Fays,
To venture so: it fills me with amaze
To see thee, Porphyro! – St Agnes' Eve!
God's help! my lady fair the conjuror plays
This very night. Good angels her deceive!   125
But let me laugh awhile, I've mickle time to grieve.'

XV
Feebly she laugheth in the languid moon,
While Porphyro upon her face doth look,
Like puzzled urchin on an aged crone
Who keepeth closed a wondrous riddle-book,   130
As spectacled she sits in chimney nook.
But soon his eyes grew brilliant, when she told
His lady's purpose; and he scarce could brook

    Tears, at the thought of those enchantments cold,
And Madeline asleep in lap of legends old.   135

It is St Agnes' eve. The poem turns on the old legend that on the night of 20 January a girl might dream of her future husband, 'If ceremonies due they did aright' (line 50; St Agnes is the patron saint of young virgins). In line 135 Porphyro himself has a tearful vision of Madeline who, having carried out the appropriate ceremonies, will become cocooned in chastely amorous slumbers. The name 'Agnes' derives from the Latin for 'chastity', which together with the idea of correct rites or conventions points us in the direction once more of chivalric or courtly love. And this romance demonstrates many of its features: Porphyro undergoing a hazardous ordeal (see line 338); Angela doubling as protective maternal nurse but also as the lovers' confidante; courtly attitudes are struck (see XXXVIII) and at line 292 there is a key reference to Provence, origins of the chivalric convention in the serenades of gallant troubadours. By playing on this medieval tradition Keats deftly sets up a tale of pulsating sexual tensions yet at the same time one of enticing moral ambiguities, which flourish on the poem's blurred margins between dream and reality.

The extract refers to at least two kinds of love: Porphyro's desire for Madeline, naturally, and Angela's protective care for her. But there are other types or examples in the poem: the family ties of the paternalistic Baron and the loyalty of his 'foemen', the beadsman's prayers to expiate the sins of mankind, while the Porter and his dog (XLI) are the personification of conventional fidelity. Thus loyalty, respect, religious obedience, fellowship and fidelity are all part of the complex love theme (whose antithesis, the immanence of hatred, helps to give the poem some extra bite).

Love in its chivalric mode is also the chief spiritual component of the poem. Although there are plenty of religious references (in the extract alone there are 'holy days', 'God', 'angels', as well as 'St Agnes'), these operate mainly as decoration and the legend of St Agnes is used as the central motif both for the motivation of the plot and for the consciousness of the narrative. Further, Keats skilfully uses the legend to 'sanctify' the relationship between the two lovers, to signal the truth of their love (and to bless their union, of course). Because Porphyro himself probably does not know of this legend or even that this night is the eve of St Agnes (see lines 132 and 166), his unexpected appearance is made to signify the honesty of his intentions. This being so, the poem, with its joyous fulfilment of love, is the antithesis of *Isabella* and *La Belle Dame*. Also, unlike the lovers in *Lamia* and 'Ode on a Grecian Urn', Madeline and Porphyro come over as warm, human and real people faced with real danger, which they overcome, thereby achieving love on credible terms.

However, at the very centre of this human love are situated its dangers. The usual uncertainty about mutual feelings is never broached since both lovers are utterly lost in each other. On the other hand the lustful attentions of the Baron's immodest cavaliers (60) remind us both of Madeline's highly desirable sexuality and of the dangerous threat to Porphyro's life should he be discovered. Encapsulated in her bedroom, the naked Madeline feels entirely safe, 'blissfully havened' (240) and blissfully unaware of the man standing only a matter of feet away. This is a nice ironic touch, of course, and one that enables Keats to eroticise the voyeuristic sight while undermining Madeline's self-possession. Eventually she herself acknowledges this when in effect she declares her complete dependence on Porphyro in breaking free of her family and the mansion.

As a romantic saga their love is perfect even given that we learn so little about them and this mysterious enchanted castle. The bedroom is a haven, a bower of bliss surrounded by the mansion's jeopardy. And beyond that? Beyond lies Porphyro's southern moors, and somewhere else, the mysterious other or alternative land.

But equally mysterious is the background to the lovers. They have no history and no context, but hover strangely in romantic space. Looked at coldly, what we have is more a premonition of rock videos and clichéd chocolate adverts, adorned with stony castles, big dogs, nasty thugs and weather effects; a young naked virgin anticipates a silky dream about her lover when suddenly he pops out of a cupboard surrounded by exotic fruits; she agrees to run away with the man from the cupboard – no food, no transport and no clean undies (so presumably they reach his remote hideout in the south by hiking across the frozen moors).

This is hard, I agree. But looking at the narrative in this way does have the merit of deconstructing the chivalric viewpoint to question the original, dreamy romanticised account (which looks at times as if it were narrated by Madeline herself). We need to question the version we have because it is only *a* version and one which, told in Keats's brilliant word magic, presents a range of different consciousnesses: visions, drunkenness, sleep and dreams. There are also many references to religious fervour, witchcraft and the supernatural (in the extract, see lines 120–1, 125 and 130). These present the reader with a great many potential traps and false turns. My version too is only that, a version.

It is the 'honeyed middle of the night' (49) and although Angela and Porphyro appear alert and rational, Madeline is a sort of sleeping beauty (a still unravished bride). Perhaps he *has* come to rescue her, and Angela as the 'other' represents the old maid that Madeline would become if he does not succeed. Realistically, however, he has come to make love to her, to 'Open thine eyes' (278), to awaken the sleeping beauty.

With a pun on his name, Porphyro's love is in a 'purple riot' (138), consumed with passion, his 'heart on fire' (75). Angela understands what he is about when she rebukes him as cruel and wicked (XVI), while his pledge about forfeiting his life (XVII) looks like a typical seducer's manoeuvre. Once he has achieved her bedroom he surprisingly starts to lay out the exotic food in a sort of wedding feast (cf. the banquet in *Lamia* II). However, the fruits have the consequence of mildly enhancing the erotic effect of Porphyro's voyeurism – in a highly perfumed arena of sexual delight. He is ecstatic at reaching the bedroom with Madeline innocently naked before him; the syrupy fruits hint too at Porphyro's sexual excitement. As he takes up 'her hollow lute' (289), Madeline awakes but remains in a trance-like state while the dream Porphyro and the real Porphyro melt together in her delicious fancy (XXXIV). She is of course 'hoodwinked' (70), in 'lap of legends old', and now Angela's word 'deceive' (in the extract, line 125) realises its full ironic force.

Is Madeline a willing (and knowing) lover or is she a victim of rape in Stanza XXXVI? Some critics have seen the bedroom episode as the rape of Madeline, the goal of Porphyro's stratagem. Jack Stillinger, for one, sees Porphyro as a villain and the rape as having a moral purpose: to teach the deflowered Madeline a clearer grasp of the reality of sex. However, the dream-state is highly concealing. Keats is typically ambiguous, a point which actually helps here to control the possibility of crude sexuality or mawkishness. The result is that his treatment of their love-making is quite sensitive and at one with the general tenor of the poem.

On the other hand this was not how the poem appeared in the first draft. Keats's initial intention was to make their intercourse more explicit (Barnard's edition of the poems contains Keats's detailed revisions) but the advice of his publishers persuaded him against it, on the grounds that it would 'render the poem unfit for ladies'. The love-making is thus presented as the ripe fulfilment and celebration of a love that is both privately carnal but publicly regulated by idealised forms of chivalry.

After the sublimely beautiful love scene, the narrator reveals significantly that 'St Agnes's moon hath set' (324), the moon as conventional symbol of virginity. Madeline fears momentarily that her lover may

> 'forsakest a deceived thing –
> A dove forlorn...
>
> (332–3)

However, Porphyro swiftly resumes the discourse of chivalry, embellished now with religious diction (XXXVIII), affirming his loyalty, and they flee together into the storm – a departure which also helps to avert a syrupy happy ending.

Describing herself as a 'deceived thing' (332), Madeline recalls Angela's prayer in the above extract, 'Good angels her deceive!' (125). However, what Angela means here is something more like 'un-deceive' her: in other words, that the angels should jolt her mind out of the St Agnes illusion (and by doing so she points up the difficulty of distinguishing truth and illusion). In line 135 Porphyro too draws attention to the image of Madeline the sleeping dreamer, the sleeping beauty. Yet, although she is physically passive for most of the poem, Madeline is described by Angela as 'the conjuror' (124), identifying her as a kind of siren who draws Porphyro onto the perilous shoals of her father's mansion (this reflection also sets off a link between this poem and *La Belle Dame*; and see *St Agnes*, line 231, where Madeline is likened to a mermaid).

Dream is both a significant theme and an important narrative technique in the poem. It is another example of Keats's continuing exploration of the exact nature of dream and its interrelationship with waking reality. With similarities to *Isabella* and *La Belle Dame*, dream or vision here has the paradoxical effect of revealing the truth where we might superficially expect the opposite. In spite of Angela's scepticism, Madeline does believe that her dream this evening will reveal her future bridegroom (as it does in fact). References to dream and deception condition the whole poem. At the same time much of the poem's imagery relates to secrecy or hiding (see lines 77, 188, 231) and thus to the occult, which strengthens the poem's texture of magic and faery (see 70, 168, 343 and so on).

These are all elements in the poem's thematic cluster of alternative consciousnesses and the possibility of escape; for example, the citations of death and sleep, elopement, drugs (237), and intoxication (364). If we add all this together with the blissful setting of Madeline's fragrant chamber and the softly eroticising fruits served by Porphyro we can appreciate in full the heady swoon of hedonistic luxury which Keats sought to generate.

What we have then is a tenuous web of sleep, dream, vision, secrecy and sorcery through which the narrative is transmitted, a story constructed through a sequence of alternating dream and reality. Death and danger stalk anxiously in the chill air of the enchanted castle. These begin to alternate from about Stanza XXIII until they merge hypnotically together in that ethereal sexual mime in Stanzas XXXIV to XXXVII where Madeline,

> Her eyes were open, but she still beheld,
> Now wide awake, the vision of her sleep.
>
> (298–9)

She seems to be at a high pitch of sexual arousal. She has in fact dreamt ardently of Porphyro (299) and when she wakes cannot at first distinguish reality from dream, but remains in a 'tip-toe' state between the two. Then, recognising the real Porphyro she is shocked to find the reality of him so inferior: 'pallid, chill and drear' (311). In this paradise of idealised love, we actually get the reverse of the Eden paradise: Eve wakes to find a poor grade male and it is he who provides the seductive fruits to turn her on again (see line 244).

Madeline spends much of the early section of the poem in excited and determined anticipation of the night's fantasy. Presumably she has been observing the appropriate 'ceremonies', which of course tautens the auto-eroticism of desire. Her eager compliance and unrealistic pursuit of dream-perfection portrays her as immature and feeble-minded. In the extract she is described as 'asleep in lap of legends old' (135) and elsewhere she is 'Hoodwinked with faery fancy' (70), 'full of this whim' (56), and a 'sweet dreamer' (334). In Keats's poetry, dreams are typically to be identified with the imagination so that they represent a redrafting of reality. But Madeline's dream is in point of fact a form of wish-fulfilment, which inevitably leads to disappointment in her double-vision of Porphyro. But this biddable dreamer seems exactly to appeal to her heroic lover, especially as it is all one with her innocence and vulnerability.

However, this said, she is not all that convincing as a character and speaks directly in only two of the poem's 42 stanzas. She is more important for what she stands for in the tale and especially in the convention of courtly love: youth, virgin, idealism, love-object of desire, angel, and novice nun. The fact of her old nurse being a co-conspirator puts us in mind of other literary virgins, such as Juliet Capulet, of course. Comparison with Isabella is perhaps not really fair and she comes off worse, lacking Isabella's vigour and presence of mind. Like Juliet, and Shylock's Jessica, she is eager to defy her family and, like Desdemona, swift to seize her adventurous lover as a life-line out of stifling confinement.

So, completely unprepared, impetuously, the two lovers escape, flee into an 'elfin storm from faery land' (343). As one of the poem's numerous antitheses (others include love/hate, youth/age, weakness/strength, warmth/cold, patience/passion), Porphyro takes Madeline out of dream and into reality – though the nature of that reality is highly ambiguous. Love is the gateway between the two realms. Once again it is the portal between the cold, hard world of mortality and the exciting, enticing world beyond time. And time is another of the poem's important concerns.

Madeline's mansion itself seems to be the very embodiment of time. A cold, solid permanent fixture in the landscape, besieged by a 'bitter chill', icy cold, in fact cold enough to make a hare limp and a beadsman's fingers numb. From this the lovers flee to the warm south (perhaps to Provence, bright with sunburnt mirth and the blushful Hippocrene) and as they do so they 'glide, like phantoms' (361). In contrast with the youthful lovers, the fortress is ancient, rooted in time and inhabited by menacingly empirical figures signifying danger. By quitting this temporal fixture with its 'sculptured dead', an ancient beadsman and the old beldame, the two lovers are also escaping the grasp of time itself, through the agency of love. Thus, as phantoms they traverse the margins between the mortal and immortal worlds.

Overall, the poem has numerous allusions to time. The above extract is typical with its 'days', 'night', 'mickle time', 'aged crone', and 'legends old'. The whole narrative is set in time too: 'it is St Agnes' Eve' (118), a strangely eternal moment flickering inviolable within the ravages of time inside the mansion. The narrator too plays with time, switching between present and past tenses even when dealing with the present moment (compare lines 127–8 and 132). The result is a mysterious and disorientating phenomenon in keeping with the faery enchantments in Madeline's own mind as well as in her bedroom. Meanwhile, Keats constantly reminds us of the immanence of time, its urgency and ravages, while the figures of Angela and the beadsman are its physical embodiment.

These ancient retainers also stand as reminders of what Madeline and Porphyro will become if they do not flee (Angela dies of palsy, or paralysis, and at line 277 Porphyro describes himself as Madeline's hermit). They symbolise the new order, the new generation, breaking out from the rocky bastion of certitude and frozen absolutes. The mansion signifies the old ways, a decadent mausoleum, in contrast to the storm in Stanza XLII with its suggestions of freedom, uncertainty and the chaos of the future. Together they seize the moment of their ripeness, both in the instant of their congress and in making this the pretext for the journey out. The moment is all. The place they quit, the Baron's world, is one of death and the withering of youth, but one where the experience of old age (in the figure of Angela) is vital to the release of the new.

For the brief period in Madeline's bedroom the lovers' situation recalls that of the happy lovers on the Grecian urn, 'For ever warm and still to be enjoyed'. However, in contrast to the 'marble men and maidens', they do achieve fulfilment and in bringing the moment to its ripeness they move it on – though we are left with the impression of that instant reverberating in stillness (XXXIV–XXXVI). The narrative form too enhances this effect. Keats is fully engrossed in the fluid account, until the time arrives to draw a close and we see again his technique of breaking off and pulling away the focus to leave the dream moment hovering but fixed in the past (370–1). The beadsman's shuffling reappearance seals off the end in a circular enclosure to the poem, a movement which encapsulates the dreamy ephemeral air of that exquisite instant.

At the end we learn that Angela's eventual fate was to die 'palsy-twitched, with meagre face deform' (376). Like the fortress she seems to represent time itself and its effects, as Keats's epithets for her reveal; she is 'old beldame' (90), 'the aged creature' (91) and 'aged crone' (129). At least three points about her are stressed by the tale: her ancient age, her role as a servant (thereby furnishing another layer, of class in addition to generation), and her moral attitude.

I have mentioned already that she prefigures Madeline's likely destiny at the mansion, namely as a wizened old spinster. At the outset Keats stresses the chill, austere, and dull lives endured by Angela and the beadsman in the service of others. As a servant to Madeline, Angela's duties include that of protectress and she is also a go-between and confidante, in short her guardian angel. She is a rational, cautious woman, practical, a balance of feeling and thought and as such a foil to the lusty, headstrong Porphyro, features which are all revealed in the above extract (and see Stanzas XII and XVIII). In fact these features, together with her problematic loyalties and affections, define her character strongly as the most fascinating and convincing in the poem. Her frequent comments on the action and people reinforce the firm sense of moral rectitude that runs through-out. For example, in the extract, line 119 demonstrates Angela's strong grasp of moral reality while, elsewhere, she berates Porphyro as a wicked man for his 'stratagem', and she agrees to her part in the deal only if he consents to marry Madeline.

She describes herself modestly, but realistically, as a 'feeble soul',

> A poor, weak, palsy-stricken, churchyard thing.
>
> (155)

Her age, her suffering but above all her firm grip on the moral realities make her a useful foil also to Madeline's dreamy flights. She is Madeline's guardian and as such her role in the action is crucial. Beneath this modestly feeble exterior Angela is a fairy god-mother too, or more. There may be more to this 'churchyard thing' than meets the casual eye.

As moral guardian Angela becomes the focal point for much of the religious imagery in the narrative. In the extract she reminds Porphyro that it is St Agnes' Eve, refers to 'holy days', 'God's help', and also to the 'Good angels'. But these are, of course, the mere accidentals of her ancient speech, its common fillers, rolling off the tongue unconsciously. Interlaced with religious diction is also that of superstition and even witchcraft: a 'witch's sieve', 'Elves and Fays', 'conjuror'; then in Stanza XV she refers to a 'wondrous riddle book' and 'enchantments'. Is Angela then a witch? There is plenty to support this thesis.

In the poem as a whole there is a plethora of allusions to magic and ghosts, as well as to the supernatural and witchcraft (for examples, see lines 168–71, 192, 343). In addition to the 'riddle book' she talks of charms (at 234 and 282), an amulet (257) and a 'steadfast spell' (287). The Baron dreams of 'witch and demon' (374) while the craggy mansion itself is beset by elves and faery, immortal figures, superstition, phantoms and charms. Those 'ceremonies' which are the necessary pretext for the St Agnes legend look suspi-ciously like occult rites for preternatural intervention, especially as the whole business seems to rely on some superstitious credence (a 'whim').

Keats too has his own subtext here. He is intent on bringing out through the drama his sceptical credo that Christian belief is no more nor less than 'pious frauds' (as he described it to his brother George). As line 70 makes clear, Keats uses the term 'faery' to be synonymous with 'religious'. He draws an equation between witchcraft or superstition and religion by interweaving the three sets of imagery. Angela's 'feeble laugh' in line 127 seems a part of this scepticism and so does the fairly clumsy simile in line 56,

> The music, yearning like a God in pain.

Like the inscrutable heraldic language in XXIV, Keats is happy to exploit religious diction for atmosphere and decoration and to imply the paranormal dimension of the weird inside the mysterious mansion.

Just as these different sets of imagery become interwoven, the mortal and immortal alternate, interlock, then finally merge through love and dream into the eternal moment of love-making when Porphyro becomes 'Beyond a mortal man' (316). As in *Endymion*, the lovers transcend this frail mortal world, passing beyond into the immortal like 'phantoms'.

But what, if any, is Angela's part in all this? That strange feeble laugh in line 127 sounds like a knowing laugh, a self-satisfied laugh at the success of wicca intervention. Is she actually a witch? Keats certainly endows her with the conventional appearance of the classic sorceress: aged crone, spectacled in the chimney corner, possessing a wand (92), and having knowledge which only the 'secret sisterhood may see' (116). Instructing Porphyro to 'hold water in a witch's sieve' (120) and become lord of the Elves and Fays points to magic, as does Keats's note about the 'riddle book' of spells and incantations (riddles and sieves being essential bits of witching apparatus, of course). Porphyro appears puzzled – as any of us might – and though he seems a rare example in Keats of an assertive male he may not be in full control. For instance, he believes himself to be saved by miracle (339), and then that mysterious 'elfin-storm' from faery land starts up (343) just in time for the escape from 'sleeping dragons' (353).

In the above extract, Angela informs Porphyro with some irony that Madeline 'the conjuror plays' (124), and while we have acknowledged Madeline's role as a siren in luring her lover across the frozen wasteland, Angela herself is the more practical 'conjuror', mover and shaker. Keats's epithet for her, 'old beldame' (90), signals a telling comparison with *La Belle Dame* and the idea of supernatural thrall (note also Porphyro's 'ancient ditty' in line 291). Pressed by the ripely urgent Porphyro, Angela at last grants his wish (lines 162 and 172).

If she is a witch then she appears to use her powers to good end (contrast the ruthless 'hell-born Circe' of *Endymion*, III). It is apt to see her as instrumental in the hoodwinking of Madeline as well as in the enthralling of Porphyro, both of which finally converge in their apparently successful love-making. Occult powers swell the elements to a hurly burly of a storm, during the silent fascination of which the phantom lovers make their getaway. Not even a feeble laugh troubles the silence about the 'footworn stones'.

The ambiguity surrounding Angela is of course all one with Keats's deliberate mystification in the whole text, with its dazzling array of brilliant effects. The poem tellingly discloses his thorough mastery in its artful manipulation of atmosphere and silence. He is himself a wizard of the piece in the easy performance of its dramatic skills: narration, lyric, character depiction, scene, theme and voice – we are now a rich universe away from the raw gropings of *Calidore* and *Endymion*'s 'one bare circumstance'.

In the manipulation of the poem's atmospheres Keats's narrator is naturally the crucial element. From the opening line the narrator himself also plays a significant role. As we begin to read he takes us by surprise with his loose, chatty construction,

> St Agnes' Eve – Ah, bitter chill it was!
>
> (1)

It looks like a conventional, even clichéd opener to a story book. That interjection 'Ah!' establishes an air of personal intimacy, taking us into his easy confidence, while imparting a sense of authoritative truth to his reminiscence. He frequently identifies himself closely with the characters in the mansion (see lines 82, 91 and 196–7), while at other times he remains apart, like the more remote narrator of *Isabella*. He achieves this detachment through his moral or satiric comments on the action (see 41, 56 or 81) and in the copious range of similes and other tropes (in the extract, see lines 124, 129 and 135). Although the overall effect is of an easy free-flowing stream, Keats's narrator successfully maintains a subtle, well-judged control with sureness of effect.

In terms of the poem's control, we have already noted Keats's fine sense of authoritative silence in the love-making section (XXXV to XXXVII). At that point Keats's silences and ambiguity were justly consonant with the episode's mood and they helped to constrain the possibility of sentiment or brusqueness. Indeed, prominent in the poem's diction is the frequency of modals like 'seems', 'may' and 'perhaps' lending a conditional, ambivalent tone to it. This contrasts with its more sharply detailed and empirical imaging, such as the frosty chapel in Stanza II and the resplendent casement of XXIV. The narrator creates many such double effects, or antitheses, not the least of which is his evocation of religious myth, which is frequently deconstructed by scepticism and irony.

The poem's richly woven arras is an accumulation of such contrasts and double effects some of which we have already listed: love/ hate, safety/danger, youth/age, narrative present and past, red or purple/white, Christian/pagan and so on. So strong are these that the whole poem pulses along such markers, continually shifting between its polarities, impelled by different intensities in a flow of sensual and almost tangible energy. Every stanza is loaded with more and still more musical and pictorial delights.

Keats's achievement in creating such a fluid masterpiece is magnified when we consider his choice of stanza form as its vehicle: eight lines of iambic pentameter with a final epigrammatic alexandrine (i.e. hexameter) in each. Keats adapts the stanza form used by the Elizabethan poet Edmund Spenser in his epic *The Faerie Queene*. A demanding form for any poet – especially in the requirements of the rhyme scheme – the biggest pitfall lies in its halting tendency, continually threatening to pause the flow in a sequence of large, self-contained paragraph units. Nevertheless, I believe Keats's system of interlocking rhyme patterns skilfully overcomes this danger. He marshals his stanzas in a sequence of related units which successively build up and swell the progress of the matter into a dynamic surge.

Unlike his earlier dramatic experiments, typically *Endymion* and *Isabella*, Keats retains our interest through to the very end, keeping the focus sharp and the tension high. There is hardly a false note or a dud line in the whole piece. By closely restraining the unities of time, place and character he not only maintains the dramatic tension but also overcomes the tricky artistic difficulty of connecting together sequences of narrative blocks.

When it was published *The Eve of St Agnes* was very highly regarded by Keats's contemporaries, particularly for its sensual images and sounds. Twentieth-century critics, however, tended to concentrate more on its meaning and narrative, especially the relationship between technical elements and interpretation.

The Eve of St Agnes is among the highest of Keats's technical and narrational achievements. It is one of his most accessible and convincing as well as fluent narratives, bringing together a wide range of stylistic and literary sources from his reading and previous poetic experiments to produce beautiful effects on the mind as much as on the ear and the eye (and as such it anticipates the major odes, which Keats composed immediately after it).

It is above all a love story and no deep metaphysics ruffle its poise – as they do in *Lamia* (though the latter also shares many of *St Agnes*'s characteristic strengths). Moreover, as a very simple and positive love story, it resembles *Endymion* in affirming and celebrating the idealism, intensity and earnestness of youthful passion . . . with a large measure of wish fulfilment thrown in for good measure (and a little help from the paranormal).

Conclusions

All three poems in this chapter tell love stories, attempt to recreate medieval settings, and focus on Keats's characteristic core themes of time, mortality, art, humanity, and truth or reality. His imaginative interest in these themes give these and the rest of his *oeuvre* a coherence that speaks of the writer's profound commitment to art and ideas.

An integral feature of the love stories is Keats's great skill in engineering atmosphere, especially for sensuous and even highly erotic effect. Also crucial to the love stories is Keats's continuing exploration and adjustment in his own attitude to women. In this respect we have seen examples of how Keats mined his own personal life, as well as his research, to provide the material for his narratives, which become the laboratory for themes and anxieties in his own life.

In terms of technique we have seen again Keats's professional readiness to experiment in new forms, including *ottava rima* and Spenserian stanza, but always with his own stamp of variation on these. We have noted the further development of his ideas in melody and prosody as well as his increasing facility in the demanding skills of narration, especially in *The Eve of St Agnes*. The rich silences of *St Agnes* and *La Belle Dame* demonstrate well his ability to learn from the unhappy misjudgements in *Isabella* when the leaves came not so readily to the poetic tree.

Further Research

At about the same time that he wrote *La Belle Dame* Keats also wrote a beautiful sonnet with the cumbersome title 'A Dream, after reading Dante's Episode of Paola and Francesca'. It is often noted that this sonnet shares some of the principal themes of *Isabella* and *St Agnes*, as well as of *La Belle Dame*. Make a close study of the 'Dream' sonnet with particular regard to these other three poems, noting comparisons and contrasts in terms of themes and Keats's attitude to them.

PART 2

THE CONTEXT AND THE CRITICS

6

Keats's Letters

Do you get health – and Tom the same – I'll dance,
And from detested moods in new Romance
Take refuge – Of bad lines a Centaine dose
Is sure enough – and so 'here follows prose.'

(Verse letter, 25 March 1818)

Keats's letters are unstudied, conversational, vivid, vital, personal and intimate. They were not written to be published and so, unlike a modern writer with a nervous eye on projecting the right image to his/her public, they are unselfconscious and disarmingly candid. This is not to say that they would only be read by the addressee – Keats's letters were passed round, copied and avidly collected by his admirers even while he was still alive. Most retained his letters out of love and respect for Keats himself, some out of love of his verse, and one or two because they saw a commercial value in them.

Keats's letters are a vast pot-pourri of scraps, orts, fragments of ideas, drafts and bits of poetry, quotations from his own and others' work, greetings, and apologies, asides, and asides to asides. For us as well as for Keats himself they constitute a journal of his daily life (he determined several times to keep a separate journal but nothing much came of the plan). They are a rough manifesto of poetic theory, an arena for thrashing out ideas, a historical document of the period, but above all a sort of slipshod autobiography, a snapshot of his life and *zeitgeist* covering just over four years of Keats's brief writing career.

Occasionally a new Keats letter turns up – and a great many have been lost – but the ones which survive probably tell us as much as we will ever discover about the poet. At the latest count, almost 250 letters exist and at least another 50 are known to have existed. Given Keats's mighty poetic output, this level of letter-writing activity of approximately 300-plus letters over about fifty-four months is astonishing – particularly when we note that some of the letters to his brother George and his wife Georgiana in America are well over twenty pages long.

However, having said that, the letters are by and large the most random, unplanned, intuitive and fragmentary compositions you could imagine, picking up and putting down topics as they flickered across his roving imagination. Usually (especially the long ones to George and Georgiana) they sound like an interior monologue, or automatic writing or sometimes even like Lucky's speech from *Waiting for Godot*. The speed of his writing is reflected in the baggy syntax, irregular punctuation – predominated by the dash and whimsical capitalisation – and his highly personalised spellings: for example, affraid, poeems, verry, coulours, rediCules, elbous (for elbows), Brittain, encrease, trowsers, moschetos. Phrases are extended beyond breaking point or simply snapped off in mid-thought as another idea cuts in.

In a letter to Charles Dilke, Keats's acquaintance and landlord, just as he is contemplating a possible career in literary journalism he breaks off to describe the sensual joy of the juicy nectarine he is just then eating – 'soft pulpy, slushy, oozy' – the description is so spontaneously fresh we can almost taste it. In another letter he breaks off to write that Mrs Dilke is knocking on the wall to say the tea is ready, and in another that his candle is almost finished.

He very rarely uses paragraphs (partly to save on expensive paper) – so a letter tends to be a single extended rambling, commodious circuit of thought. And this lack of order, of rule and line, accords well with his subjective Romantic viewpoint.

His vocabulary is, as we would expect of a writer, highly revealing. He takes great pleasure in word-play and a high delight in punning: 'I have been looking out my dear Georgy for a joke or a Pun for you', and later he hopes to 'bandy back a pun or two' with his brother across the Atlantic. He delights too in the informality of his exchanges – so that his lexis is rich in contemporary vernacular – puffy, rout, pig (a drenching), bever (a snack), a wet (a drink). His use of neologisms points to his close contact with the times and gives a fresh glimpse into the period; for example, he notes that the latest craze in the spring of 1819 is the 'Velocepede', an early form of bicycle, and in the same letter he refers to an 'electric fire', that is, a sort of moral intuition inside people. And there is his own rich favourite vocabulary some of which we have come across already: 'to smoke', 'smother', 'gusto', 'sweet', 'pouncing rhymes' and 'grotesque'.

If Keats wrote so many letters and so intensively then we need to ask why he took on such a massive obligation; in other words, what function did letter-writing fulfil for Keats and what, loosely speaking, was his purpose?

Letter-writing was quite often a relief from composing verse and it filled a perennial urge to write and 'speculate'. Letters helped Keats to try out ideas on his friends in the knowledge that his letters would be passed around. They also let friends, but chiefly his brothers, know what poetry he had written lately. Keats was a great socialiser and letters enabled him to keep in touch with associates, of course, and most importantly, to lessen the gulf of separation between himself and George. It allowed him to keep his social contacts with friends, especially given the problems of transport in the early nineteenth century. Following the death of their parents, Keats as the eldest of the siblings felt a great love and sense of responsibility for his sister Fanny and his two brothers, George and Tom (and later to Georgiana too). Letters helped him to hold the family together and to maintain a sort of balance between them, habitually providing advice and support, quite often with financial help (in one letter he warned George to 'be careful of those Americans . . . [they will] fleece you').

There are three principal periods of letter-writing in Keats's mature years. The first period covers the year from mid-1817 to mid-1818, it is dominated by correspondence with two of his closest friends (Benjamin Bailey and John Reynolds) and closes with Keats's journal letters vividly describing his walking tour of the Lake District and Scotland with another close companion, Charles Brown. The middle period spans Keats's great creative year, September 1818 to September 1819; it is characterised as his most successfully fertile era, by the lingering death of Tom, and by the three massive letter-journals which Keats wrote to his brother and sister-in-law in America. The final period reveals his devotion to his fiancée and his increasing fears about his own declining health; with premonitions of death.

Throughout all of the letters we get references to what was going on during the nineteenth century, especially in literary matters. As we might expect, Keats comments freely (and critically) on major literary figures such as Wordsworth, Charles Lamb, Coleridge, Scott, Byron and Shelley (most of whom he had met) along with the shapers of literature at this time, particularly the highly influential William Hazlitt and Leigh Hunt. There are references to the recent past too – obliquely to the French and American revolutions, Arctic explorations, Mozart, Napoleon Bonaparte, the death of Queen Charlotte in 1818; and to the general feeling of the age – socialising, fashions, pastimes (for instance, in a letter to George, Keats proclaims that he has managed 'very nearly quite' to give up taking snuff – then bemoans the fact that 'I have none though in my own snuff box'; 2 January 1819).

Although for most of Keats's life Britain was either at war or preparing for war there is very little of this in his letters, very little sense of the tension we might have expected. Instead the letters tell us more about Keats's close circle of friends and naturally about the poet himself, his attitudes and his great range of interests in this tumbling stream of consciousness. Although he is most free with his criticism of, say, Wordsworth and latterly Leigh Hunt, Keats saves his greatest spleen for himself, particularly in his letters to America. As a 'severe critic of his own Works' he smokes out his own 'insufficiency' and frequently falls victim to self-doubt about his poetic ability. This naturally exacerbates his tendency towards melancholy and spells of inertia. In politics he is centre-left but hardly anything comes through about this. In ethics Keats thought that a poet could not be a moral agent because ideally 'he has no Identity' (27 October 1818). In matters of religion he despises the established Church ('the pious frauds of Religion') but admires Christ, whom he holds up as a supreme example of what Keats calls 'disinterestedness of Mind'. This was an ethical ideal for Keats, the refinement of a mind beyond self-interest and towards mankind as a whole, and he admitted disconsolately his own failure to come up to this high ideal (19

February 1819). However like most of us, Keats's views were, over a period of time, inconsistent. His attitude to women is a good case in point. In a letter to Bailey he writes:

> When I am among Women I have evil thoughts, malice spleen. . . . I am full of suspicions.
>
> (18 July 1818)

But two months later he writes to George and Georgiana that he has met Jane Cox, and

> I always find myself more at ease with such a woman. . . . I forget myself entirely because I live in her.
>
> (14–31 October 1818)

But he flatly denies that he is in love. It is not until he meets Fanny Brawne that he manages to make some tentative reconciliation between the two attitudes.

However, Keats is a great socialiser and one thing he cannot forgo (apart from composing) is company, male as well as female. He loves walking and talking with people, social gatherings of all sorts: dinner parties, card schools, visits to clubs, coffee houses and theatres, or simply chatting with an acquaintance. The vast majority of letters are filled with details about visits to or from friends, ladies' circles, encounters with strangers on the Heath or in Town (strangers who generally turn out to be the friend of a friend). But these cosmopolitan accounts are rarely pure fact. Above all, they betray Keats's great interest in people, sympathy for others' problems, social issues, romances, rivalries, the motives of people, the dynamism of changing relationships, money problems and comedy. In fact probably the single most obvious impression that emerges from the whole corpus of this prose is humanity itself: Keats's great interest in, love of and regard for the whole spectrum of mankind in all its good and bad. The only occasion on which he demonstrates anything like true hatred for any individual is when Keats finds the 'Amena letters' after the death of Tom. These were love-letters sent to Tom as a 'cruel hoax', signed by the fictitious 'Amena Bellefila' but traced to Charles Wells, and Keats felt strongly that these had expedited his brother's death.

> It was no thoughtless hoax – but a cruel deception on a sanguine
> Temperament. . . . I consider it my duty to be prudently revengeful.
>
> (14 February–3 May 1819; 'Letter C')

As much as it is a token of his great family loyalty, this can be seen
as evidence of Keats's capacity to be moved to intense feeling. These
moments he made no apology for, and in fact he seems to have
regarded this capacity as a healthy symptom (passionate intensity was,
as we noted, one of his pathways to truth). To his friends he was
quite open about the primacy of feelings, and he was especially
candid to Bailey and Reynolds and, naturally, to his brothers and
sister. In later life his greatest and most spontaneous intimacy was
reserved, of course, for his correspondence with Fanny Brawne.
When Keats's letters to Fanny were published in the late nineteenth
century, the intimacy of his love embarrassed many readers (one
critic scorned them as 'vulgar' and lacking in true passion). But to
our age it is difficult to see them as other than the purest affirmation
of the most tender feelings simply and honestly articulated,

> You cannot conceive how I ache to be with you: how I would die for
> one hour. . . . I am in deep love with you . . .
>
> (25 July 1819)

It is interesting to look back too at Keats's first impression of Mrs
Brawne's 'daughter senior' soon after they had moved in, next door –
'I think beautiful and elegant, graceful, silly, fashionable and strange'
(16–18 December 1818). Great affiliations have been forged on less
propitious beginnings.

The openness and intensity of devotion in these letters are made more
poignant by the premonitions of death that became increasingly apparent to Keats. While the co-existence of death and love is a recurrent
theme in his poetry, the imminence of his own demise makes these final
letters a deeply moving experience. With unknowing irony he writes in
1819 of his intention to compose, 'if God should spare me' (compare
Sleep and Poetry, line 96), but it is only in his final letter, when he concedes

> I have an habitual feeling of my real life having past, and that I am
> leading a posthumous existence
>
> (30 November 1820)

that we get any real suggestion that the magnificent energy and joy of life is about to fail.

While Keats's letters are justly celebrated as perhaps the most complete personal statement of any nineteenth-century writer's context and social setting, it is as a poet first and last that he is esteemed. As he himself famously predicted, 'I think I shall be among the English Poets after my death' (14 October 1818; 'Letter A'). Accordingly our discussion of the letters should focus on what they reveal of Keats's views on poetry itself, his 'theory' of poetry in general and the composition of his own poetry.

On 18 April 1817 Keats wrote to John Reynolds in rapture:

> I find that I cannot exist without poetry – without eternal poetry – half the day will not do – the whole of it. . . . I had become all in a Tremble from not having written any thing of late.

At such moments poetry filled Keats's whole being like a sacramental spirit taking him out of his immediate self, lifting his spirits, especially when he was in a spell of composing. As this entry reveals, too, a dry season could have serious emotional implications for him, he could become anxious and irritable. Sometimes writing was like a drug for him.

Poetry was something that was well under his skin and he could not understand why this was not so for others too. Literature was of great significance in his life and he longed to feast on it, not only English literature but also the literature of other languages. He had some Italian and less Greek but felt it a deficiency in himself that he had not mastered languages sufficient to read the classics, such as Homer, in the original (though at school he did begin a translation of *The Aeneid*). However, of literature in general he took poetry 'to be the Chief', of course, and he thought that people ought to become thoroughly absorbed in it, telling Reynolds again that they should 'read a certain Page . . . untill it becomes stale'. But why? One answer can be found in one of Keats's enormous letters to George and Georgiana in America. Writing from Chichester where he began *The Eve of St Agnes* he declares:

> The great beauty of Poetry is, that it makes every thing every place interesting – The palatine venice and the abbotine Chichester are equally interesting.

> (17–27 September 1819)

Then he prefaces some lines from *The Eve of St Mark* with the promise that 'it will give you the sensation of walking about an old county town in a coolish evening'. To give the poem an air of medieval authenticity he tags on some lines in 'imitation of the Authors of Chaucer's time'.

But such joy in poetry was not always evident in Keats. In March 1818 he told Bailey of his fear that Poetry was, compared with religion or metaphysics, just a mere ephemeral toy unlikely to penetrate the mysteries of life. And in July 1819 in his great creative year, his *annus mirabilis*, he wrote to Fanny Brawne disheartened, 'Poems are as common as newspapers', and later to Dilke he expressed his mystification as to why the public was so interested in poetry: 'I have no trust whatever on Poetry – I dont wonder at it...' (22 September 1819); though he did confess that he was 'fit for nothing but literature'. It was at this point that he broke off to describe the sublime oozy joy of that slushy nectarine.

In the letter to Fanny Brawne he also pointed out that he could not and would not write poems merely to a timetable. They must evolve naturally, he thought. This sentiment recalls a letter to his publisher, John Taylor, in which he asserted that for poetry he had only a few axioms. This was in that anxious period just before *Endymion* appeared in book form in early 1818. He insisted that poetry should involve the 'highest thoughts' and that these and the images of a poem ought to arise naturally, from within the subject matter of the poem. A third axiom is that 'if poetry comes not as naturally as the Leaves to a tree it had better not come at all' (27 February 1818); in other words, that poetry comes naturally from within, evolving under proper inspiration. Or as he explained to a partner in the publishing firm J. A. Hessey, poetry is an autonomous sort of gift and 'must create itself' (8 October 1818).

It is as though poetry in its pre-verbal state has a life of its own, within the poet but apart from him or her. It is as though the poet is merely a sort of vessel for incubating the verse, and as we have already noted, Keats believed that the poet has no character of his or her own, he is the 'camelion Poet'. His own view of the poet is therefore of a man of integrity – at least where his art was concerned. He believed it a form of prostitution for a poet to write to order or to make money out of his sacred gift. But, perhaps ironically, he felt it was reasonable to write out of motives of fame and reputation. Especially early in his career, the prospect of 'poetical fame' was a great spur to his writing and we have seen already how he hoped, after his death (or even before it), to be among the pantheon of great writers, to be 'among the English Poets'. And you would not be reading this book if this had not proved true. However, he seems to have had an invidious attitude toward fame – in December 1818 he told a friend, the painter Benjamin Haydon, that 'love of effect and admiration' was a vice, even though earlier that year he had claimed, somewhat ingenuously possibly,

> I never wrote one single Line of Poetry with the least Shadow of public thought.
>
> (9 April 1818)

As well as suffering bouts of melancholy, Keats was victim to frequent crises about his status as a poet. Having abandoned a career in medicine in autumn 1816 to dedicate himself to poetry he was tormented by self-doubt. Partly disillusioned by his motives and partly disheartened by some of his early compositions, especially after the clobbering that *Endymion* received, he seriously considered alternative careers such as ship's surgeon, as well as vague altruistic projects for the benefit of mankind. In autumn of 1819, fed up with living a life of penury and devoid of luxuries, he seriously contemplated a career as a literary journalist; he declared to Brown,

> I will write ... for whoever will pay me.
>
> (22 September 1819)

This was quite a fanciful scheme, involving renting a flat in London and getting involved in the drama of literary debate and the glamour of the Press. But it was a pipe dream, a chimera, and nothing at all came of it.

Keats did feel deeply that his verse never attracted the sort of remuneration that Wordsworth and Byron could command, and felt a mild personal resentment against both of them. Towards the end of his life he rapped the 'new' poets for selling out. He told Shelley that the moderns wrote not only to express an explicit purpose but also to 'serve Mammon', and with deep sarcasm he advised his fellow poet to:

> curb your magnanimity and be more of an artist, and 'load every rift' of your subject with ore.
>
> (16 August 1820)

As we have seen, Keats's own poetry more often than not loads every rift with ore. It is one of its great delights, but it does spring from an utterly different credo, largely that of Keats's worship of beauty. I mentioned above that among the many attractions of the letters is that of revealing something of Keats's own poetic creed. In addition to exploring the role of the poet and his motives for writing, Keats uses his correspondents to sound out ideas on Beauty and the Imagination, two of the cornerstones of his writing.

The early letters are a great testimony to Keats's total, almost erotic, fascination with beauty 'in all things'. His love of beauty throbs through almost all of his existing letters for 1817–18. To Bailey he sings joyously for beauty, the 'poetical in all things' (3 November 1817), and a month later to his brothers he proclaims, 'with a great poet the sense of Beauty overcomes every other consideration' (21 December 1817). And he wished above all to become a great poet.

The three pillars of his poetical manifesto are beauty, the emotions and the imagination. They were not just the bedrock of art but also of understanding and truth. In a letter to Bailey he also proposed a further axiom, one that has by now become a familiar part of Keatsian lore,

> I am certain of nothing but of the holiness of the Heart's affections and the truth of the Imagination – What the Imagination seizes as Beauty must be truth – whether it existed before or not...
>
> (22 November 1817)

Keats renounced any poetry that 'has a palpable design on us' (3 February 1818) and those other extraneous motives. In their stead, beauty was placed centre-stage among his principles, acknowledging no aesthetic responsibility to anything else than 'the eternal Being, the Principle of Beauty' (9 April 1818). Alternatively, it is fair to say that Keats was never tempted to go all the way down the road of art solely for art's sake; his temperament, his friends and his environment made sure of that. His poetry is firmly rooted in the worldly, the empirical, even when he is discoursing on gods and goddesses. Recall too, Keats's great faith in the power and inspirational effect of 'a Life of Sensations rather than of Thoughts' (22 November 1817). As a highly sensitive man he could certainly perceive the 'beauty in all things', in art of course, but especially in the poetry of Shakespeare and Thomas Chatterton. He yearned for and pleasured in the beauty of nature and the human in humanity, especially female beauty. The momentous walking tour of Scotland and northern England with Charles Brown planted in him a new love of nature and of the sort of wild landscapes that had moved Wordsworth so much. Reporting back by letter to his brother Tom he exulted,

> What astonishes me more than any thing is the tone, the coloring, the slate, the stone, the moss, the rock-weed.
>
> (27 June 1818)

It was probably the beauty of this countryside more than anything else that convinced him of the rightness of his belief in seeking beauty in verse. Love of Fanny Brawne too gave such a great intensity of commitment to his life and his art. He told her so in his letter to her of 8 July 1819 and he humbly suggested that it was this which had enabled him to come through his prolonged moments of depression. When he proposed that her beauty had been the start point of his love, Fanny protested that perhaps this was all he loved her for. His reply was that while this was true, it was also his belief that outer beauty reflected an inner concord of other positive qualities and values (March 1820).

While such a naively moral point of view might well be the sort of ingenious remark to get a lover out of a tight corner it does give some idea of Keats's view of beauty: beauty is considerably more than the accidental rhythm of superficial features. To Reynolds, Keats argued that a love of beauty enabled a poet to be a 'severe critic' of his own writing (22? September 1818). And then, at a mature period in his

poetical life, he re-iterated his early belief in beauty, writing to George
on the final day of 1818,

> I never can feel certain of any truth but from a clear perception of its
> Beauty.
>
> (31 December 1818)

Not only did he reassert this belief to himself but the thesis finds a
strong (and controversial) poetical expression in the closing lines of
'Ode on a Grecian Urn'.

The earlier expression of this thesis (again in his letter to Bailey, 22
November 1817) also sets out the role which the imagination would
play in the process. It is, of course, the imagination that sizes beauty,
and thereby truth. For Keats, truth is never completely an intellectual,
coldly rationalistic question, as for example *Lamia* and the Hyperion
poems attest. It was never to be arrived at via 'consequitive
reasoning' alone. Instead he replaced the *a priori* approach with a
holy alliance between mind, intuition, sensations, and the imagination. The imagination could be likened to a dream ('Adam's dream',
Keats wrote to Brown) in which the sense data of physical reality is
reorganised along subjective lines, to *create* a waking perception of
reality. It is an active faculty in shaping perceptions but also, for
the artist, in exploring other moods and conditions (8 March
1819).

Keats never refined his ideas on Imagination to the great extent
that Coleridge did but like him he often contrasted it with the Fancy,
and both agreed that it was a highly active and powerful function. In
an early letter Keats distinguished them with regard to their roles in
poetic inspiration:

> Fancy is the sails, and Imagination the Rudder.
>
> (8 October 1817)

By which he appears to say that Fancy is the power or driving force
while Imagination gives poetic direction and form or order.

In seeing the imagination as an active, expansive function Keats
could also see its vital importance from the other side: the reader's

point of view. Ideally, he wrote to George in America, a work of art should not seek to supply all the details but give enough to stimulate the reader's imagination and omit enough to allow that imagination to fill in the gaps (31 December 1818). Of course, this is a very difficult matter for artistic judgement and Keats did not achieve such a fine balance from the outset. Not until 1819 with the subtle lacunae of the major odes and the vacant, eluding atmospheres of *Eve of St Agnes* and *Lamia* does he get this judgement exactly spot on.

The letters tell us a great deal about Keats's social life, its currents and pressures, and about his attitudes to a great wealth of topics – love, people, theatre, food, fashions, nectarines and of course himself. As a poet Keats also reveals great anxieties about composing: his fears, aims, delights along the way and then his response to the finished text. The course of composing never runs smooth, as the letters reveal. Even so, when he is working on a composition, especially an extended poem, he is characteristically excited and fully engaged.

We have here, alas, space enough only to give a faint whiff of the flavour of Keats's letters and to focus on one aspect of the great diversity of enthralling topics. Sufficient in themselves, they are nevertheless a vital complement to the verse, which they enrich immeasurably – as well as revealing much of the man behind them. Throughout his correspondence he shares his exuberance with friends (and with us), and his running commentary to the verse reveals both its great interest to him and also their interest and commitment to him. Nowhere is there the slightest hint of self-indulgence or duplicity, only large measures of self-criticism, modesty, his great good humour and, above all, a zest for all the life that moved within and around him.

> Mrs Dilke is knocking at the wall for Tea is ready – I will tell you what sort of tea it is and then bid you – Good bye – This is monday morning – nothing particular happened yesterday evening, except that just when the tray came up Mrs Dilke and I had a battle with celery stalks – she sends her love to you...

(4 January 1819)

7

Keats and Nineteenth-Century Romanticism

In this chapter I want to set Keats's poetry within the context of the period in which he lived, and particularly with regard to Romanticism, the revolutionary movement in art that emerged towards the end of the eighteenth century. It will be useful to see how Keats's contemporary poets worked with some similar themes and literary interests, and with this in mind I have arranged the chapter under the following headings: (i) The Origins of Romanticism, (ii) Nature, (iii) The Imagination, (iv) Feeling, (v) The Writer, (vi) Language, (vii) Romanticism after Keats.

The Origins of Romanticism

Before we attempt to define the characteristics of Romanticism I would like first to consider what preceded this movement. This will allow us to introduce some of the principal features of Romanticism but, just as important, it will also allow us to examine some of the characteristics that led to Romanticism itself, which was a radical revolution against the manners and literary theories of its predecessors.

For practical purposes we can take 1789 as the starting point of Romanticism, when French revolutionaries seized the Bastille prison in Paris, and the year in which William Blake's *Song of Innocence* was published (other critics point to 1798 as the significant starting point, the year of the publication of the highly influential *Lyrical Ballads* by William Wordsworth and Samuel Taylor Coleridge).

I have described Romanticism as a revolution, but it is, of course, the eventual climax of a gradual development, of changes in ways of thinking and regarding the world that evolved over a period of time. While the Romantic poets were united in their resistance to the literary culture of the eighteenth century, it would be misleading to describe them as a combined 'school' as such. Although each of the six major poets of English Romanticism (Blake, Wordsworth, Coleridge, in the first wave; and Byron, Shelley and Keats in the second) were aware of the work of the others they did not form a recognisable group with anything like a united artistic manifesto. In fact, in many ways they were a quite disparate collection of writers – and paradoxically one of the concepts they did jointly embrace was that of pluralism, the refusal of standardisation in aims or agenda. (It is worth noting too, at this point, that the term 'Romanticism' itself was not used about these poets until about the middle of the nineteenth century when most of them were already dead.)

In respect of their pluralism the Romantic poets were radically different from the movement that preceded them. Neo-Classicism, the dominant movement of much of the eighteenth century, was a unified doctrine rooted in the aesthetic ideas of ancient Greece and Rome. Above all, eighteenth-century authors showed a marked inclination to generalise about people, a belief predicated on the assumption that all people were in essence uniform.

The Age of Enlightenment was an age of great confidence, following on the discoveries of Isaac Newton among others, in which the pursuit of scientific laws encouraged thinkers to discover universal laws supposed to exist behind all things, including art and ethics.

Standardisation and fixed patterns were their keynotes, and this fostered a fixed frame of reference for artistic judgements. Neo-Classical writers saw themselves as members of a close-knit coterie, centralised on London, with common roots and a conformity of vision. In English literature, it is the age of Dr Samuel Johnson (whose famous dictionary attempted to standardise the language), of Pope, Sheridan and Swift.

An important consequence of Neo-Classicism's heavy reliance on rationality was its disregard for significant areas of human interest. Indeed it ignored what we might today regard as crucial areas of artistic interest, namely the imagination, inspiration and intuition. But chiefly it diminished the importance of individual perception and expression, in exchange for conformity and mechanistic formalism.

It is in the decline of Neo-Classicism that the roots of Romanticism lie. Two key pioneers in the new movement here are the Swiss philosopher Jean-Jacques Rousseau (1712–78) and the English essayist and political radical William Godwin (1756–1836), father of Mary Shelley.

Rousseau was *the* seminal force in the revolution of thought that produced the Romantics. His own writing is passionate, free and (for a philosopher) written in a style of charismatic simplicity. His work gives full expression to nature, to the spontaneous inner world of the emotions, stressing organic rather than mechanistic forms, with a sensitivity to individual visions and to authentic action, in contrast to Neo-Classicism's artificial manners. Rousseau fervently advocated the return to nature as a source of inspiration and truth, and encouraged the discovery of childhood as a truly discrete realm separate from the life of adults. His humane, liberating attitude to mankind looks on people as essentially good, not as innately brutish or aggressive (as Thomas Hobbes had seen them):

> The fundamental principle of all morals … is that man is naturally good, loving justice and order; that there is absolutely no original sin in the human heart, and that the first movements in nature are always right.

In literature Rousseau launched the return to nature both as a source of inspiration and as subject matter and his politics spawned new utopian visions (such as Blake's vision of a Golden Age and Coleridge's 'Pantisocracy', an ideal community founded on the notion of equal power).

William Godwin explicitly acknowledged the influence of Rousseau on his own thoughts. A political idealist, Godwin aligned himself with Rousseau's attack on the dominant political system, the autocrat rule of the monarchy and aristocracy. He took up the Neo-Classical preoccupation with rationality and used it as the raft for a logical system of justice rooted in the nobility of mankind.

A mercurial and fearless crusader in the cause of humanity, Godwin had a notable influence on the youthful idealism of the Romantic poets. This was felt most directly by Shelley but also, through Leigh Hunt and William Hazlitt, by Keats himself. Hazlitt, a noted critic and essayist, acclaimed Godwin as 'the spirit of the age', whose reforming zeal held out the hope of a better world based on a positive view of mankind, stressing the community as the basis for progress and justice.

Under the influence of Rousseau and others the revolution eventually spread across Europe but, in literature at least, it made its earliest and greatest impact on British literature. Here Romanticism caught on essentially because of its human appeal: the rigorous strait jacket of Neo-Classicism had eventually stifled its own vitality and become moribund. Moreover, increasing social upheaval, in the form of industrialisation and urban expansion together with a fear of growing mechanisation, led to a reappraisal of the Enlightenment's tenets.

The search for new areas of truth opened up new artistic concerns and emphases: gradually, the subjective took over from the objective, while a new interest developed in the writer's individuality and perceptions. There rapidly grew up a renewed concern with nature, together with a fascination for the primitive rather than the highly cultured. In addition there were revolutionary new areas of stimulus and exploration such as the strange and the supernatural, the foreign, as well as interest in the sphere of childhood.

The new paradigm also meant a shift in the poet's perception of his own function and role in society, which brought new freedoms along with it. The poet becomes the artist as hero, the conscience of his society, a sage or prophet in search of the genuine voice of humanity. And, significantly, the new approach stressed the importance of detailed first-hand observation instead of the stale and gestured commentaries of Neo-Classicism.

Because the new poets did not view themselves as part of a formal movement and did not discuss 'Romanticism' as such, we need to look a little deeper to see how some of its features actually manifested themselves in their work. To do this we should examine the principal areas of interest for the Romantic poets, beginning with 'nature', and reflect on how Keats and his contemporaries responded to each.

Nature

The Romantics were not the first to celebrate the delights of nature. It has been the traditional stuff of literature in one form or another. However, the image of nature in the work of Neo-Classical writers is something lifeless and quite dull. Seen through the eyes of their Greek and Roman models, the pastoral was a fairly conventional, flattened vision of bucolic life. This produced the unmistakable impression that many writers of the period had never actually witnessed the countryside at anything like first-hand but more distantly from the safe haven of the Georgian library. Accordingly, for most Neo-Classical writers, nature in literature quite often had a background or allegorical function, as in the work of Pope and Swift. In other words, nature was regarded as a garden, interesting only as long as it remained at a safe distance and was groomed in accordance with good taste.

But not all eighteenth-century poets saw nature in this flattened way. The work of William Cowper (1731–1800) shows a remarkable sensitivity and close intimacy with nature, while James Thomson's *The Seasons* (1726–30) is a dynamic depiction of the grandeur and often awesome workings of the forces of nature, blending closely-observed details of natural settings and mood together with his own very subjective responses to those details. Where eighteenth-century poets saw nature merely as the picturesque and graceful handiwork of a benevolent and magisterial God, the Romantic poets looked at the physical world in terms of its powerful moral force, as a deep source of inspiration and, above all, as a mysterious and sublime entity.

William Wordsworth (1770–1850) was one of the first to become interested in the complex effects of nature on the human mind, especially its moral power. His poetry often centres on the ways in

which an individual's consciousness interacts with that of nature, for
instance in terms of perception:

> for she can so inform
> The mind that is within us, so impress
> With quietness and beauty, and so feed
> With lofty thoughts...
>
> ('Lines Composed a Few Miles above Tintern Abbey', lines 125–8)

Wordsworth's friend Samuel Taylor Coleridge (1772–1834) took this
idea even further, to regard nature as potentially the reflexive landscape of the mind itself.

In this sacramental attitude, in which nature takes on mystical or
religious significance, possessing power and radiance, nature becomes transfigured into something actually beyond the power of
man to comprehend or rationalise. It becomes transfigured into a
portentous entity and it is the duty of the poet as seer or sage to
translate and express this mystery through art.

It is a power that could be deeply overwhelming in its effect, as
Keats found when he became engulfed in a mist on Ben Nevis during
his Scottish walking tour in 1818:

> I felt it horribly – 'Twas the most vile descent – shook me all to pieces
> – Over leaf you will find a Sonnet...
>
> (Letter to his brother Tom, 6 August 1818)

And from the sonnet referred to,

> Here are the craggy stones beneath my feet –
> Thus much I know, that, a poor witless elf,
> I tread on them, that all my eye doth meet
> Is mist and crag, not only on this height,
> But in the world of thought and mental might.
>
> 'Read me a lesson, Muse, and speak it loud'

But nature is interpreted in many other ways too. It is often linked
with the poet's search for identity, as in the above example from

Keats. Typically, this relates the poet's loss of Christian faith with his personal quest for something genuinely spiritual. For Keats himself, nature is also frequently manifested in beauty and time, with his special perception of 'beauty', the sublime dimension of being, beyond time and mortality. As we have also seen, his verse regularly dwells on the theme of time: its passing, a season or a moment, mortal or natural beauty contrasting with the eternity of immortal beauty (as in 'Ode to a Nightingale' and in the Hyperion poems).

The Imagination

To see such profound matter in nature requires more than just the passive observation of a landscape, of course. Wordsworth observed in detail the cyclical process by which nature tutors the mind before it becomes fully sensitive to nature. For Wordsworth, Keats, and the Romantics as a whole, a crucial element in the process is the imagination, one of the principal distinguishing marks of their poetry.

In fact if there is one point in which Romanticism differed from its antecedent it was in the prominence given to the imagination. The critic M. H. Abrams has suggested that the change from the eighteenth century to the nineteenth century is epitomised by a switch from the mimetic conception of the imagination towards the expressive; in other words, away from merely imitating faithfully what was observed and towards dynamically formulating a personal interpretation of it.

For William Blake (1757–1827) especially, and the Romantics that followed him, the imagination is never objective, like a photographic plate, but always subjective and active. Uniquely the Romantics see their world with a special sort of vision that allows them to look beyond the immediate reality of physical surfaces into the internal, intrinsic truth, to what Keats called the 'truth of imagination'. Which does not necessarily mean that they lost touch with reality, but it does mean that the external world was only the starting point for the exploration of reality through the imagination; as Wordsworth wrote,

> While with an eye made quiet by the power
> Of harmony, and the deep power of joy,
>   We see into the life of things.
> ('Lines Composed a Few Miles above Tintern Abbey', lines 47–9)

The Romantics were indeed acutely aware of the gulf between the outer, everyday world of appearances and the inner, esoteric realm of immortal truths of goodness and beauty, a realm accessible only through the imagination.

Wordsworth described poetry as 'works of imagination and sentiment', while Keats claimed simply, 'I describe what I imagine' (letter to George, 18 September 1819). In a letter already cited, Keats reproaches his friend Benjamin Bailey on his objections to the reliability of the imagination, asserting instead that,

> I am certain of nothing but of the holiness of the Heart's affections and the truth of the Imagination – What the imagination seizes as Beauty must be truth – whether it existed before or not.... The Imagination can be compared to Adam's dream – he awoke and found it truth.
>
> (22 November 1817)

The point is reflected in action in his 'Ode on a Grecian Urn' and also in *Endymion*, where he links this truth with joy,

> Wherein lies happiness? In that which becks
> Our ready minds to fellowship divine,
> A fellowship with essence.
>
> (I.777–81)

Coleridge, who gave the early Romantics much of their philosophical backbone, made an important distinction between the 'vital' imagination and the 'idle' fancy.

> The primary imagination I hold to be the living power and prime agent of all human perception, and as a repetition in the finite mind of the eternal act of creation in the infinite I AM.... It is essentially *vital*... Fancy, on the contrary, has no other counters to play with, but fixities and definites. The Fancy is indeed no other than a mode of memory emancipated from the order of time and space.
>
> (*Biographia Literaria*, chapter 13)

The point Coleridge is seeking to make here, I think, is that the imagination is active (he stresses the word 'vital'), a shaping force, drawing together images for unity of effect. Fancy on the other hand is passive, less a force for creativity than merely for idle day-dreaming (as it is in Keats's poem 'Fancy'). The imagination for Coleridge directs and leads, asserts and controls towards the end of creativity.

So what we have are two distinct, but nevertheless integrated, aspects to the Romantic imagination: on the one hand it is *insight*, opening into that truth beyond the immediate surfaces in the world, and on the other, it is the active genius of the artistic mind to *create* anew, forging the symbolic truths of this insight into artistic creations. And the imagination has the power to unlock new areas of interest. Hand in hand with the 'discovery' of the imagination, the Romantic period sees a growth in the non-rational as a legitimate realm for literature: this includes subjects such as the dream, the fantasy-macabre, sexually charged settings of evil and danger, the Gothic, the supernatural, and the past (especially the medieval period).

Keats himself was foremost among those taking a serious interest in medievalism, or 'Gothic' as we have seen in *Isabella* and *The Eve of St Agnes*. Coleridge too attempted something similar in his narrative *Christabel*. In the field of the novel, Walter Scott (1771–1832) had mined a rich Gothic vein with his historical novels, while Jane Austen's *Northanger Abbey* attempts to satirise the fashion. But perhaps the most striking of poets who sought to recapture or at least redraft the medieval past is Thomas Chatterton (1752–70), whose short, tragic life became the archetype of the Romantic tragic genius. Although he died (probably by suicide) before the age of 18 his poetic output was both prolific and dazzling. He had set out to meticulously pastiche a medieval style in a series of satirical 'forged' verses, though these are now regarded as brilliant productions in their own right. Keats in particular was deeply inspired by Chatterton, describing him as 'the purest writer in the English Language' and dedicating *Endymion* to his memory. He also emulated his pastiche with some Chaucerian lines in *The Eve of St Mark*.

Dreams too were an adjunct to the new cult of the imagination. The appeal of dreams as a subject for the Romantics lies chiefly in that they focus on the consciousness (and what today we would call the subconscious). In this dream-realm they discovered the psyche as a mental theatre in its re-shaping of the past – and the past as an element of memory also opened up a new interest in the theme of childhood. At the same time, because dreams can operate in the realm of symbols, they became most apt as poetic subject matter *per se*, especially with their visionary associations, and these are discussed below.

Keats himself uses dream extensively to probe the nature of reality, namely in the relationship between what is physically real (senses) and what is ideal (Platonist truth, beyond the senses). Indeed he often ventures to probe how the imagination connects both of these realms, for instance in 'Ode to a Nightingale' ('Was it a vision or a waking dream?') and in *Lamia*:

> It was no dream; or say a dream it was,
> Real are the dreams of the Gods, and smoothly pass
> Their pleasures in a long immortal dream.
>
> (*Lamia*, I.126–8)

But even fanatics 'have their dreams'. Like Keats, Shelley was very much attracted to this visionary aspect. *Alastor* explores this area of dream-life, for it is in a dream that the young poet of the story sees, loves, and enjoys – though he is ultimately disappointed.

In addition, dream figures strongly in Romantic poetry simply in terms of theme and setting and is often associated with escape – as we have seen repeatedly in Keats. It represents an alternative world for the Romantic poetic, exciting, mysterious in operation, the antithesis of the mechanical world of rationality and everyday reality. It is a world made complex and multi-layered by the action of symbolism, continually offering fresh possibilities of interpretation. In fact dream in its creative function closely parallels the mysterious processes of art itself, enigmatic, occult, unpredictable, evanescent.

But dreams had other attractions. They can express, metaphorically, the mysterious or blissful nature of experience – or simply the uncertainties of existence. At the same time, they may represent the world of the spirit, a quasi-religious province – which is also important when we consider the fact that most of the Romantic poets abandoned conventional Christianity (though they did continue to use the diction of Christianity; for instance, the words 'holy' and the 'soul' occur repeatedly).

Feeling

As we have seen, the decline of Neo-Classicism was in part due to its neglect of key areas of human interest. It was widely held that, as Alexander Pope claimed, 'Reason alone countervails all the other faculties' (*An Essay on Man*, 1732–4). Reason, in holding all other faculties under firm restraint, suppresses such treasonable elements as the imagination and the feelings, regarding them as capricious and volatile. The Enlightenment view was that the feelings had to be drilled or trained out of the everyday life, so that emotional responses to such events as bereavement, hardship, and the splendours of nature were to be stifled or transmuted through set social rituals and clichéd manners.

Alternatively, the newly awakened interest in the vitality of nature aroused interest in fresh attitudes to nature; for instance its ability to draw out hidden emotions and its powers of moral education, following the lead of Rousseau and Wordsworth. Thus the psychology of mankind and the mysteries of the outer world could be explored and united through the emotions or 'sensibilities'. The emotions, working through the imagination, could become the gateway to the enigmatic power of nature itself.

So when Wordsworth ecstatically declares,

> My heart leaps up when I behold
>   A rainbow in the sky:
> So was it when my life began;
> So is it now I am a man....

'My heart leaps up...'

his intense feelings are a response to the spectacular phenomenon of the rainbow, of course, but also to the mysterious symbolic effect of the rainbow, uniting his adulthood with his youth.

This expansion in focus can readily be seen in Keats's letters too. Even a cursory reading reveals what free emotional expression was typical – at least for the new generation. These are mapped out graphically on the page by outbreaks of euphoric 'O', and the spate of exclamation marks. Shelley's work too helped to fill the vacuum created by the shift away from rationalism, though we are now less likely to go along with some of the nebulous experiences in which his emotions are generated.

As we might anticipate, the Tory literary magazines were not eager to embrace this new cultural paradigm. *Blackwood's* and *The Quarterly Review* stubbornly defended traditional rationalism against the revolutionary spirit, sometimes brutally, as in the case of *Endymion*. Blake too, who associated strong emotions with a healthy mind, was an early object of their venom while Wordsworth and Coleridge's stress on compassion also made them prime targets.

Wordsworth set the keynote for the period in his famous preface to the 1802 edition of *Lyrical Ballads*:

> For all good poetry is the spontaneous overflow of powerful feelings.

And because he believed that rural people most freely expressed their feelings then they and their environment were the most appropriate subjects for poetry. In the same paragraph he goes on to clarify this view by saying that while all good verse begins in the outflow of feeling it would not be good if it contained feelings exclusively: hence emotion ought to come under the supervision of thought. Later in life, when Coleridge reflected on what had made Keats's poetry so great, he concluded that it was 'the union of deep feeling with profound thought': in other words, deeply felt emotions harnessed and shaped by the creative power of the Imagination.

The Writer

> *... sure a poet is a sage,*
> *A humanist, physician to all men ...*
>
> (*The Fall of Hyperion*, I.189–90)

Having examined the attitude of Romantic poets towards nature, imagination and feeling, we need to turn to their attitude about themselves: how did they view the role and position of the poet and of poetry and what, if any, was the poet's special function?

In *A Defence of Poetry* Shelley wrote:

> Poets, according to the circumstances of the age and nation in which they appeared were called, in the earlier epochs of the world, legislators or prophets: a poet essentially comprises and unites both these characters .... A poet participates in the eternal, the infinite and the one.

Clearly Shelley sees the role of the poet as a double one: possessing the powers of a seer or prophet while at the same time acknowledging moral responsibility for them. Both of these features devolve upon the important idea in the final sentence in this quotation: that poets have a special genius for seeing behind or beyond everyday reality into some abstract, perhaps sacred realm of immortal truth.

It is a concept of the poet which echoes that outlined by Blake in his statement 'The Nature of my Work is Visionary or Imaginative .... This World of Imagination is the World of Eternity' (*Vision of the Last Judgement*). Blake is also a model of the new spirit of individualism in terms of wisdom and morality, in contrast to the rigid conformities of the eighteenth century. To a great extent Blake had withdrawn from the social context of polite London society (and was in turn rejected by it) and this enabled him to explore more fully the visionary aspects of his work. We have already noted the great emphasis that Blake placed on the full expression of the emotional life, and, as herald of the new age, he also experimented in the realms of the imagination and the unconscious (frequently in hallucinations). He began to turn his attention towards new spheres of interest such as the primitive and childhood, investing them with integrity and mystique.

Coleridge took this even further, regarding the poet as a deity, a demi-god (cf. Keats's 'To see as a God sees'). And again it was in terms of the imagination that he envisioned this idea. Since the imagination is active and, above all, creative, the artist re-enacts the role of God, the creator of the universe, and like many fellow

Romantics, he often used religious diction for the phenomena of poetic creativity.

Like Keats and Shelley, Coleridge had been influenced by the school of philosophy known as 'idealism' (or Neo-Platonism), which stressed the notion of seeing beyond this world of material objects into a transcendental zone of truth. In this way these poets also affirmed the role of subjective knowledge; in other words, emphasising the individual as the source of his or her own truths, rather than simply trusting to the received and 'established' truths which society passed down to them.

Blake also took this line. He referred to Romantic knowledge as seeing 'through the eye', implying both an active and subjective faculty, which he contrasted with seeing 'with the eye', the passive and (ostensibly) objective method of Newtonian science. He took the idea further than most of the Romantic poets by conceiving the external world as actually *created* through the workings of the mind, operating fully through the imagination and its accumulated experience. While Wordsworth stops short of such an advanced position, something of the same theory is at work in his *Tintern Abbey*, quoted above.

In *Lamia* Keats defends the special place of the poet-as-visionary against the scientific rationalists by pointing out how the latter had reduced a rainbow to a 'dull catalogue' of parts, dismal and mundane,

> Philosophy will clip an Angel's wings,
> Conquer all mysteries by rule and line,
> Empty the haunted air, and gnomed mine –
> Unweave a rainbow...
>
> (*Lamia*, II.234–7)

And he also uses his idea of Negative Capability to support the visionary notion as a counter to the dispiriting commonplaces of science; only the artist can reach beyond the realm of the everyday:

> For Poesy alone can tell her dreams,
> With the fine spell of words alone can save
> Imagination...
>
> (*The Fall of Hyperion. A Dream*, I.8–10)

Typically, then, the poet is an individual who is exalted with a dual consciousness: of the senses and of the artistic imagination. And it is the mystical energy of the imagination that imbues the poet with the authority of a visionary seer. For this reason the Romantic sees himself as less concerned with producing imitations of reality than with creating his own versions of reality. In this approach, often called 'expressionism', the vital roles are carried out by emotion, imagination and symbolism. Together they coalesce within the poetic soul to draw out the archetypal essence from physical reality; or to put it more plainly, the poet first experiences the physical world, and then through his uniquely gifted imagination transforms those experiences into his private vision in the form of literature.

The Induction to *The Fall of Hyperion* reveals that Keats did not go all the way with this idea of the poet's gifted imagination. But elsewhere he shows some sympathy for it, especially in his concept of the 'vale of soul-making' (and compare *The Fall of Hyperion*, I.172). What encouraged most of the Romantic poets to see themselves as visionary is the importance they placed on two features principally: namely the high status of the imagination and the idea that the poet is gifted with extraordinary sensitivity. What interested Keats, for instance, is not just a vision of nature in itself, but of *himself* in nature; that is, concerned with understanding his own special reality or vision through the working of the imagination.

Keats thought this individualism was most extreme in the case of Wordsworth, and mocked his 'egotistical sublime', in a letter of 27 October 1818. As we have already considered, this letter goes on to make it clear that in the role of the visionary, the poet gradually becomes empty of self-identity, almost entirely refined out of existence. Under the shimmering power of the Romantic vision he becomes its medium or instrument.

Accordingly, for the Romantic there exists a constant tension between realism and idealism. And yet the very appeal of Romantic poetry arises most powerfully from the friction between the two, especially when the two sides become energised through highly charged symbolism. Thus, later Romanticism manages to accommodate both Keats's intimate affinities with realism and, at the other extreme, Shelley's visionary idealism.

As a result of these complexities, Romanticism is distinguished by an astonishing variety of poetic expressions. So much so that we really should not regard it simplistically as a narrow literary term or merely as a nostalgic experiment to catch at something of the medieval past (or even as an exclusively nineteenth-century phenomenon). It became a wholly new paradigm, a profound shift in culture, with a revolutionary new aesthetic.

Yet, while this revolution inspired a powerful upsurge in imaginative poetics it was anything but universally popular. The Romantics scandalised the literary establishment of their day with its ideals of 'good taste' – and as a result they were pilloried (as we have seen already with John Keats). This gave rise to the symbolic figure of the outcast in Romantic poetry and Keats's poetry often portrays the alienated hero (for example, the figures of Endymion, Hyperion, Isabella, and the knight-at-arms of *La Belle Dame sans Merci*, 'Alone and palely loitering'.

The Romantics are sometimes satirised by their opponents as effete or ineffectual emotionalists locked up in their private feelings. But it is worth bearing in mind that most of them shared a strong responsibility in the moral and political issues of their day. Romantic verse was often considered as, at best, perverse, and at worst seditious. Blake was strident in his defence of the poor and the uneducated, and protested against slavery, child labour and the squalor of the London slums. William Godwin and Leigh Hunt were both energetic in radical social politics, while Wordsworth's poetry is just as vivid about rural poverty as it is about haunting natural beauty. Lord Byron spoke passionately in support of unemployed Nottingham lace workers, and in later life actively campaigned for Greek independence from Turkish occupation. Shelley supported the Italian national rising and he too was a frequent pamphleteer against injustice (*The Mask of Anarchy* is an ardent response to the 'bloody Peterloo massacre' in Manchester, in 1819).

From early adulthood Keats, too, was vitally interested in contemporary politics and was staunchly republican in his affiliations. One of his earliest published poems was composed in defence of Leigh Hunt, 'shut in prison' for a denunciation of the prince regent. A lover of mankind and sociability, Keats's early inclination towards a medical career is a manifestation of his concern for the welfare of others, and though he rarely makes his poetry the rostrum for explicit political comment, it does contain a host of political references (for example, his famous denunciation of capitalist iniquity in Stanzas XIV and XV of *Isabella*).

The press, too, politicised Keats as poet. From a lower middle-class background, he was frequently the victim of the right-wing literary press, which baited him for these 'lowly' origins and dismissed his circle sneeringly as the 'Cockney School' of poetry. It may seem odd today that someone should use verse as the platform for strong political views and the fact that the Romantic poets did so attests to the vitality and enormous influence of poetry in their day. And yet about the social life they held somewhat paradoxical views. Where Blake and Keats worked in predominantly urban settings, most early Romantics often sought escape and solitude from their fellow man. Furthermore, the whole corpus of Romantic poetry reveals an uneasy marriage between its social conscience and its emphatic insistence on individualism. At the same time, the Romantics' commitment to expressionism has a tendency to blur these social realities.

Language

As we might expect, such a revolution in aesthetics required new modes of expression, a new approach to language. Most influentially, Blake and Wordsworth each advocated the style and diction of 'modern' language, as well as the adoption of everyday scenery and events. The Romantic poets also sought to make their verse lines less contorted, adopting as much as possible the rhythms of conversational English.

There is not space here to discuss the new modes at length but it is worthwhile to compare the two following extracts to give some idea of the differences. The first was written by Alexander Pope in 1735, and the second by John Keats in 1819–20. Note how in the Pope each line contains a separate and complete thought, whereas in the Keats we see the thoughts run more naturally from one line over into the next in enjambement. Keats's poem flows more easily, in a more modern idiom, and note too the differences in diction and word order.

> Ladies, like variegated Tulips, show,
> 'Tis to their Changes half their Charms we owe;
> Their happy Spots the nice admirer take,
> Fine by defect, and delicately weak.
>
> ('An Epistle to a Lady', 41–4)

> It was the custom then to bring away
> The bride from home at blushing shut of day,
> Veiled, in a chariot, heralded along
> By strewn flowers...
>
> (*Lamia*, II.106–9)

In this respect, compare the end-stopped lines of Keats's 'Imitation of Spenser' of 1814 with *The Fall of Hyperion*, written five years later. But not all of the Romantics, nor all of their verse, used the contemporary idiom. Byron preferred to perpetuate eighteenth-century styles, while Coleridge and Keats also occasionally experimented with poetic diction and archaic forms of language, most notably medieval and Miltonic styles.

To some extent the poet's use of language was determined by his imaginative vision or by his view of himself as a prophet-figure. This can mean that the poet is less interested in the construction of explicit or definitive statements, and more with the creation of symbolic effects and evocative moods. Moreover, the Romantics are often deeply concerned with the complexities of nature, its subtle and mysterious energies, and their language usually conveys shadowy and uniquely individualistic impressions, making full use of figurative diction.

Two key ways in which this concern is manifested in Romantic poetry are the use of symbol and the lyric form. As we have noted already, the symbol is a major device in the Romantics' handling of imaginative visions of nature and humanity. One of their shared characteristics is the constant awareness of the transcendental, that is, the *other* world, the divine reality lying within or beyond mundane physical objects (for an example, examine again Keats's 'Ode on a Grecian Urn'). And the symbol is the poet's way of making this spiritual presence become almost palpable. Typical Romantic symbols are the harp and song (as the poet's labours or simply as poetry itself), the rose (as beauty), the soul (sensitivity and receptiveness to impressions), mountains (ancient time), fountains and rivers (as the regenerative power of nature).

The new interest in nature and in the authentic expression of emotional responses to it also led to the widespread adoption of the lyric verse form. Originally a poem designed to be sung, the lyric has come to mean any short poem presenting intimate thoughts and feelings, usually with rich musical resonances; it includes the ballad as well as the ode and the sonnet. Thus, because of the newly awoken interest in the imagination and the focus on the individual, the lyric became the natural vehicle for personal reflection. And while the Romantic poets experimented with practically all verse forms (including verse dramas) the lyric became the quintessentially Romantic mode. Its flexible, organic form suited well the need to express profound responses to experience.

All of the poets under consideration explored the diverse manifestations of the lyric; from Blake's *Songs of Innocence and Experience*, through Wordsworth and Coleridge's *Lyrical Ballads*, to the great mature odes of Shelley and Keats. Even Byron, who in many respects was happy to continue in the received style and wry ironies of the eighteenth century and who was most at home with epic narratives, was sometimes moved to smaller-scale intimacies.

Romanticism after Keats

By the time of Keats's death in 1821 Romanticism had become firmly established. What had begun as a reaction to Neo-Classicism became a significant force in its own right, and its effects are still with us – in fact many would say that we are still living in the tail of Romanticism's comet.

In this chapter I have tried to argue that Romanticism evolved into something larger than a literary movement, into a wide cultural outlook. Indeed, evidence of its continued presence in Western culture today is not difficult to find; for example, a dynamic if exploited youth culture, individualism in politics and lifestyles, bohemianism in art, a fascination with the supernatural and an interest in alternative wisdoms (in medicine, philosophy and music, among other things). All of these owe much in their attitudes to Romantic origins.

And Keats's own reputation? There is no doubt that it has continued to grow – so much so that he has, of course, fulfilled his hope to be 'among the English poets'. In fact in the period since his death his fame has rarely wavered and his inspiration in British literature has been remarkably pervasive.

The Victorian poet Tennyson was among the first of his disciples. His verse contains unmistakable echoes of Keats's musicality, though his tone is invariably moralistic and he never quite achieves Keats's subtle wit or his intensity of vision. Arnold and Swinburne were very much influenced by Keats's sensibilities and the Pre-Raphaelite movement took a large measure of its inspiration as well as its material from *The Eve of St Agnes* and *La Belle Dame*. Another great Victorian, Gerard Manley Hopkins, was an open admirer of Keats and his lyricism has strong affinities with the 'great odes'. Although written from the perspective of deep religious conviction, Hopkins's poetry also often displays the same exhilarating 'gusto' as Keats's and he has the same verbal agility. Most of these points can equally apply to the Great War poet Wilfred Owen, another great admirer of Keats, though it would be fair to say that neither Owen nor Hopkins achieve either the range or versatility of their mentor.

By the beginning of the twentieth century Keats's unique poetic lyricism had already become an intrinsic presence in British poetry. His 'eternal whispering' has been an inspirational voice for a long tradition of writers of widely varying poetic backgrounds and diverse perspectives, ranging from English and Celtic poets such as Owen, W. B. Yeats and Dylan Thomas to international voices as those of Joseph Brodsky, Derek Walcott and Seamus Heaney. There are no signs either that his 'fame to nothingness do sink', or is likely to.

8

Some Critical Approaches to Keats's Writing

At the end of the previous chapter I indicated that Keats's reputation has gradually become established in the galaxy of great English poets. His work has been subject to (and sometimes victim of) modulations in literary opinion and literary theory. These modulations have focused on differing elements in the verse as succeeding generations have opened it up to new viewpoints and theoretical positions. To get some idea of the changing critical landscape, I would like to look in brief at the views of four influential critics, each from a different period, noting the characteristic features of these views. They are Matthew Arnold, H. W. Garrod, F. R. Leavis, and Susan J. Wolfson.

Matthew Arnold (1822–88)

Matthew Arnold towers as one of the giants of late Victorian letters and was highly influential on the practice of literary criticism. Because literary study was a component of his wider social and cultural philosophy, it will be useful to begin by getting a feel for his general intellectual attitude.

The son of the famous Thomas Arnold, headmaster of Rugby, he was himself greatly interested in education systems and eventually became Inspector of Schools. He had a fascination with the workings of society in general, its classes, religious beliefs and intellectual attitudes and values, in particular the role of 'culture' in the intellectual life of a community. In the early part of his life he was also a reasonably popular poet: 'Dover Beach' and two other elegiac pieces, 'The Scholar Gypsy' and 'Thyrsis', are his most well-known, and exhibit a strong Keatsian influence.

'Dover Beach' is a beautiful lyric, balancing feeling and intellect, and fusing deep personal feelings with a sincere, earnest concern for social attitudes. In particular, it speaks of a wistfulness over what he thought was the decline of religious faith in contemporary society. This preoccupation with the intellectual life found expression increasingly through prose and even before he was appointed to the Chair of Poetry at Oxford University in 1857 he had begun to turn from composing to criticism. Prose became his chief literary medium and his two most influential essays are probably 'The Function of Criticism at the Present Time', which first appeared in1865, and his book *Culture and Anarchy*, first published in 1869. In the former, he held that the literary creativity of a society can flourish at its most vigorous best when it emerges from and is nourished by a healthy intellectual life. In other words, the function of 'criticism' is to underpin the artistic life by feeding into it and into society in general a stock of inspirational ideas. As a result, he believed that the Romantic poets were weakened by the absence of a thoroughgoing intellectual and spiritual basis (though he himself seems to have come strongly under the influence of Coleridge's philosophy).

To achieve its function, criticism had to become, he believed, dispassionate, and free of 'ulterior, political, practical considerations' (though, of course, his own criticism was just as much a reflection of his deeply held convictions and Romantic preconceptions).

Broadening this view, he argued that criticism, in this intellectual drift, could and should be applied to society in general as well as to art; in fact as Arnold himself put it, 'poetry is the criticism of life'. The ideas germinated in the 1869 essay blossomed years later in his liveliest and most widely known book, *Culture and Anarchy*. Briefly, the main thrust of his thesis is that given the rise of democracy and increasing freedom (together with a decline in religious faith), unrestrained individualism is likely to sink into anarchy unless it submits itself to a more wide-ranging social responsibility. The function of culture is to promote and disseminate a deeper appreciation of social issues: in other words, education's vital role lies in encouraging social cohesion.

However, the essay I want to look at in more detail is one on Keats, which first appeared in 1880 as the preface to a selection of Keats's poems (reprinted in Arnold's *Essays in Criticism: Second Series*, in 1888). Prior to writing this well-known essay Arnold had occasionally referred to Keats in his letters, where he set out his belief that Keats had 'a very high gift' but was over-ambitious and paid too much attention to 'expression', which Arnold usually held to be less important than subject matter. He thought Shakespeare and Milton masters of both whereas Keats and Shelley managed only to create some superficial features of rhetoric and style, especially exuberance and richness. Arnold tried to argue that, because Shakespeare was so powerful a writer, 'lesser' poets including Keats, Shelley and Browning had become blinded by the charm of his manner. Taking *Isabella; or, The Pot of Basil* as example, he conceded (if that is the right word) that it was a 'perfect treasure-house of graceful and felicitous words and phrases' which surprise and thrill the reader in almost every stanza, and yet the whole was feeble and loose in construction:

> although undoubtedly there blows through it the breath of genius, [it] is yet as a whole so utterly incoherent, as not strictly to meet the name of a poem at all.

One of the key themes running through Arnold's criticism is that a good work of art reveals 'character'; that is, it reveals or affirms what Arnold regards as acceptable moral facets in the writer. This view is also strongly evident in his essays on Keats in *Essays in Criticism: Second Series*. He sets up two models of poets who demonstrate the 'right' properties and virtues, namely John Milton and Shakespeare, and begins by quoting Milton's axiom that poetry should be 'simple, sensuous, impassioned'. In judging Keats as a poet Arnold accepts that he is 'abundantly and enchantingly sensuous' but asks if he were anything more than this? Behind the quotation from Milton lie the properties Arnold expects to find in a poet: simplicity of style, a feeling for sensuous beauty, but also a firm intellectual dimension. Arnold is really asking, Was Keats anything more than a flashy sensationalist full of rich sounding music?

The answer to his question then follows in two main parts; first he attacks Keats the man and then in the second part he salvages from his picture some redeeming features about the poet. He begins his assault on Keats's character by quoting the opinions of the poet's friends as well as Keats's own letters, to put forward a view of him as a decadent man lacking the necessary qualities of 'character' and self-control, a hedonistic sensualist, one who as 'passion's slave' abandoned 'all reticence and all dignity'. Regarding his 'love letters' to Fanny Brawne, where we might see these as beautifully tender, humane but essentially private, Arnold finds them as proof of Keats's lowly social caste, 'the sort of love-letter of a surgeon's apprentice...badly bred and badly trained'. Poets were expected to come of the upper middle class, or at least to affirm the lofty values of it!

In spite of the 'unwholesome' and 'questionable' nature of the man, Arnold detects signs of 'character and virtue', which are the true marks of a 'very great poet'. However, he regards these as more obvious in Keats's promise than in the actual performance, the verse itself. So Keats fails to convince on social and moral grounds and on a third too – his manliness and courage are also doubtful, a 'charge' which perpetuates the nineteenth-century accusation that Keats's work was essentially 'feminine'. Having said this, Arnold does admire some of the virtues apparent in his writing: his strong sense of a community among friends, a self-critical awareness of the limitations in his early poetry, and evidence of artistic integrity. He concludes this section of his article by saying (somewhat incongruously) that 'Keats had flint and iron in him...he had character.'

The second section begins to redeem Keats by noting his lucidity and detecting something of a moral dimension (recalling Arnold's love of 'simple' unadorned poetry),

> But indeed nothing is more remarkable in Keats than his clear sightedness, his lucidity; and lucidity is in itself akin to character and severe work.

(page 113)

The reference to 'severe work' here prepares for a more difficult hurdle that Arnold has to leap across. Beneath Keats's sensuous music and his plea for a 'Life of Sensations' he discovers a faint voice of earnestness, implicit in his shared admiration of Milton. This implies that Keats had after all realised that the best sort of poetry *ought* to embody a rational and intellectual dimension (points which he had rejected in the early verse and letters). He records that Keats had an addiction to 'the best sort of poetry' but is perplexed at why this addiction left him cold. Arnold's conclusion is that Keats's 'feel' matters less than his 'know'.

We get the strong impression that in spite of the fact that Keats's poetry does not meet the strict conditions for the 'best' or the 'right' sort of poetry, Arnold desperately seeks to make out a case for advancing it to these realms. To achieve this and to prove Keats's worth, Arnold seizes on the very element that ought to disbar him:

> The truth is that 'the yearning passion for the Beautiful,' which was with Keats, as he himself truly says, the master-passion, is not a passion of the sensuous or sentimental man, is not a passion of the sensuous or sentimental poet. It is an intellectual and spiritual passion.
> (115)

After all, Arnold concludes, Keats was acutely passionate about beauty not as a 'sensuous weakling', a sentimental hedonist, but out of intellectual inquiry. For Arnold this detected strain is what rescues Keats, advances him to the top echelon of great English poets, and at last 'a dignity and a glory shed gleams over his life'.

Arnold has great sympathy for Keats's struggle against the 'consuming disease' of tuberculosis ('throttling and unmanning', he says early on). However, this is not from some sentimental conception of the tragic poet but something more rationalistic. He strongly believes that it was the inception of his fatal illness that robbed Keats of the chance to refine the intellectual implications of beauty in its special relationship with truth (hinted at in *Endymion* as well as 'Ode on a Grecian Urn'). And further, Arnold actually believes this potential intellectual capacity, together with the great 'natural magic' of the poetry (what Keats himself calls 'gusto' and by which Arnold probably also means something like earnest endeavour), raises Keats to the same rank of genius as Shakespeare. He concludes his essay by writing that while the shorter poems are 'perfect', the longer ones are unsuccessful, the reason being that Keats's poetic sense of control ('architectronics') as well as his 'power of moral interpretation' were not, he believes, fully ripened.

The strengths and weaknesses of Arnold's approach are readily apparent to anyone reading the essay. He wishes fervently to elevate Keats's verse to that level of greatness they deserve but his rigid Victorian morals find something in Keats the man that irks him. This is probably on account of the received version he had of him rather than the actuality, so he seeks to praise Keats on technical grounds such as lucidity, self-criticism, and the 'seriousness' of his project.

On the other hand, he slams Keats for chiefly irrelevant aspects – his sensuality in the love letters and for the idea that he came from the wrong class. At the heart of Arnold's own weakness is his tendency to ignore the texts. Today we would be more likely to focus on the texts themselves, if we wished to highlight them, rather than on the private life of the writer. He very rarely offers a detailed, close analysis of the poetry, tending instead to generalise and over-simplify, with a personalised overview based on 'taste' (though, unusually for a Victorian critic, he makes some effort to place his comments on a rational foundation).

He speaks too with a tone of great authority. Sometimes quite perfunctory, he hands down verdicts and sentences in high, judicial overtones. Compared with the twenty-first century, he is profoundly certain of his values and his mission, as well as of the absolute order of his universe (he has no doubts either in the efficacy of language as a medium for precise communication). As such he has a classical view of art and poetry in that before something can be admitted to the status of literature it *ought* to embody specific prescribed properties and reach a certain standard in them; for example, it should project 'correct' moral qualities and conform to ideals of artistic control. In these areas, Arnold clearly believes that Keats fell short – but only just.

H. W. Garrod (1878–1960)

Like Arnold, H. W. Garrod was an academic and he too held the Chair of Poetry at Oxford University. Garrod is well known as the first modern editor of Keats's verse, which he collected and established on scholarly principles in 1939 as *The Poetical Works of John Keats*.

However, the book I would like to examine is Garrod's extended critical essay, titled simply *Keats* and first published in 1926, the edition I have used here. His essay – about half of which was delivered as lectures – appeared at a time when scholarly interest in the poet was becoming more serious, raising Keats into the canon of English literature. To a large extent Garrod's book is a highly organised response to Arnold's thesis that Keats can be taken ser-iously only when his work is more than merely 'feel' or 'sensuous-ness' and that Keats died before he was able to realise his potential to fuse together feel and philosophy in his poetry. Arnold had by and large set the agenda for the discussion.

The plan of Garrod's essay is quite simple; he examines the poems in turn, chronologically, to develop his thesis, except that about half its 137 pages deal with the 'great Odes', and are placed at the end as the crown of Keats's achievement.

We do not read poetry with sufficient 'attention', he claims, or 'take pains' over it. This is important because by these terms he really means reading with attention to detail, to the actual and individual words. So already this is a major difference from Arnold. Garrod though is interested only in a certain type of poetry: 'There is a great deal of poetry in the world not worth reading' (page 9). This is the opening sentence, and while in its day it might have attracted an approving ripple of laughter it points to the prescriptive ideas of a literary elite, an exclusive sort of club to which poetry with the correct attributes may be admitted. Garrod never actually makes clear what qualifies as 'poetry worth reading' but by the end some of these attributes are at least implicit.

Anyway, Keats's poetry *is* of the right sort. There is also a right, or ideal, sort of reader – one who has diligently trained him/herself to become 'disinterested' (an idea borrowed from Keats), meaning not distracted by moralising considerations. This too conflicts with

Arnold's explicitly moral attitude as does the idea that a critic should be trained in particular academic skills and principles. To give extra support to his argument he reminds us that Keats himself was a 'student of his art' in spite of being surrounded by plentiful examples of 'bad poetry' (12).

However, in spite of this latter, quite vague concept, Garrod now begins to focus more sharply on Keats himself. His starting point in this section of his essay is Sydney Colvin's statement that Keats's poetry always faces up to the realistic horrors of life. Garrod agrees, while adding that his best poetry is that which also explores a world of idealism steered by the active Imagination (not the passive, dreaming Fancy or pure fantasy):

> Only in that world…does Keats move easily, with the divine ease of poetry.
>
> (27)

In other words, Keats produces his best poetry when it fuses reality with an imaginative ideal world. Garrod believes that Keats preferred to remain with 'poetry of reality', eschewing this 'world of idealism', and that Keats thought the remedy was to dabble in the politics of republicanism, more evident in his early verse. He brands Keats's republican politics as 'strongly tinged with what we call pacifism' (25). This again perpetuates the nineteenth-century reproach that there was something weak, unmanly or 'feminine' about Keats (remember that in 1926, in the aftermath of the First World War, 'pacifist' was still a term of abuse). Instead of 'republicanism' Garrod is convinced that Keats's most germane kind of reality, from which his best poetry draws its strength, is suffering, and to support this view cites *The Fall of Hyperion*. But he does not intend everyday, routine suffering but something more metaphysical and noble. He is not clear on what this is but he hints that such suffering is an exquisite pain of the 'five senses', akin to the poetic truth discovered by Wordsworth and Coleridge in *Lyrical Ballads* and which made them great revolutionaries (30–2).

On this issue of suffering he especially takes Matthew Arnold to task. Where Arnold believed that the proper fulfilment of Keats's

brilliant promise was dashed by his early death, Garrod is convinced
that had he lived longer he would have wasted it with more of the
shallow sensuous luxury into which he was sometimes distracted
(29). Garrod also detects in Keats another source of weakness: that
he could not finally decide between, on the one hand, verse of the
senses or emotions and, on the other, that of the mind (and politics),
and spent his poetic career vacillating between the two. Arnold's
opinion, of course, was that the poetry of the mind was Keats's best.

Garrod's analysis is, naturally, very much 'of its time'. Running
through his essay is an implicit idea that as well as *judging* Keats's
actual output our task as critics is to try to excavate the writer's
intentions. To do this, we need to look at the writer's letters, comments
of his friends, as well as at biographies and the internal evidence
within the poetry itself. The reader must adjust himself or herself to
the poem in order to discover the authorial meaning, which is then
authoritative too. It is less a matter of interpretation and what the
reader brings to the text than of deciphering the single truth or truths
of the text. In order to achieve this, Garrod quotes copiously from
Keats's letters and the biographies, aiming to find support for his
prior hypothesis. However, this is a step forward, I think, from
Arnold's highly personal approach in which we get the strong impression that he wished to bend Keats's verse to suit the needs of his
own prior ideological purposes. Another advance is that Garrod is
careful to seek precise evidential facts to support his evaluation.

Between them Arnold and Garrod help to set the agenda for
literary discussion of Keats's *oeuvre* throughout the first half of the
twentieth century. As leaders of the dominant force in literary theory
they, and others in the same liberal tradition, determine how readers
should conceive of what makes 'good' poetry and what the function
of criticism as well as of poetry ought to be. Which is not to say that
Arnold and Garrod agree on their preferences with regards to Keats.
On *Isabella*, while Arnold abjures its sensuous luxuries, its 'feel',
Garrod acclaims it as

> a piece full of his *characteristic* perfections ... a piece with as little
> promise, or threat, of philosophical powers as could be conceived.
>
> (44)

The very opposite in fact. Garrod also celebrates *The Eve of St Agnes* for springing from the 'same exquisite sense of the luxuries' as *Isabella.*

However, Garrod generally rates Keats's narrative poems quite low – preferring to call them works of 'continuous writing'. Drama and narrative, he feels, are alien to Keats's perfect poetry, which, he asserts, is 'the lyric of personal passion' (58). So, although many critics would regard *Lamia* as appearing at the height of Keats's creative powers, Garrod laments its 'tolerable poetry' (63), considers it 'somewhat overrated' (61), and is also troubled by its moral (63). On the other hand he does (incongruously, since it includes four narrative poems) acclaim the 1820 volume of *Poems* as the 'most marvellous' of all the world's books, each poem 'in its kind, a masterpiece' – but adds in the same breath, 'I do not say the greatest' (64).

Garrod reserves his brightest garlands for the odes, the 'great Odes'. In terms of Keats's whole work they are his apotheosis, the perfection of what he was meant to be, a 'poet of lyrical feeling'. Significantly, it is at the start of his erudite analysis of the odes that Garrod gives some idea of what he sees as the point of literary criticism, almost *sotto voce*: admiration and approval of texts should be backed up by scholarly, rational analysis,

> they deserve to call forth in us some better element than our faculty for gush.
>
> (74)

Garrod's reticence on this point, the purpose or aim or even practice of criticism, is not unusual. Only relatively recently has Literary Studies seriously confronted itself over what questions it does or should answer, and the jury is very much still out.

In more general terms, Garrod projects a very strong awareness of his building on the work of others, especially Matthew Arnold. Garrod is also aware that his submission is part of a dialogue (though the dialogue takes place within a relatively exclusive circle). Without doubt his mode of analysis refines the practices of criticism beyond Arnold's personal and more visceral adjudications and, overall, his method is much more discriminatory. For instance, where Arnold writes of Keats's poetry, Garrod refers to Keats as a lyric, narrative, dramatic, philosophical, or feeling poet – so instead of one we have five or more Keats.

Perhaps one of the most manifest differences between the two men and their critical attitudes is in the support material. Arnold supports his views with hardly any reference to the texts of Keats, whereas by comparison Garrod's citations are copious. Garrod is of course most famous for his editing of *The Poetical Works* and he uses the full panoply of his scholarly research to back up his judgements with quotations and references to individual works. Frequently too, he makes cross-references and comparisons between poems and often brings in points of contact with other Romantic poets.

Another sign of his discriminating approach is that Garrod adopts or adapts a range of literary technical terms (e.g. heptasyllabic, Pindarics, dixaines, apostrophe), much of them deriving from the study of Classics. No bibliography is provided but other scholarly furniture has appeared, such as detailed footnotes and academic citations or referencing. We get the feeling that the infant subject of 'English Literature' is at last emerging from its dark chrysalis, even if its ultimate shape is somewhat pre-ordained rather than free to develop.

At the same time, he shares with Arnold a disciplined, organised methodology towards this new discipline. I have mentioned Garrod's largely chronological plan, in which he sets out to trace the development of Keats's intended views on poetry, especially in the 'feel' versus 'philosophy' dispute. In this diachronic approach he also sets out to discover the compositional sequence of the poems (again from external as well as internal evidence) as part of his other aim of tracing developments in the poet's technique (this is especially evident in his discussion of the major odes). To this end, Garrod attempts to discover changes in Keats's moods, health and relationships and as a result he interestingly reads the individual poems through Keats's own commentaries in the letters – though he never allows Keats to dictate the terms of his analysis.

His most detailed and incisive technical scrutiny is dedicated to the 'great Odes'. He looks in fine detail at Keats's formal innovations, drawing on the work of Shakespeare, Petrarch, Spenser and Dryden, and links these with developments in theme. Indeed, Garrod gives a convincing argument for an extremely coherent ode sequence in which form and subject are in perfect symbiosis. So detailed is Garrod's research and so meticulous is the stepping of his argument that when he weds these factual elements to his evaluation we also begin to get a glimpse of the type of approach more usually associated with the New Critics in the early part of the century, among the first to put literary studies on a firmly intellectual, and linguistic footing.

Garrod's long essay first appeared in 1925 at about the dawning of the sort of literary method with which we are familiar today: close scholarly textual exegesis based on an awareness of the transmission and implications of the writer's text. As editor of Keats's collected poetry he was aptly placed to achieve these. This said, however, his is a highly personalised view, framed inside an air of authority, speaking among like-minded people of a singular social class, culture and moral values. It is very much a personal view and because of this his critical evaluations are often vague; words such as vivid, perfect, supreme, courageous, difficult, timid, jarring and blurred are common and reflect matters of taste (where Arnold is morally prescriptive, Garrod is aesthetically prescriptive). Perhaps because of the nature of their shared backgrounds, Garrod is often evasive or imprecise – both in unpacking his terms ('imagination' is typically vague) and, importantly, in his principles of literary criticism. Talking to a coterie of colleagues and students at Oxford in the 1920s he imparts the impression that on these matters there was of course an unquestioning consensus.

F. R. Leavis (1895–1978)

In his influence and reputation F. R. Leavis is to twentieth-century literary discussion what Matthew Arnold was to the nineteenth. Both saw a vital and privileged function for literature in bolstering the life of British culture and both set out with missionary zeal to put English Literature at the forefront of British intellectual consciousness. For both critics, literary study was never merely a narrow dilettante concern but something central to the very national life itself.

Leavis's views were and still are controversial. His name stands for a particular attitude both towards what analysis should be and also towards the relationship between the reader and the writer. Most of Leavis's academic life was involved in teaching at Cambridge University and his highly stimulating 'theory' was disseminated chiefly through his many critical books and his co-editorship of *Scrutiny* as well as through his lectures and tutorials. *Scrutiny* was published for twenty-one years (1932–53) and was probably the most influential literary journal of the century. Its success and longevity were largely due to the persistence, among readers, contributors and editors, of an essential consensus on the function and direction of English literary criticism. *Scrutiny* also became something of a loosely formulated manifesto of Leavis's theory, himself its chief driving force; the emphasis was, like Arnold's, on practical analysis ('the words on the page') rather than theory, in which its chief tasks were to distinguish the proper functions of criticism; that is, recognising serious literature and deciding on the nature of a proper response to it.

Both Arnold and Leavis conceived of the role of poetry as vital in uniting the culture of British society in the face of what they regarded as a decline in the influence of spiritual values. Among Leavis's favourite authors and those of his 'great tradition' are Milton, Tennyson, Yeats, Keats, T. S. Eliot, Pope, and the novelists Dickens, Lawrence, Henry James, George Eliot and Conrad.

The essay I have chosen for discussion is from one of Leavis's early books, *Revaluation* published in 1936. The title does not refer to reflections on previous judgements of his own but to the appraisal of authors who had become accepted as part of a traditional canon of English Literature especially as it was taught in university and school. He wanted to step back and have another look at them but not to question their position so much as to place them under the scrutiny of his particular method of analysis. In other words he wished to look in detail at the works of writers such as Milton and Pope to see what it was that had led to their high reputation in specifically English culture.

The final sentence of his essay, called simply 'Keats', is revealing of this aim and is a good starting point:

Keats, as has been generally agreed, was beyond any doubt gifted to become a very great poet.

(273)

Note the confidence (some might say arrogance even) in the phrases 'generally agreed' and 'beyond any doubt' plus 'a very great poet'. But while this confidence is indicative of Leavis's attitude it was not in itself aimed at bolstering Keats's image. Instead it explains the essay's strange opening sentence, in which he points out that he has nothing new to say about him:

The excuse for writing at the present day on Keats must lie not in anything new to be said about him but in a certain timely obviousness.

(241)

Leavis has nothing to add in terms of inflating, or boosting Keats's high literary reputation but, crucially,

what a critic may still propose to himself is a sharper explicitness; a recall, that is, to strict literary criticism.

(241)

And this reveals the point of his essay, namely to apply a sharper explicitness, a more rigorous type of literary analysis than has hitherto been applied, one that pays strict attention to the words as they appear on the page. Although Leavis's essay on Keats is one of the briefest in his book it offers an excellent insight on his 'method'. The plan of his essay is approximately along these lines: (a) a critique of the traditional adulation of Keats; (b) the need to make detailed textual analysis of the poems; (c) Keats's influence on Victorian literature; (d) the central features which account for Keats's high place in the traditional literary curriculum.

Siding with Matthew Arnold (but against Garrod), Leavis agrees that the consensus is that Keats's greatness rests on his promise rather than his achievement – on the poetry that Keats 'might have written'. He cites two authors who have extolled this 'greatness' in the highest terms – John Middleton Murry and Arthur Symons – but he berates them both because he feels they merely present us with a woolly, personalised account, perpetuating received reputations with-out explaining. Instead of searching vaguely for the poet's 'soul', literary criticism should adopt a greater 'particularity' in its accounts.

In the second and longest section of the discussion, Leavis takes 'Ode to a Nightingale' and 'Ode on a Grecian Urn' to illustrate this 'particularity' of his own method. His initial purpose is to try to account for why 'Nightingale' is usually rated highest of the odes by determining how it is 'finer and more vital'. This idea of ranking poetry is a characteristic of Leavis's hierarchical approach and is a development of Garrod's assumption that there is good (or 'proper') poetry as well as bad. In a general statement Leavis proposes that what makes 'Nightingale' superior to, say, Shelley's 'To a Skylark', is that its detail reveals delicacy of touch and intensity but above all a skill in organising its different parts into a rhythmic whole. He then launches into a detailed scrutiny of these parts in context.

What follows is a running analysis with Leavis closely tracing, through the two poems, the ways in which individual words affect and alter a response to the poem as we read it. He is at pains to illustrate how one word can take up another and reinforce its associ-ations or effect, and he makes a detailed analysis of diction and syntax to bring out their subtle influence in building up an overall impression. As an example of this method he takes the word 'forlorn' in 'Nightingale' and reveals how at first it seems hackneyed, but when repeated in the final stanza it produces a strange reversal of the reader's expectations.

Throughout Leavis's essay and individual analyses the words 'con-crete', 'movement', 'direction' and 'keyword' continually reappear and the personal lexicon is indicative of both his conception of poetry and his method of its analysis. A poem is to be understood as a dynamic, fluid organism in which the power of a key word (which can be any single word in fact) may suddenly alter the direction or tone or mood of the poem as we proceed through it. And the word 'concrete' usually refers either to the material words as printed on the page or to Keats's characteristic resolve to fuse his verse with the real physical world. The fact of Keats's verse being rooted in actuality is a facet of Keats's subject matter greatly valued by Leavis but, further, it is of course one which shows a strong affinity with this critic's own critical approach.

Furthermore, this facet of actuality, which 'gives a firmer stay to fancy' (252), is one more reason why he believes Keats's verse is among the best. Although, he feels that Keats makes 'major poetry out of minor' (i.e. great poetry out of minor material), Leavis acclaims Keats's attempt to make his poetry relate to actual life as a sign of his serious endeavour.

Leavis concludes his discussion by saying that Keats's high reputation is well deserved because what qualifies him as a true poet is his ability to translate his life's experiences symbolically into art. While Leavis makes no detailed reference to events in Keats's life – there is no attempt at biographical or any other context – it is implicit in his argument that the verse is a direct and public correlative of Keats's particular experiences. Thus the verse dramatises the poet's inner life as a 'profound tragic impersonality' without self-pity, under the strict control of a 'critical intelligence' (271).

At the start of his analysis, Leavis's point of departure from previous eras is to use J. Middleton Murry and Arthur Symons as the foil to his new methods. He clearly wishes to put some distance between himself and the past, and the critics who tended to pontificate from lofty privileged towers on matters of taste. While he is quite blunt in his admonition of 'Mr Murry' and 'Mr Symons', Leavis himself can be seen as one point along a steady trend in literary criticism extending back through them, through Garrod and on to Arnold. Like Arnold and Garrod, Leavis tries to give the impression that his is an impersonal, objective analysis, using the words of the poet as his 'facts'. He also uses the same evaluative parameters in his discussion as did his predecessors, namely ideas like seriousness, moral engagement with life, connecting with actuality, and so on. All of which have a fine and noble resonance, of course, but are not particularly precise. In fact these rhetorical phrases tend to be used strategically, working as climaxes to detailed sections of analysis: for example, 'perfection attained within a limiting aestheticism' (264) and 'profound tragic impersonality' (271). It is quite a compressed style and one which gives the impression that Leavis felt that the critic ought to try to match the author in eloquence.

One important contrast with Garrod and past critics is the change in point of view here. Leavis's line of attack moves away from a consideration of the writer's intentions and towards the reader's response to the specific text under examination. He continues to see much of the commentary by way of Keats's own attitudes and aspirations but now there is a very strong attention to what these words might mean or do to 'me', the reader. For this reason, and in spite of any attempts at objectivity, Leavis's response is really that of Leavis himself – he records what the poem does for him. However, he presupposes that we are all alike as sensitive people and so each of us can expect to get a more or less similar reading of the poem. Accordingly, this assumption draws him nearer to his predecessors because his view of English culture makes him see all readers as essentially the same, deriving from an 'enlightened', liberal and unified community of educated readers, each of us bringing to the poem basically the same cultural experiences. Eventually he has an unwavering faith in the referential efficiency of language itself; namely, that words and grammar constitute a more or less stable and transparent medium – not only for the poet but also for the critic and the readers of the critic. Like Arnold and Garrod he is fully persuaded of the absolute moral and semantic stability of the language.

However, more than these other critics Leavis is also concerned with what the function of criticism should be, and even more, what its methods must be. It is, of course, prescriptive in this respect (and in respect of his expectations of literature itself). His aims are clear and by and large he conscientiously and rigorously applies these through his method. He is explicitly modest regarding the novelty of his conclusions on Keats but this seeks to disguise a sense of authority about his technique as well as the rightness of his observations. By omitting the context of Keats's history, contemporary life etc. he implies either that it does not matter or that we are already aware of it. In which case there lingers the irritating air that Leavis's dialogue is basically a measured and relatively cosy chat with like-minded chaps.

Revaluation is an early outline of Leavis's personal method but it did not vary markedly over the extent of his lifetime. His injunction to precise and detailed analysis and exegesis of the 'approved' texts had a huge influence on the practice and conduct of English Literature up to and after the Second World War. He became an icon for a type of cultural approach, one that has become undermined by wider changes in cultural attitudes, textual theories, general intellectualism and the globalisation of literary studies; slated by New Criticism.

Susan J. Wolfson

The final piece I would like to discuss is an essay by Susan J. Wolfson, 'Feminizing Keats', which first appeared in 1990 in *Critical Essays on John Keats*, edited by Hermione de Almeida. The essays in this collection are all relatively modern and approach Keats from a variety of critical directions and backgrounds. Some belong to what we might call a traditional critical viewpoint while others are distinctly post-modern in their assumptions and aims.

Post-Modernist or Post-Structuralist study has been, like Romanticism in its day, a sort of quantum revolutionary change in the way that critics regard writers and their works. Since the 1960s, Literary Studies has undergone a period of profound reappraisal. It is impossible to generalise on the nature of Post-Modernism more than to say that as a radical reappraisal of the foundations of literary criticism, all of its presuppositions, values, aims and even its texts or canon have become subject to change. Following New Criticism, modern literary study has tended to split into factions, which approach textual analysis from various theoretical positions. For example, Linguistic analyses (after Saussure and Derrida), Psychoanalytical (after Kristeva and Lacan), and Historicist/Neo-Historicist. These are only a few of the major movements or groupings which have emerged and are still emerging. In general terms the revolution in Literary Studies has been vigorously controversial, sometimes polemical, and often disruptive but it has highlighted some disproportions endemic in the discipline and has galvanised a new type of intellectualism in it.

Historicism and Neo-Historicism have sought to examine closely the context of the writer, and by 'context' is meant not only the close psycho-biography of a writer but very nearly everything, including their social class, political system, precursors, and gender. A strong sense of determinism runs through this approach, regarding the writer, his or her work, and its reception as the product of its context,

the conditions of its generation. Feminist literary study has developed
as a feature of this 'school', one of whose consequences has been a
radical readjustment of which writers and works are to be included in
the 'canon' of the subject, as well as the critical attitudes underlying
its study. In many ways feminist criticism is the epitome of Neo-
Historicism since it refuses to accept the values and strategies of a
poet, for instance, on his/her own terms, placing texts within the
wider symbolic and ideological tensions of their day (and ours, for
that matter). On a simple level, too, it has tried to open up the subject
to include more female authors and critics.

In the essay under review, Professor Wolfson's primary focus is
not on Keats at all but on the history of the critical reception of his
work. In a highly stimulating, closely researched paper she discusses
the preoccupation of nineteenth- and twentieth-century critics with
feminine aspects of Keats's style, attitude and subject matter.

She begins with a general exploration of what the 'feminine' usually
means in literature and criticism: it has represented the 'other' in a
system which tends to privilege the masculine. Crucially she points
out that whereas 'sex' is a matter of biology, 'gender' is more one of
prevailing ideology (in other words, what makes behaviour etc. 'feminine' depends on social culture and political values). Critics discussing
Keats's writing have frequently questioned his gender, especially in a
normative way, by noting either what is typically 'effeminate' about it
or where it is deficient in expected masculine features. Her aims in the
essay are broadly to outline Keats's practices as a poet in order to
examine how the language of gender operates in the literary and
social culture in which Keats worked.

This is essentially a historically based strategy, relying heavily on
the detailed examination of reviews over the past two centuries. At
the heart of the issue is what Wolfson considers to be an obsession of
nineteenth-century critics to legislate on the definitions of the terms
'masculine' and 'feminine'. Nineteenth century critics who regarded
Keats as effeminate included John Lockhart (who as 'Z' berated
Keats over *Endymion*), Byron, Coventry Patmore, Swinburne, Alfred
Austin, and Gerard Manly Hopkins. And the 'effeminate' characteristics which they and later reviewers identified in Keats were such
things as gentleness, tenderness, sympathy with suffering, unworldli-

ness, a 'passive intellect', and amazingly a too detailed description of dress in *The Eve of St Agnes*. One reviewer entitled her article 'Keats – The Daintiest of Poets', while another wrote that 'In poetry his was the woman's part.'

Wolfson argues that Keats himself actually sets out to question and blur the distinctions in received gender labelling as part of an exploration of social and psychological attitudes.

> [Keats] imagines the masculine self being feminised or rendered ef-feminate by women exercising power and authority; and still at other times, he projects feminine figures as forces against manly self-possession and its social validator, professional maturity.
>
> (325)

This is a very persuasive light in which to view Keats's figure of the dominant and active woman (such as Moneta and La Belle Dame), and which opposes the interpretation of it as exclusively the projection of a male erotic fantasy. In crediting Keats with a head-on confrontation with the gender values of his own time, she also highlights the deeply entrenched and prescriptive attitudes against which he was swimming. Further, she proposes that in his verse Keats allows woman to stand as the symbol for 'fulfilment' and thus the poet's problematic relationship with her symbolically betrays his deepest anxieties about his profession.

These observations are significant in themselves, of course, but there is a political dimension too. Wolfson argues that gender issues in Keats were important to Victorian critics because they believed art, and culture in general, played such a big part in forming the consciousness of men and women. It was the area of public life most likely to effeminise men; as one Victorian critic worried, pursuit of ideal beauty and other intensities had the dangerous potential to drive 'the pith and manliness out of the national idiom'. A weak, unmanly poetry could be subversive, undermining the nation's imperial, masculine might.

In the late Victorian period two attitudes to Keats's 'feminine' voice can be identified: the majority one was to attack this as a weakness and use it as a warning, while much the minority view was to defend Keats as an honourable explorer in the realms of gender psychology. In both camps of this 'binarism', though, the existing definitions of 'masculine' and 'feminine' prevailed as an attempt to 'secure stable and legible codes of manly conduct' (333).

Wolfson goes on to show that these deep-seated attitudes manifested themselves in an obsession with Keats's physical appearance. Such features as the poet's voice, physique, hair colour, eyes and facial contour were scrutinised for evidence, but since such things tend to be a matter of subjective judgement, observations tended to reinforce the prejudices of the commentators. The essay reproduces some of the portraits of Keats produced from memory or 'fancy' after his death, to show how these perpetuated stereotypical views of him as effeminate (342–3). However, in her delineations of these portraits, Wolfson herself succumbs to some gender stereotyping (339–40).

She concludes her essay with a brief survey of critical attitudes in the twentieth century. In the early part of that century the 'contest' between the two parties continued explicitly, but towards mid-century it became sublimated through the language used about the verse; so a critic might talk of a 'virile idiom', or the masculine strength of his language. She adds that modern feminist critics have been as guilty of stereotyping as the Victorians, prolonging the gender polemic by applauding what they regard as the feminine in Keats: in other words, Keats is still being treated as an exception to traditional expectations of a male poet by referring to conventional definitions of the two genders (definitions which she believes were actually created and handed down by male 'authorities'). Her final point is that to do this, repeatedly using Keats to support one ideology or another, is to continually misread a poet who sought to blur gender distinctions.

> If Keats continues to animate discussions of gender in literary and social experience, he continues, just as surely, to confuse the terms. Even as he provokes us to describe and differentiate among what is 'masculine', 'feminine', 'effeminate', or 'feminist', he confronts us with the need to complicate and redefine the judgements that underlie these categories.

(349)

The central difference between Wolfson's thrust and those of the three previous critics is quite apparent. Clearly she sidesteps the terms on which they had determined the historical debate on Keats; that is, whether he was a poet essentially of 'feel' or 'know', whether he had fulfilled himself as a poet, or whether he embraces and reinforces the moral values that make for good poetry, and so on. The poetry is still important to Wolfson but it is important also in her deconstruction of critical attitudes towards it. It is in this function, of making us aware of critical constraints inherent in the system, that such approaches derive much of their strength and appeal, since these constraints are frequently silent manifestations of an ingrained bias in the culture.

Her view about the aim of literary study, however, is not particularly explicit and its function is left open. Compared with the grand designs of Arnold and Leavis, Post-Modernist critics tend to have less crusading or definitive ambitions and more limited aims. But at one point Wolfson does hint at the point of her own literary discourse here as 'to investigate the multiple and often conflicting interests that animate men's writing within a patriarchal culture' (349). Also, in spite of a generally objective approach, her own view on the gender issue comes forcibly forward, both implicitly and explicitly: Keats is essentially an androgynous figure, exhibiting characteristics from both masculine and feminine genders, as we have usually conceived them, and it is not valid to propose that any one side or trait is *intrinsically* more valuable than the other.

Her essay derives from a prior theory, of course, and some will argue that it has less to do with Keats or even with literature than with sociology. However, Post-Modernist writing is less likely to make such a traditional distinction. Unlike most theory-driven theses, Professor Wolfson's essay is presented in a thoroughly engaging and provocative style. We are likely to dislike criticism that has a palpable design upon us but this is not only an example of top flight modern scholarship but also extremely valuable both in its particular insights and, more importantly I think, in challenging the reader over his/her received paradigms.

Further Reading

Primary Texts

John Keats: The Complete Poems, edited by John Barnard (1988; 3rd edition).
The Poetical Works of John Keats, edited by H. W. Garrod (1956).

Biographical

Gittings, Robert (ed.), *Letters of John Keats: A Selection* (1970).
Rollins, H. E. (ed.), *The Letters of John Keats, 1814–21* (1958).
Rollins H. E. (ed.), *The Keats Circle: Letters and Papers* (1948).

Gittings, Robert, *John Keats* (1968).
Hilton, Timothy, *Keats and His World* (1971).
Motion, Andrew, *Keats* (1997).

Critical Studies

Arnold, Matthew, *Essays in Criticism: Second Series* (1888).
Barnard, John, *John Keats* (1987).
Christensen, Allan C. et al., *The Challenge of Keats: Bicentenary Essays, 1795–1995* (2000).
de Almeida, Hermione (ed.), *Critical Essays on John Keats* (1990).

Fraser, G. S. (ed.), *John Keats: Odes – A Casebook* (1971).

Garrod, H. W., *Keats* (1926).

Hill, John Spencer (ed.), *Keats: The Narrative Poems – A Casebook* (1983).

Jones, John, *John Keats's Dream of Truth* (1969).

Leavis, F. R., *Revaluation: Tradition and Development in English Poetry* (1936).

Matthews, G. M., *Keats: The Critical Heritage* (1971).

O'Neill, Michael, *Keats: Bicentenary Readings* (1997).

Pettet, E. C., *On the Poetry of Keats* (1957).

Ricks, Christopher, *Keats and Embarrassment* (1974).

Roe, Nicholas (ed.), *Keats and History* (1994).

Stone, Brian, *The Poetry of Keats* (1992).

Wolfson, Susan J. (ed.), *The Cambridge Companion to Keats* (2001).

Nineteenth-Century Romanticism

Abrams, M. H., *The Mirror and the Lamp* (1953).

Everest, Kelvin, *English Romantic Poetry: An Introduction* (1990).

Mellor, Anne K., *Romanticism and Gender* (1992).

Watson, John, *English Poetry of the Romantic Period: 1789–1830* (1992; second edition).

Index

(Refer also to 'Principal Events in John Keats's Life', p. xii)